BLACK BELT KARATE

BLACK BELT KARATE

by Jordan Roth

CHARLES E. TUTTLE COMPANY
Rutland . Vermont : Tokyo . Japan

Published by the Charles E. Tuttle Company, Inc.
of Rutland, Vermont & Tokyo, Japan
with editorial offices at
2-6 Suido 1-chome, 112, Bunkyo-ku, Tokyo

Library of Congress Catalog Card No. 73-87677
International Standard Book No. 0-8048-1851-7

First printing, 1974
First paperback edition, 1992

PRINTED IN JAPAN

TO BRIAN AND HEIDI

■ Table of Contents

■ Acknowledgments

The author is indebted to many people for their assistance in the preparation of this book. Limitations of space prevent the enumeration of every name. A special word of thanks is due to Ed Parker for his encouragement and to John Ritterath for his many kindnesses. A note of appreciation is also due members of the Southern California Karate Association for their cooperation, as well as to Jerry Emory and Bob Rechtsteiner for their invaluable technical criticisms. Also, to my wife, Susanne, whose thoughts along the way have been so helpful. Finally, my profound gratitude to Tsutomu Ohshima, who has taught me karate as a way of life.

TSUTOMU OHSHIMA

"The ideal in karate is to one day say, 'I ask my mind and find no shame.'"

■ Foreword

by Tsutomu Ohshima

There are few karate practitioners in this country worthy of the title "instructor." These few have achieved this distinction only after long years of hard training. I would hope in the years to come to be able to see more and more *real* instructors bring the true spirit of karate to their students.

It is sad to see big tournaments and trophies come to mean so much that good form is no longer important. It is only through drilling and working in the old way that real progress is made.

Hard training has direct results: the student improves and progresses, and it becomes easier for him to polish his character and strengthen his will power. The individual who gains a high level of technical skill without the moral integrity to support it is not yet a true karate man.

Jordan has been my pupil for eleven of the fifteen years he has studied karate and has seriously kept at his training without thought of personal gain. In this book I see an honest approach to karate.

Los Angeles, California

■ Preface

Today karate stands unique among sports and invites the bold athlete. The Western world, in its eager and inquiring zest for innovation, has welcomed this new challenger to the world of sports. New indeed to Occidental thought, but in truth centuries old, karate is a system of unarmed self-defense wherein those portions of the body capable of being utilized as weapons are employed to their fullest potential.

A decade and a half ago, when the author first became aware of karate, there was little information available regarding this exciting and fascinating sport. Today this original interest is shared by the growing enthusiasm of others around the world. The magic word "karate" is being publicized and promulgated through television, magazines, books, and other media. What does the novice learn from these sources? In the main, arts of the showman such as board, brick, and tile breaking.

To help acquaint the public with karate, its assimilation and application, photographs and textual material have been designed to encompass all requirements for a Black Belt First Degree.[1] The blackbelt karateist as well will find considerable material to augment his continuing study since many points of particular interest to the advanced student have been added to the basic prerequisites. In the interest of unimpeded study Japanese terms have been for the most part omitted; thus the student need not constantly have his attention diverted from the lesson. Choice of language is optional, but in translation instructors should choose words whose sounds and pronunciations are markedly explosive.[2]

Never in our nation's history has the need for stalwartness been so critical as it is today. Dynamic physical fitness programs, far-reaching in their effects, will prove a strengthening, revitalizing force. This will be reflected in a drop in juvenile delinquency, a

[1] In the interest of succinctness and without sacrificing clarity, various photographs which are merely repetitious have been omitted.
[2] See Training Hall Glossary.

decline in lost man hours due to ill health, a slackening of the mental health problem, and a multitude of other ways.

Prospective students frequently ask, "If I learn karate, can I beat a boxer or wrestler?" Provocative as this type of speculation may be, emphasis in karate should never be placed on such an issue, for its real value lies in the health-building and enjoyable activities which lead toward a better understanding and control of one's own inner weakness. Adherence to rigid mental discipline is the program that sets karate apart from most other sports. Consequently, the question of who can win a match ceases to be important. Unlike other methods of self-defense, karate eventually means to the student not merely defense against an aggressor but, in the larger sense, a growing conditioning against the various pitfalls of life. Through a strengthened spirit made manifest we develop the ability to resist temptation.

Three features are emphasized in the text:

1. Healthful physical exercise.
2. An effective form of self-defense.
3. Character development through perseverance, integrity, and self-control.

Beyond the mere assimilation of self-defense techniques, the training methods shown in this book will expedite the student's attainment of a healthy and vigorous physique, quick in response to emergencies. While the author does not necessarily endorse a late start he has seen several students begin training in their fifties. It is safe to assume that anyone who actively enters karate should be able to continue to an advanced age. Karate offers this opportunity for conditioning throughout one's lifetime.

Do not allow yourself to be misled by opportunists who prey on the glamour of karate. Know your source of information and be sure of the authenticity of a prospective instructor before reaching a decision.

—JORDAN ROTH

■ PART 1

INTRODUCTION

The ultimate aim of the art of karate lies
not in victory or defeat, but in the perfection
of the characters of its participants.

—GICHIN FUNAKOSHI

■ History

The clenched fist is a popular symbol of karate.[1] To anyone realizing its significance this symbol becomes an inspiring and forbidding trademark. Although its origins are obscure it is generally believed that karate has evolved from a system of self-defense taught to monks at the Shaolin Monastery in northern China many centuries ago by Daruma (Bodhidharma), a Buddhist monk from India.[2] Because of religious beliefs, weapons could not be carried by monks. Thus Daruma reasoned, so the legend goes, that to protect oneself against the local bandits various parts of the body, principally the arms (hand and elbow) and legs (knee and foot), could be fashioned into offensive weapons. In this way the fist becomes a hammer or mace; the open hand can slash as a sword, thrust as a dagger, or rip like a tiger's claw. These techniques were reinforced by various exercises designed to harden the striking surfaces. Consequently a blow delivered by anyone having a pronounced buildup of the striking surface produced a most devastating effect.

After Daruma introduced this system, it spread throughout China, and with modifications became known as *kung-fu* and also as *kempo*. Following upon the heels of commerce, these methods made their way to Okinawa, where they attained a high degree of perfection during many decades of Japanese occupation when arms were forbidden there. The Chinese methods undoubtedly underwent a metamorphosis upon continued contact with the native Okinawan fighting form known as Okinawa-te.

Master Gichin Funakoshi, the man most responsible for the systematization of karate as we know it today, was born in Shuri, Oki-

---

[1] Karate, translated literally, means "empty hand." The clenched fist is the symbol of the Goju style.

[2] Be this as it may, one thing is certain: unarmed self-defense began when the first caveman lifted his arm to ward off a club or rock wielded by an unfriendly neighbor. This natural reaction was modified an infinite number of times through countless centuries. Today we find this same ancient, instinctive response appearing in different cultures under names like boxing, wrestling, savate, and so forth.

nawa, in 1868. As a boy of eleven he began a study of the precursors of karate, mastering both of the major existing styles in Okinawa. These schools were known as Shorei and Shorin and are still in evidence. The Shorei approach is characterized by heavy, powerful movements; the Shorin method utilizes lighter, quicker techniques. Master Funakoshi then molded aspects of these techniques into the school of karate today known as Shotokan. Shoto was the pen name of Master Funakoshi, who was also well known as an author. Hence, the word "Shotokan" simply signified the training hall of Funakoshi. Today, however, it has grown to mean the style of karate as taught by his disciples in major universities in Japan, and as it was subsequently taught to members of the Southern California Karate Association by Tsutomu Ohshima, the Association's founder.

The Shotokan school is therefore adaptable to all body types. The heavier Occidental is particularly favored by the slightly slower but more powerful techniques adapted from the Shorei school, whereas the lighter individual may find the swift, agile techniques of the Shorin school more suitable.

Master Funakoshi left Okinawa for Japan in 1922 at the invitation of the Ministry of Education to teach karate at various universities throughout Japan. Six years prior to this move, Master Funakoshi had had occasion to give a series of demonstrations in Japan. This was probably the first formal presentation in Japan of what came to be called karate. The years that followed saw the inevitable interaction among the various systems, both native and imported. Master Funakoshi's system, as it evolved, bore the eventual imprint of other contemporary forms of self-defense. With the transfer of this teaching to Japan came the eventual substitution of the word *kara* for the "Okinawa" in "Okinawa-te," thus forming the word *kara-te*.

Following the U.S. occupation of Japan at the close of World War II, the U.S. military command in Japan, under General Douglas MacArthur, considered the practice of judo and kendo overly militant and it was strictly forbidden. Karate, being relatively obscure, temporarily escaped notice and as a result flourished. Tsutomu Ohshima, then a student at Waseda University, was fortunate in having Master Funakoshi as his instructor during the period from 1948 to 1953. He progressed under Master Funakoshi's tutelage to the rank of Black Belt Third Degree. (In the years since he has achieved the ultimate fifth degree.)

In view of present ranking trends, it is worth while recalling that Master Funakoshi himself never awarded a degree higher than fifth. Within these traditional guidelines each rank represents a comprehensive and specific level of performance. The trend in many quarters toward a runaway mode of ranking serves only to distort the intrinsic value of each degree.

During the 1952 All Japan Collegiate Sandan (Black Belt Third

GICHIN FUNAKOSHI

Degree) promotional, Tsutomu Ohshima accumulated the highest score.[3] The format of this tournament covered forms and sparring. Shortly before Master Funakoshi's death, Ohshima visited the United States as an exchange student to do graduate work at the University of Southern California. At the request of interested persons, Ohshima began to teach karate at the Konko Temple in Los Angeles in 1956. On December 5, 1959, at the second promotional examination under Ohshima's direction, the author was one of six awarded the rank of Black Belt First Degree.[4] These early participants were the pioneers of Shotokan Karate in the United States. Tsutomu Ohshima instructed the new black-belt holders to further advance the art of karate at an academic level. It is felt that in this manner karate may soon evolve as an art form and become recognized for its character-building potential rather than exclusively for its unique properties as a martial art.

Shortly after, Ohshima had the opportunity to visit Brazil and then France. He reported that there were enthusiastic karate students in those countries. He later returned to France for an extended visit of a year's duration, during which he did much to organize the various groups throughout the country and to refine their training programs.

[3] In those early years there was no formal title of collegiate champion or any series of tournaments through which one could be determined. Therefore the winner of this tournament was tacitly recognized as such.

[4] During the preceding year the first promotional examination of the Southern California Karate Association had been held. At that time no one had achieved black-belt rank; different degrees of brown belt were the highest to be conferred.

Returning to the United States at the end of 1962, he has continued in his original capacity with the Southern California Karate Association.

The opportunity presented itself in February 1967 for Tsutomu Ohshima to revisit Japan, and he took with him a small group. This became the first organized band of karateists from the United States to tour Japan. The author was fortunate in being one of their number. The itinerary was planned so that the group would be able to meet several revered masters in the martial arts. Among these was Master S. Sato, who treated everyone to a demonstration of judo at the Kodokan. Master Isao Obata, Gichin Funakoshi's senior active pupil, addressed the group at Keio University, where he is head instructor of its karate club. Master Uyeshiba's son Kisshomaru, who is himself a master, demonstrated aikido, and later, in Nagoya, the group observed a demonstration of karate by Master Hironori Otsuka, the founder of the Wado-Kai style. The visitors also were privileged to meet Toshiro Kamata, Shigeru Egami, and Hiroshi Noguchi, each a master of karate. During the brief two weeks sojourn exchange practices were held with karateists from Waseda, Keio, Toyo, Hosei, Takushoku, Meiji, and Nihon universities. The sociability of all those connected with the experience, in addition to the benefits acquired from an exposure to high-level karateists in a distant land, made this a deeply rewarding experience. The spirit of karate can function as a cohesive force in the world through international participation in its activities. Anyone who has seen the camaraderie which emerges from such a gathering can understand its potential in this regard.

■ Mental and Physical Development

Karate training must necessarily be strenuous, each session lasting perhaps two hours and repeated several times weekly. Very brief rest periods should be provided (above and beyond those intervals between individual exercises) to separate the main phases of training. Unseemly jocularity is out of place and a serious demeanor should be encouraged. The ability to concentrate full attention on the immediate task is highly stressed at all levels of training. All extraneous thoughts are to be erased from the mind. During workouts, the instructor may feel it necessary to order, "Tighten your mind!" when it becomes obvious that some students are not serious enough or too readily manifest fatigue. The ripening ability to utilize our powers of concentration, when applied in a broader sense, will help to alleviate the practical problems of daily living. This particular facet of mental control and direction is more or less inherent among Asiatics, with their centuries of philosophic disciplines, such as Yoga and Zen Buddhism. On the other hand, this ability must be painstakingly cultivated by the Occidental. The student starting training has in effect given his instructor and seniors the right to train him as rigorously as they feel necessary to increase his skill and make a better person of him. The student should fix an image in his mind of the perfect man and, through his karate experience, endeavor to reach that goal.

Once in condition, unless something is physically wrong, a student should not stop exercising at the first signs of fatique, but rather should push on to the phase called "second wind," which will leave him relatively refreshed and able to proceed with renewed vigor. If, for example, it normally takes a student thirty minutes of exertion to feel fatigue, with determination he will find that this period of time can be considerably lengthened. During sparring there frequently comes a time when both contestants feel completely exhausted. This condition usually manifests itself by a weakened stance (that is, standing too high in order to relieve leg tension), using ineffectual technique, and otherwise exhibiting a disheartened attitude. The student who "grits his teeth" at this point and remains in a low stance, attacking strongly and forcing himself to continue, will not only gain his "second wind" but will very probably win the contest. The physically superior student who utilizes only a portion of his strength will in reality not register as much power as his weaker counterpart who uses his entire strength in combination with superior mental conditioning. It seems that when we begin to tire, we commence a rationalization. We then imagine that we labored especially hard that day, or obtained insufficient sleep the previous night, etc. At this point the karate student should purge such thoughts from his mind and reach out for prolonged activity with new determination.

Because of the Spartan nature of karate training, the dedicated instructor will frequently urge his students beyond the normal limits of endurance. He may, for instance, demand a given number of additional repetitions of an exercise or form when the class appears exhausted. In an effort to mobilize his reserve power some student may *kiai* (yell) spiritedly at the outset of each succeeding exercise. Others will often pick up the challenge, building in unison to a crescendo of sound on which the entire group is swept irresistibly along.

Considering the increasing popularity of karate and the current emphasis on physical fitness, it is important that an evaluation be made of its worth as a physical training program. A serious difficulty in evaluating the benefits of karate training is that when the following tests were administered the number of available students having studied this sport in the United States long enough to be considered as a basis for comparison was unfortunately limited. Any conclusion, therefore, must necessarily be speculative.

During the summer of 1962, various physical tests were given to fourteen karate students who had been training for a period of at least one year. Since karate emphasizes the importance of exerting maximum concentrated strength, the first series of tests were a measurement of total proportional strength.

These tests were conducted by Dr. Phillip J. Rasch, California College of Medicine, assisted by Eugene R. O'Connell, Department of Physical Education, University of California at Los Angeles.

The TPS (Total Proportional Strength) test was given in a manner identical to that previously administered to a group of fourteen collegiate wrestlers comparable in age, experience, and other factors. A simple metered tension device was squeezed in order to provide data for right-hand grip and left-hand grip. In measuring back lift, the participant bent forward keeping his knees straight, grasped a bar under tension attached to a meter, and attempted to raise it as far as possible. Leg strength was tested by the same bar. In this case the participant squatted, grasped the bar, and attempted to lift it as far as possible. The resulting data was reduced to strength per pound of body weight. The analysis of the data indicated that the karate group was significantly stronger in the legs per pound of body weight, and consequently scored markedly higher in the total score than did the wrestlers. This is a result of the emphasis on vigorous and extensive training of the legs in all phases of karate instruction.

Actually, a considerable number of different kicking techniques are practiced during training sessions, and the legs are rigorously exercised through their full range of motion in various ways. The differences between the two groups tested, in right-hand grip, left-hand grip, and back lift, however, were not significant, and combined results compared favorably with the scores reported for athletes in other sports.

As stated previously these results cannot be considered conclusive because of the limited number of participants. The author will, however, venture the opinion that further studies will confirm that karate students develop stronger legs than are characteristic of participants in other combative sports.

The principal maneuvers in karate are based largely on techniques employing the kick and straight punch. Some throwing and grappling maneuvers are practiced, however. These are utilized primarily to disrupt an opponent's defenses preparatory to launching an assault and are therefore of secondary importance. Contemporary karate masters place great emphasis on the necessity for speed in the execution of these movements.

A more recent series of tests examining comparative reaction and movement time between a group of karate students and certain participants in the 1960 A.A.U. Wrestling Championships was administered. Reaction time and movement time were recorded in one continuous test on a single device consisting of a lever, a light bulb, and an electric eye. When the operator switched the light on, the participant whose hand had been depressing the lever would quickly thrust his hand forward, intercepting the beam. When the differences between the scores of the karate students and those of the wrestlers were analyzed, it was found that there was no appreciable difference in either the reaction or movement times of the two groups. Significantly though, the mean age of the karate students (31.6) was considerably higher than that of the wrestlers (24.5).

If it is assumed that the reaction time of the karate students reflected the normal deterioration consequent upon aging, this suggests that at age twenty-four they would have been markedly faster than the A.A.U. wrestlers. The question arises whether emphasis on extension movements of the arms and legs is associated with faster reaction and movement times than is characteristic of American amateur wrestlers, who emphasize flexion movements of the extremities. An alternate explanation is that the karate students were actually no faster when younger, but constant training has offset the normal deterioration of the aging process, or that specialized training in reflexive-type exercise has resulted in an advantage in this particluar phase of testing. No decision can be reached until the practice of karate has expanded to the point where advanced students no older than the A.A.U. wrestlers previously tested are available.

Future tests are proposed which will compare athletic performance in the specific areas of endurance and punching power. In both cases the author is confident that the superiority of karate training will be proven.

TOTAL PROPORTIONAL STRENGTH
(Comparison of College Wrestlers and Karate Students)
(*TPS scores: body weight in pounds*)

STRENGTH TEST	WRESTLERS				KARATE STUDENTS			
	Number tested	*Mean scores*	*Standard deviation*	*Classification*	*Number tested*	*Mean scores*	*Standard deviation*	*Classification*
Right grip	13	.74	.09	average	13	.68	.12	average
Left grip	14	.70	.14	average	14	.64	.07	fair
Back lift	15	2.47	.41	very good	14	2.47	.48	very good
Leg lift	14	2.20	.26	fair	14	4.33	.59	excellent
Total score	12	6.15	.63	above average	14	8.11	1.08	excellent

REACTION AND MOVEMENT TIME
(*Mean response in seconds*)

SUBJECT	REACTION TIME			MOVEMENT TIME		
	Number tested	*Mean scores*	*Standard deviation*	*Mean scores*	*Standard deviation*	*Mean age*
Karate students	12	.240	.026	.127	.012	31.6
(Karate students adjusted to age 24)		(.240)		(.097)		
A.A.U. wrestlers	32	.241	.034	.130	.021	24.5

Each summer several days of intensive group training will prove extremely beneficial (see schedule, page 60). The class should train rigorously for several hours each day, preferably outdoors in the country. For best results, the curriculum should include running as well as all standard aspects of karate. The theory behind the serious and particularly strenuous activity associated with special summer training is that only dedicated students worthy of the sport will remain active. Instructors and students alike should prepare themselves to meet what will at times become an ordeal, physically and mentally, by dwelling upon the conditioning (again both physical and mental) which they will receive. Many demands will be made upon the endurance of the participant, but the inherent challenge in this type of discipline will always be not only to endure but to overcome.

Unlike most methods of self-defense, karate, in its broadest sense, means to the sincere student not merely defense against any human assailant but also protection against the more elusive evils. The strengthening of the spirit which evidences itself in the advanced karateist will enable him to stand firm against the suggestions of wayward companions and to overcome other obstacles in his path as well.

The ability to break boards, bricks, or tile with the fist or foot, etc., however impressive, is relatively unimportant. Anyone strong enough can learn to do these spectacular stunts without having to acquire the slightest knowledge of karate.

Although our involvement at the outset may be as simple an objective as the mastery of self-defense per se, we must make a broader commitment somewhere along the way. With the gaining of more and more physical skills should come a growing awareness of karate as a way of life. Understood as a philosophy it provides a far more meaningful program for those interested in a broader interpretation. The thoughts once focused upon one's adjustment to a specific training schedule will now turn inward, and here the ground to be gained and the victory won will be in individual discipline and self-mastery.

It becomes apparent that the highest level a karateist will reach is actually spiritual in nature, the ultimate goal being the absolute subordination of the body to mental discipline. "Harmony is Supreme" reads the motto of the Southern California Karate Association, referring specifically to individual search and fulfillment. Briefly, it is recognized that modern man very often develops feelings of inferiority, which in turn produce jealousy, distrust, or fear, resulting at times in violence. The karate-trained athlete, who has reached a high degree of excellence in this paradoxically lethal sport, will have progressed beyond this pattern of behavior to a state of inner harmony. Anyone allowed to continue this far would have successfully suppressed antisocial feelings of either inferiority or superiority and thus would maintain an inner equilibrium. In defending himself against an aggressor he would feel no hostility toward his assailant, but instead would show restraint and try to understand the reasons causing his antagonist's display of force. In short, karate is never to be used aggressively. We must studiously attempt to avoid violence to the point of accepting insult. If, however, after exhausting all efforts at settlement, we find we are forced to defend ourselves, we attempt to dissuade our adversary by the use of formidably efficient blocking techniques and a rigid, resolute demeanor. If this does not prove convincing enough, then only at this time would we progress to the extreme measure of the attack. Remember always, victory in an altercation that could have been avoided may result in a lifelong enemy.

■ Rules of Conduct

1. The use of vulgar language is discouraged both within and without the training hall. Besides denoting possession of an inferior vocabulary and lack of culture, such indiscriminate word usage brings discredit upon our art.
2. Aside from its incongruity within the confines of any sport, smoking should be prohibited within the training area. Smoke-laden air reduces the quality of oxygen available to participants, who use a prodigious amount while training. Outside the training hall this simply becomes a matter in which to exercise individual discretion.
3. Alcoholic beverages are never allowed within the training hall, and their consumption outside should be held to a minimum. When indulging in alcohol, it may seem that the more we drink the stronger and wiser we become. Unfortunately the reverse is true.
4. The training uniform should be kept fresh and clean and in good repair at all times. Outside the training hall it should be neatly folded and carried over the arm as follows (see facing page):
    (a) Place jacket, back down, on floor and stretch smooth.
    (b) Fold one side back and place neatly doubled pants inside. Smooth and fold, extending pant legs just within bottom of jacket.
    (c) Fold jacket-front back to original position.
    (d) Fold sleeves in.
    (e) Fold jacket over once.
    (f) Fold again lengthwise.
    (g) Fold from the bottom up and place on the outstretched belt, one third of the way down. Then neatly wind the belt around the uniform, ending with a simple knot.
    (h) Place the forearm through loop of the uniform.
5. To prevent injury all students are requested to keep their fingernails and toenails carefully clipped. Neither glasses nor rings

should be worn by any student during sparring. Students having insufficient vision without resorting to glasses should not be permitted to participate in sparring.

6. A clean-shaven, well-groomed appearance is always proper. A dignified approach to karate by every student will engender a like attitude toward our sport by nonparticipants.

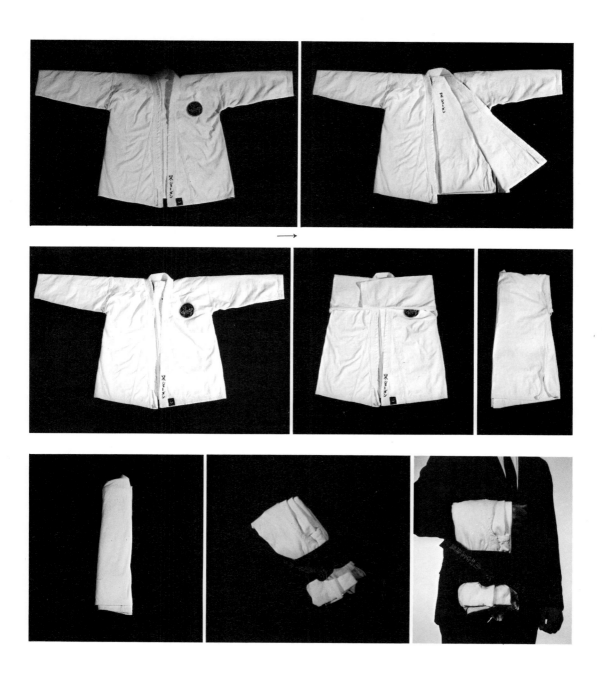

■ The Training Hall

The training area should consist of a well-lighted and airy enclosure, preferably with a wooden floor. When we jump on a concrete floor during training sessions, the accompanying shocking power thus generated is at the moment of contact almost wholly reversed with resulting ill-effect to the student. To minimize this shocking power and to render it tolerable the excellent absorptive quality of a wooden floor produces the ideal surface. There are no other prerequisites, but equipment such as punching boards and mirrors is helpful. If available, at least one large mirror should be placed in an area where it will not distract the group during training sessions. This aid will prove invaluable in individual self-corrective drill.

Because so much of karate is a community effort, the membership must share in training-hall housekeeping. When everyone, regardless of rank, takes part in the care of the training hall, this becomes a means of self-immolation. The training hall, symbolically speaking, mirrors forth the modesty and purity of individual students. A statement of principles and rules of conduct for the guidance of all who enter the training hall should be prominently posted.

The discussion of dues, financial policy, etc., is not befitting the position of head instructor. These matters are more appropriately left to one of the senior students.

■ Formalities

Descriptive examples of situations encountered will be given to aid the novice in forming a karate club. Through the study of judging techniques and other procedures the student will be made more aware of the traditions behind karate and will become acquainted with various formalities involved.

Whenever entering or leaving the training hall, students should pause momentarily in the entrance to bow. Every serious student knows that he is learning something here upon which he can place great value, especially since this knowledge will prove beneficial throughout his lifetime. We bow at this time to demonstrate our awareness of this concept.

At the beginning of each training session the class lines up, with the highest ranking members on the right, and then kneels facing the instructor. Our eyes are lightly closed, and at this time we endeavor to drive all worldly thoughts from consciousness to achieve a state of complete concentration on the ensuing lesson.

At the command to bow, given by the one on the extreme right, the students place their hands on the floor, and bend forward until the forehead is just above the floor. We pause momentarily at this time to show gratitude to our instructor for the benefits we are about to receive. Then we reassume the kneeling position, remaining in a state of attentiveness.

After examining the students and satisfying himself as to their appearance, the instructor gives the command to rise. This formality is repeated at the completion of the training period. This time, when we close our eyes, we attempt to normalize our labored intake of air by deep abdominal breathing, and also to readjust our thinking processes to the outside environment.

Whenever students are paired off prior to and after any exercise, they will bow to each other from a standing position, normally at least two feet apart. As students change partners this gesture will be repeated. This conveys mutual confidence and respect. In effect the student is saying, "I am allowing you the use of my body for this exercise to improve your skills. Therefore, I expect you to take care of it."

When the instructor calls upon a student to assist him in demonstrating a particular technique, the student will approach him, stopping approximately four feet directly in front, and execute a standing bow, which will simultaneously be returned. At the conclusion of the demonstration this courtesy will be repeated before the student returns to his position within the group.

Frequently, when bowing to each other at the end of a mutual exercise, or when bowing to the instructor at the completion of the training session, appreciative students will express verbal thanks.

It should not be too difficult for us to understand these formalities. In boxing, fencing, and tennis, along with many other sports, we in the Western world are familiar with various courtesies. The formalities of karate moreover have a deeper significance, as the new student will soon come to realize.

1. In opening and closing the training session, perform the following in unison with instructor (see facing page):
   (a) Assume closed-leg stance.
   (b) Kneel on left knee.
   (c) Kneel on right knee with knees a shoulder-width apart and feet crossing one over the other. Place each palm on the corresponding thigh.
   (d) Lightly close the eyes.
   (e) Open eyes.
   (f) Bow.
   (g) Resume kneeling position.
   (h) Raise right leg, and then place right foot down.
   (i) Raise left leg, and then place left foot down and return to closed-leg stance.
2. The instructor and an assisting student preparing to demonstrate a technique will perform the following in unison:
   (a) Assume closed-leg stance.
   (b) Bow.
3. Two student partners immediately prior to basic or free sparring perform the following in unison:
   (a) Assume closed-leg stance.
   (b) Bow.

■ Grading

Students are graded according to their proficiency, perseverance, attitude, and record of attendance. Their progress is indicated by the belt color they are permitted to wear.

In all, there are thirteen ranks which one may acquire in Shotokan Karate. It should be noted that the Black Belt Third Degree represents the highest degree awarded on the basis of technical skill alone. The higher fourth and fifth degrees are somewhat honorary in that they are normally given on the additional basis of service to the community and the advancement of karate in general.

Beginners start with white belt (no rank), and within one year may progress through five additional levels of white-belt ranking to arrive at brown belt, third degree. With the proper display of perseverance, coupled with an acceptable attitude and improved proficiency, a student will in due time be graded brown belt, second degree, and perhaps at the end of two to two and one-half years will be ready for brown belt, first degree. The next step becomes the most difficult and most significant: advancement to Black Belt First Degree. The dedicated student should normally be considered ready for this important move within two and one-half to three years.

It should be noted that in other schools of karate ten or more ranks of black belt are awarded, while in many of the Chinese martial arts belt ranks are not used. No one of course moves higher until he has first mastered all the prerequisites of his present category.

■ Shotokan Rank Structure

The standard approved progression is from white to brown to black belt. In some schools, however, other belt colors were recently added to spur flagging interest due to the lengthy time interval between the ranks of white and brown belt. The reason for not conferring intermediate colors beyond the classic white, brown, and black is that anyone who might tend to capitulate to discouragement or other negative attitudes is in the final analysis unworthy of the black belt. The development of patterns of self-discipline which lead the student to persevere with no thought of immediate reward is far more desirable than the mere opportunity to display additional belts.

Then, too, the student must command a working knowledge of the three phases of karate: basic training, forms, and sparring. He will

SHOTOKAN RANK STRUCTURE

WHITE BELT	WHITE-BELT RANK	BROWN-BELT RANK	BLACK-BELT DEGREE[1]
Beginner without rank	8 7 6 5 4	3 2 1	1 2 3 4 5
	Comments: A student should be well seasoned as a white belt and holder of the three brown-belt ranks as well. During this more or less probationary period any serious flaws will have risen to the surface, and should therefore have terminated the training of a student not worthy of karate.		1 Advanced level 2 3 Instructor level 4 5 Expert level[2]

[1] The fourth and fifth black belt degrees represent honorary bestowals in the main, while the first, second, and third degrees are awarded on the basis of skill.

[2] Although various groups now provide higher black-belt degrees, the traditional system instituted by Master Funakoshi himself consists of only five.

be tested and graded competitively, as well as individually, on his ability as a karateist. The standard used in grading him will be predicated upon the capabilities of the best competing student. All other participants will be judged accordingly.

The color of the belt a student is permitted to wear should never be cause for disparagement by others or self-depreciation any more than it should be cause for inordinate pride. The ultimate or ideal evaluation should embrace the student's total gains in technique and self-mastery. Thus, for example, the attainment of any one of the lower ranks might well reflect more praiseworthy dedication and effort during some specific period than a student may later express.

Learning the fundamentals, assimilating the basic philosophic outlook, premises, attitudes, and techniques, and being able to give and take in sparring lead eventually to becoming an adequate karateist of black-belt level. By contrast the master has brought to his practice of karate a very vital spark that sets him apart from his fellow students; his is a formidable courage powered and directed by conviction, yet tempered by that humility which is indispensable to true greatness.

Using the following as a guide, students preparing themselves for participation in promotional examinations must review every requirement in their category. A minimum of five repetitions of each specified exercise should be performed on all days when not attending the training hall. This program, when practical, should be started no later than two weeks prior to the examination date and continued up to the day preceding it. This day should remain free for relaxation.

BASIC PROMOTIONAL EXAMINATION[1]

GRADE	FORM	BASIC TRAINING		SPARRING
		Hand Techniques	*Foot Techniques*	
White Belt 8th	Demonstrate: a) Various block and counter-attack combinations as called for b) Heian 1	Demonstrate: Lunge punch Reverse punch Rising block Inward block Outward block Downward block Knife-hand block	Demonstrate: Front kick Side-thrust kick Side-snap kick	Demonstrate: a) Various block and counterattack combinations as called for to be executed with an opposing student b) Three consecutive attacks: lunge punch, upper level; lunge punch, lower level; front kick, lower level

[1] It should be understood that this outline is somewhat skeletal. Individual instructors will want to augment this framework with additional techniques at their own discretion.

GRADE	FORM	BASIC TRAINING		SPARRING
		Hand Techniques	*Foot Techniques*	
White Belt 7th	Demonstrate: a) Various block and counter attack combinations as called for b) Heian 2	Demonstrate: Lunge punch Reverse punch Rising block Inward block Outward block Downward block Knife-hand block	Demonstrate: Front kick Side-thrust kick Side-snap kick	Demonstrate: a) Various block and counterattack combinations as called for to be executed with an opposing student b) Three consecutive attacks: lunge punch, upper level; lunge punch, lower level; front kick, lower level
White Belt 6th	Demonstrate: a) Various block and counter-attack combinations as called for b) Heian 3	Demonstrate: Lunge punch Reverse punch Rising block Inward block Outward block Downward block Knife-hand block	Demonstrate: Front kick Side-thrust kick Side-snap kick	Demonstrate: a) Various block and counterattack combinations as called for to be executed with an opposing student b) Three consecutive attacks: lunge punch, upper level; lunge punch, lower level; front kick, lower level
White Belt 5th	Demonstrate: a) Various block and counter-attack combinations as called for b) Heian 4	Demonstrate: Lunge punch Reverse punch Rising block Inward block Outward block Downward block Knife-hand block Right lunge punch—left front kick	Demonstrate: Front kick Side-thrust kick Side-snap kick Right front kick—left lunge punch	Demonstrate: a) Various block and counterattack combinations as called for to be executed with an opposing student b) Three consecutive attacks: lunge punch, upper level; lunge punch, lower level; front kick, lower level
White Belt 4th	Demonstrate: a) Various block and counter-attack combinations as called for b) Heian 5	Demonstrate: Lunge punch Reverse punch Rising block Inward block Outward block Downward block Knife-hand block Right lunge punch—left front kick	Demonstrate: Front kick Side-thrust kick Side-snap kick Right front kick—left lunge punch	Demonstrate: a) Various block and counterattack combinations as called for to be executed with an opposing student b) Three consecutive attacks: lunge punch, upper level; lunge punch, lower level; front kick, lower level

GRADE	FORM	BASIC TRAINING *Hand and Foot Techniques*		SPARRING
Brown Belt 3rd	Demonstrate: a) Various block and counter-attack combinations as called for b) Tekki 1	Demonstrate: Lunge punch Right lunge punch—left front kick Right front kick—left lunge punch Right lunge punch—left reverse punch Right side-thrust kick—right back-fist		Demonstrate: a) Various block and counterattack combinations executed with opponent as called for b) One attack each: lunge punch, upper level; lunge punch, lower level; front kick, lower level; side-thrust kick, middle level
Brown Belt 2nd	Demonstrate: a) Various block and counter-attack combinations as called for b) Tekki 2	Demonstrate: Lunge punch Right lunge punch—left front kick Right front kick—left lunge punch Right lunge punch—left reverse punch Right side-thrust kick—right back-fist strike		Demonstrate: a) Various block and counterattack combinations executed with opponent as called for b) One attack each: lunge punch, upper level; lunge punch, lower level; front kick, lower level; side-thrust kick, lower level
Brown Belt 1st	Demonstrate: a) Various block and counter-attack combinations as called for b) Tekki 3	Demonstrate: Lunge punch Right lunge punch—left front kick Right front kick—left lunge punch Right lunge punch—left reverse punch Right side-thrust kick—right back-fist strike		Demonstrate: a) Various block and counterattack combinations executed with opponent as called for b) One attack each: lunge punch, upper level, lunge punch, lower level; front kick, lower level; side-thrust kick, lower level
Black Belt 1st	Demonstrate: a) Various block and counter-attack combinations as called for b) Independent forms: choices by examiner and examinee	Demonstrate: Right lunge punch—left front kick Right front kick—left lunge punch Right lunge punch—left reverse punch Left side-thrust kick—left back-fist strike Left side-thrust kick—right lunge punch Round kick Left side-thrust kick—right front kick		Demonstrate: a) Various blocks and counterattack combinations executed with opponent as called for b) One attack each: lunge punch, upper level; lunge punch, lower level; front kick, lower level; side-thrust kick, lower level. Semi-free.

The following examination form is presented with the thought that it may serve as a guide for judging promotional examinations.

INDIVIDUAL EXAMINATION FORM [SAMPLE]

(Student to write in bold-bordered section only)

Last Name	First	Middle		Basic Training	Form	Sparring	Other	Average	Result
Smith	John	James							
Date	*Age*	*Membership Card No.*		3	2	3	3	3+	3rd Kyu
April 25, 1967	26	73							
School				3	3+	3	3	3+	Remarks: Level of attack not on a par with that of block; needs more emphasis. Stress kiai. Side-thrust kick strong but slow in execution.
City Karate Club									
Present Rank		*Time in Rank*		3	2	3−	3	3	
4th Kyu		6 months							
Rank Attempted									
3rd Kyu									
Special Training Attended:		*When?*		3	3+	3−	3	3	
Summer: One		1967							
Winter: None									
Membership Dues				MORIKAMI [signature]					
Paid to date				*Chief Examiner*					

Grading is calculated on the basis of an average derived from scores in the above categories. The numerical grading (indicated in the chart) employed in judging each category represents the rank equivalent of the student's performance and is entered by each of the judges. The category termed "Other" includes such sundry items as overall performance during the preceding months and general conduct. At the termination of the student's examination the panel makes known its evaluation, and the consensus is then reached and recorded in the "Result" column.

The promotional examination is given twice yearly by the Southern California Karate Association in commemoration of Master Funakoshi's birth, November 10, and of his death, April 26. It is presided over by a panel of several judges and a chief examiner, all of black belt rank. The chief examiner should be that person who holds the highest rank and often is, as well, the head instructor at a training hall. Candidates for the black belt, first degree, must have completed at least one special training session. The panel of examiners should consist of at least one person no lower than black belt, third degree. In order to vote each official must be at least one rank higher than the rank being considered.

■ Basic Training

Basic training, forms, and sparring constitute the three indispensable components of karate. Basic training alone includes the study of the various stances, blocks, and attacks, requiring countless repetitions until the student becomes well grounded in these essential techniques.

The record shows that within the first three months of training the student-dropout rate is greatest. Many Occidentals are apparently searching for self-defense systems that are quickly and easily mastered. The skillful application of karate techniques is painstakingly developed. Therefore, traditionally exacting training methods, although not sound commercially, will soon cull out the fadist. The student who is tempted to give up karate because of the rigorous training routine may be better off in some other sport that is not quite so demanding, while those who remain can in time prove themselves worthy of karate.

The new student will be revitalized both physically and emotionally. Physically he will soon become agile, tough, and capable of extreme endurance. While cultivating a compassionate attitude, he will be building a reserve of courage and strength upon which to draw when necessary.

Any student passing lightly over the basic techniques (thinking only of learning advanced methods) will develop a structure with a poor foundation, reminiscent of the Biblical story "The House Built Upon the Sand."

The course presented in the following chart is suggested as a guide to promote standardization of karate-training methods and the comprehensive approach expected of each instructor. It is basic and should therefore be supplemented by special exercises. There should be three practice sessions weekly, each of two hours duration.

Avoid overexertion! It is likely that at the outset the student's high enthusiasm will lead him to overextend himself. The student new to such rigorous exercises should pace himself carefully until the physique is able to withstand greater demands upon it.

The methodical process of assimilation is best aided by a patient long-range commitment.

In general, the class should be arranged according to the following alignment:

· · · · · ·
· · · · ·

The significant advantage of this formation lies in the added freedom of movement and unimpeded vision gained by both instructor and student.

BEGINNERS' BASIC COURSE

MONDAY	WEDNESDAY	FRIDAY
First Week		
Explain:	Demonstrate:	Opening calisthenics
Preface	Vital areas	
History	Natural weapons	Review
Development	Kiai	Rising block
Training hall	Calisthenics	Downward block
Rules of conduct	Miscellaneous notes	Close punch
Formalities	Stance: open-leg, forward	Vertical punch
Grading	Balance	Straight punch
	Slide-step	
		Closing calisthenics
Second Week		
Opening calisthenics	Opening calisthenics	Opening calisthenics
Review	Review	Review
Outward block	Front kick	Lunge-punch preparation
Inward block	Close-leg stance	Lunge punch
Reverse-punch	Forward stance	Lunge-punch development
preparation	Knife-hand block	Block and slide-step
Reverse punch	Cross-arm block	Front kick
Closing calisthenics	Closing calisthenics	Closing calisthenics
Third Week		
Opening calisthenics	Opening calisthenics	Opening calisthenics
Review	Review	Review
Combination blocking	Lunge-punch variation	Demonstrate use of:
and hand attacks	Rising punch	punching board
Front-thrust kick	Hook punch	heavy punching bag
Side-thrust kick from:	Side-thrust kick	Sparring: five times
open-leg stance,		Form: Heian 1
forward stance	Closing calisthenics	Demonstrate each individual
		technique
Closing calisthenics		Emphasize tempo
		Instruct in progression of
		above form
		Closing calisthenics

Fourth Week

MONDAY	WEDNESDAY	FRIDAY
Opening calisthenics	Opening calisthenics	Opening calisthenics
Review	Review	Review
Block and slide-step	Block and slide-step	Block and slide-step
Reverse punch	Reverse punch	Reverse punch
Lunge-punch development	Lunge-punch development	Lunge-punch development
Punching combinations	Punching combinations	Punching combinations
Combination blocking and hand attacks	Combination blocking and hand attacks	Combination blocking and hand attacks
Front kick	Front kick	Front kick
Side-thrust kick	Side-thrust kick	Side-thrust kick
Sparring: five times	Sparring: five times	Sparring: five times
Form: Heian 1	Form: Heian 1	Form: Heian 1
Closing calisthenics	Closing calisthenics	Closing calisthenics

At this time the class should pause to reflect and evaluate their karate experience. The instructor should stress rules of conduct and formalities and carefully point out and note any potentially serious character flaws during private discussion with the affected student. It should also be emphasized at this point that not only many thousands of repetitions of the past month's activities lie ahead on the road to the coveted black belt but that much more is to be learned and similarly practiced.

The following basic-course outlines, both intermediate and advanced, do not pretend to be as inclusive as the beginners' course. They are merely guidelines within which satisfactory programs can be improvised. The techniques presented, however, are essential and are considered worthy of special stress during whatever month is indicated.

INTERMEDIATE BASIC COURSE
For White-belt Students in Grade 8 through Grade 4

First Month

Opening calisthenics

BASIC TRAINING
Review
Blocking   Emphasize:
 Rising   Slide-stepping with hips low and tucked forward,
 Outward   buttocks tensed
 Inward   Keeping lower abdominal and latissimus dorsi tensed
Hand attacks   Keeping elbows close to the body
 Bottom-fist strike

FORMS
Review   Emphasize the correct: Demonstrate:
         Attitude; breathing; stance; Each individual technique:
Heian 2   balance; kiai   tempo; power fluctuation

(First month cont'd)

SPARRING
Five-time attack, upper level

Emphasize:
 Study opponent's eyes
 Attack smoothly with one unbroken movement and a single
  steady exhalation of breath
 Perform correct block efficiently

SPECIAL EXERCISES
Punching speed

Closing calisthenics

Second Month

Opening calisthenics

BASIC TRAINING
Review

Blocking
 Rising
 Knife-hand
 Outward
 Inward
Hand attacks
 Lunge punch

Emphasize:
 Perform each technique precisely, step by step
 Constantly correct stance to insure equilibrium
 Utilize strong positive hip movements

FORMS
Review

Heian 3

Emphasize the correct:
 Attitude; breathing; stance;
 balance; kiai

Demonstrate:
 Each individual technique:
 tempo; power fluctuation

SPARRING

Five-time attack, upper level

Emphasize:
 Correct attitude
 Counterattack control

SPECIAL EXERCISES
Reaction speed

Closing calisthenics

Third Month

Opening Calisthenics

BASIC TRAINING
 Review
 Hand attacks
  Reverse punch
  Bottom-fist strike
  Knife-hand strike
 Combination: blocking and hand attacks
  Inward block—reverse punch
  Outward block—reverse punch
  Downward block—reverse punch
  Knife-hand strike—reverse punch
 Shifting
  Back stance; forward stance; recover

Emphasize:
 Speed; power;
 shoulders relaxed;
 low, strong stance

FORMS
  Review
  Heian 4

SPARRING

  Five-time attack, upper level

Emphasize the correct:
  Attitude; breathing;
  stance; balance; kiai

Demonstrate:
  Each individual technique:
  tempo; power fluctuation

Emphasize:
  Correct distance between opponents;
  tempo; coordinated breathing and body movement

SPECIAL EXERCISES
  Endurance

Closing Calisthenics

Fourth Month

Opening Calisthenics

BASIC TRAINING
  Review
  Hand attack
    Lunge punch; reverse punch
  Blocking
    All blocks
  Foot attacks
    Front kick; side-thrust kick

Emphasize:
  Precise application of techniques

FORMS
  Review
  Heian 5

Emphasize the correct:
  Attitude; breathing;
  stance; balance; kiai

Demonstrate:
  Each individual technique:
  tempo; power fluctuation

SPARRING
  1. *Attacker:* Delivers lunge punch, lower level
     Defender: Executes downward block;
     reverse punch, lower level

Emphasize:
  Low stance; control; distance; form

  2. *Attacker:* Delivers lunge punch, upper level
     Defender: Executes inward or outward block; reverse punch, lower level
  3. Repeat with defender substituting the following where applicable:
       Knife-hand block; spear-hand attack, lower level
       Rising block; reverse punch, lower level
       Knife-hand block; reverse punch, lower level
       Inward block; bottom-fist strike, upper level (same hand as used in
       block); reverse punch, lower level
  4. Five-time attack, middle level; downward block

SPECIAL EXERCISES
  Punching power

Closing Calisthenics

Fifth Month

Opening Calisthenics

BASIC TRAINING
  Review
  Blocking
    All blocks
  Foot attacks
    Front kick—side-thrust kick;
    round kick
  Hand attacks
    Lunge punch; reverse punch

Emphasize:
  Technique
  Balance
  Breathing
  Tension

(Fifth month cont'd)

FORMS
    Review
    Tekki 1

SPARRING
    Five-time attack, lower level

SPECIAL EXERCISES
    Abdomen

Closing Calisthenics

Emphasize the correct:
    Attitude; breathing;
    stance; balance; kiai

Emphasize:
    Proper timing

Demonstrate:
    Each individual technique:
    hand thrusting forward;
    tempo; power fluctuation

End of Fifth Month: EXAMINATION AND CRITIQUE

At this point a little extra time given to critical analysis of individual students (in group or private conference) will reap rewards. The student should be alerted to any salient weaknesses; special self-help exercises can then be suggested to remedy any such shortcomings. Along these lines, if it is possible to take movies, they will prove highly beneficial in pinpointing for the student himself those areas requiring special attention.

Sixth Month

Opening Calisthenics

BASIC TRAINING
    Review
    Blocking
        Outward block—reverse punch
        Knife-hand block; spear-hand attack; reverse punch
    Stance
        Straddle-leg

Emphasize:
    Keep elbows close to sides;
    speed; power

Emphasize:
    Knees tensed outward

FORMS
    Review
    Tekki 2

Emphasize the correct:
    Attitude; breathing;
    stance; balance; kiai

Demonstrate:
    Each individual technique:
    tempo; power fluctuation

SPARRING
    Five-time attack, upper level

Emphasize:
    Rising block; bottom-fist
    counterattack

SPECIAL EXERCISES
    Legs

Closing Calisthenics

Seventh Month

Opening Calisthenics

BASIC TRAINING
    Review
    Hand attacks
        Reverse punch; lunge punch
    Foot attacks
        Front kick; side-thrust kick

Emphasize:
    Speed of retracting hand; shoulders relaxed;
    swift initial movement of foot to knee and snap
    back to knee after kick

FORMS
Review
Tekki 3

Emphasize the correct:
Attitude; breathing;
stance; balance; kiai

Demonstrate:
Each individual technique:
tempo; power fluctuation

SPARRING
Three-time attack, upper level

Emphasize:
Correct breathing

POWERFUL PUNCH DEVELOPMENT
Basic punching exercises

Closing Calisthenics

Eighth Month

Opening Calisthenics

BASIC TRAINING
Review
Stances (various)

Emphasize:
Balance; weight distribution—in place, moving
forward, moving backward

FORMS
Review

Emphasize:
Outside practice of forms[1]

SPARRING
Three-time attack, upper level

Emphasize:
Blocking power; attacking precision

POWERFUL PUNCH DEVELOPMENT
Intermediate punching exercise

Closing Calisthenics

Ninth Month

Opening Calisthenics

BASIC TRAINING
Review
Blocking
Rising, inward, outward,
downward, and knife-hand blocks
Stance
Forward; back; straddle-leg
Hand attacks
Reverse punch; lunge punch
Foot attacks
Front, side-thrust, side-snap, and round kicks

Emphasize:
Body tension; low stance;
continuous breathing

FORMS
Review

Emphasize:
The practice of forms outside the class
session

SPARRING
Three-time attack, upper level

Emphasize:
Peripheral vision; controlled direction of gaze

POWERFUL PUNCH DEVELOPMENT
Advanced punching exercise

Closing Calisthenics

[1] Referring to individual practice in addition to the regular class session.

Tenth Month

Opening Calisthenics

BASIC TRAINING
    Review
    Foot attacks
      Front, side-snap, side-thrust,
      and round kicks

Emphasize:
    Elevation of kicks;
    speed of retracting foot

FORMS
    Review

Emphasize:
    The practice of forms outside the class session

SPARRING
    Three-time attack, lower level

Emphasize:
    Slide-stepping backward on the diagonal

SPECIAL EXERCISES
    Leg stretching

Closing Calisthenics

Eleventh Month

Opening Calisthenics

BASIC TRAINING
    Review
    Stance and hand attacks
      Straddle-leg stance
      Straddle-leg stance—alternate
      reverse punches
      Straddle-leg stance—multiple
      reverse punches in sets of two
      through five inclusive

Emphasize:
    Straddle-leg stance,
    held rigidly for 15 minutes

FORMS
    Review

Emphasize:
    The practice of forms outside the class
    session

SPARRING
    Three-time attack, lower level

Emphasize:
    Correct form in attacks, blocks,
    counterattacks; power; speed

SPECIAL EXERCISES
    Blocking speed and distance control

Closing Calisthenics

End of Eleventh Month: EXAMINATION AND CRITIQUE

Twelfth Month

Opening Calisthenics

BASIC TRAINING
    Review
    Hand attacks
      Punching board
    Foot attacks
      Front, side-snap, side-thrust,
      and round kicks

Emphasize:
    Sustained dynamic workout

FORMS
    Review
    Heian 1–5

Emphasize:
    The practice of forms outside the class session

SPARRING
Three-time attack, lower level;
block and counterattack

Emphasize:
Effective blocking and strong counterattack

SPECIAL EXERCISES
Muscle toners

Closing Calisthenics

Thirteenth Month

Opening Calisthenics

BASIC TRAINING
Review
Hand attacks
Reverse punch
Foot attacks
Side-thrust kick

Emphasize:
Speed; power; body tension; kiai;
extended kicking leg locked at knee;
rotate hip to support kicking leg

FORMS
Review
Tekki 1–3

Emphasize:
The practice of forms outside the class session

SPARRING
Attacker: Basic one-time attack, lower level
Basic one-time attack, upper level
Defender: Block and counterattack

Emphasize:
Realistic feeling

SPECIAL EXERCISES
Blocking power

Closing Calisthenics

Fourteenth Month

Opening Calisthenics

BASIC TRAINING
Review
Hand attacks
Back fist; bottom fist strike
Foot Attacks
Side-snap; round kick

Emphasize:
Low stance; speed; power;
stable balance on supporting leg

FORMS
Review
All Heian and Tekki

Emphasize:
The practice of forms outside the class session

SPARRING
Three-time attack, upper level

Emphasize:
Strong stance, attack, and block

SPECIAL EXERCISES
Kicking development exercises

Closing Calisthenics

Fifteenth Month

Opening Calisthenics

BASIC TRAINING
Review

(Fifteenth month cont'd)
   Blocking
      Downward, rising, inward,
      outward, knife-hand blocks

Emphasize:
   Low, strong stance; hips tucked firmly forward

FORMS
   Review all Heian and Tekki

Emphasize:
    The practice of forms outside the class session

SPARRING
   Basic one-time attack

Emphasize:
    Timing; strong stance

SPECIAL EXERCISES
   Leg stretching

Closing Calisthenics

Sixteenth Month

Opening Calisthenics

BASIC TRAINING
   Review
   Combination block and hand attacks
      Downward block—reverse punch,
         lower level
      Inward block—knife-hand strike
         (using same hand), upper level; reverse punch, lower level
      Knife-hand block, lower level; spear-hand attack, lower level
      Rising block—reverse punch, lower level
      Knife-hand block—reverse punch, lower level
      Inward block—bottom-fist strike (using same hand), upper level;
         reverse punch, lower level

Emphasize:
   Low stance; correct form; power; speed

FORMS
   Review
   Heian 1

Emphasize the correct:
   Attitude; breathing;
   stance; balance; kiai

Demonstrate:
   Each individual technique:
   tempo; power fluctuation

SPARRING
   Three-time attack, lower level

Emphasize:
   Maximum effort; good form

SPECIAL EXERCISES
   Wrist and forearm

Closing Calisthenics

End of Sixteenth Month: EXAMINATION AND CRITIQUE

Seventeenth Month

Opening calisthenics

BASIC TRAINING
   Review
   Continuous hand attacks
   Continuous foot attacks
   Combination of continuous hand and foot attacks

Emphasize:
   A smooth powerful style;
   precision of form

FORMS
   Review
   Heian 2

Emphasize the correct:
   Attitude; breathing;
   stance; balance; kiai

Demonstrate:
   Each individual technique:
   tempo; power fluctuation

SPARRING
Three-time attack, upper level

Emphasize:
Forward speed; keeping low;
outward block; reverse punch counterattack

SPECIAL EXERCISES
Roadwork

Closing Calisthenics

ADVANCED BASIC COURSE
For Students in Brown-Belt Grade

First Month

Opening Calisthenics

BASIC TRAINING
Review
Hand attacks
Lunge punch

Emphasize:
Speed of slide-step;
knees tensed outward

FORMS
Review
Bassai

Emphasize the correct:
Attitude; breathing;
stance; balance; kiai

Demonstrate:
Each individual technique:
tempo; power fluctuation

SPARRING
Attacker: Basic one-time attack, lower level
Basic one-time attack, upper level
Defender: Block and counterattack

Emphasize:
Precise form throughout

SPECIAL EXERCISES
Neck

Closing Calisthenics

Second Month

Opening Calisthenics

BASIC TRAINING
Review
Hand attacks
Lunge punch, jumping in
Back-fist strike, jumping in

Emphasize:
Extended range of attack;
work on balance and precise stance

FORMS
Review
Kanku

Emphasize the correct:
Attitude; breathing;
stance; balance; kiai

Demonstrate:
Each individual technique:
tempo; power fluctuation

SPARRING
Attacker: Basic one-time attack, lower level
Basic one-time attack, upper level
Defender: Block and counterattack

Emphasize:
Concentration;
eye and breath control

SPECIAL EXERCISES
Wrist and forearm

Closing Calisthenics

Third Month

Opening Calisthenics

BASIC TRAINING
  Review
  Hand attacks
    Reverse punch—lower level,   Emphasize:
      upper level   A fully completed block
    Lunge punch—lower level,   before commencing
      upper level   counterattack
  Block and Counterattack
    Downward block—reverse punch, lower level
    Outward block—reverse punch, lower level
    Inward block—reverse punch, lower level
    Knife-hand block—spear-hand attack, lower level
    Rising block—reverse punch, lower level
    Inward block—bottom fist strike; reverse punch, lower level

FORMS
  Review   Emphasize: Demonstrate:
  Jitte   Attitude; breathing;   Each individual technique:
                       stance; balance; kiai   tempo; power fluctuation

SPARRING
  Semifree one-time attack   Emphasize:
                         Strong demeanor and
SPECIAL EXERCISES   vigorous counterattack
  Free-style sparring   even when block fails

Closing Calisthenics

Fourth Month

Opening Calisthenics

BASIC TRAINING
  Review
  Foot attacks   Emphasize:
  Side-thrust, side-snap, round,   Maintainance of low stance
    continuous, and combination kicks during multiple kicks

FORMS
  Review   Emphasize: Demonstrate:
  Ganka-ku   Attitude; breathing;   Each individual technique:
                       stance; balance; kiai   tempo; power fluctuation

SPARRING
  Semifree one-time attack   Emphasize:
                         Proper timing; swift,
SPECIAL EXERCISES   powerful attacks
  Free-style sparring

Closing Calisthenics

Fifth Month

Opening Calisthenics

BASIC TRAINING
  Review
  Foot attacks   Emphasize:
    Front, round, and side-thrust kicks Using knee as fulcrum; hips thrust
                         forward solidly supporting the kicking leg

FORMS
Review
Empi

Emphasize:
Attitude; breathing;
stance; balance; kiai

Demonstrate:
Each individual technique:
tempo; power fluctuation

SPARRING
Attacker: Semifree one-time attack
Defender: Downward block—front kick
Inward block—reverse punch

Emphasize:
Counterattack: speed,
power, low stance

SPECIAL EXERCISES
Free-style sparring

Closing Calisthenics

Sixth Month

Opening Calisthenics

BASIC TRAINING
Review
Stance and slide-step
Body, hip control; balance

Emphasize:
Feeling of projection of
attack through rather than
to the opponent

FORMS
Review
Jion

Emphasize:
Attitude; breathing;
stance; balance; kiai

Demonstrate:
Each individual technique:
tempo; power fluctuation

SPARRING
Semifree one-time attack

Emphasize:
Dynamism of technique

SPECIAL EXERCISES
Free-style sparring

Closing Calisthenics

End of Sixth Month: EXAMINATION AND CRITIQUE

Seventh Month

Opening Calisthenics

BASIC TRAINING
Review
Closing the distance
lunge punch

Emphasize:
Use of rear leg to catapult
hips forward

FORMS
Review
Han-getsu

Emphasize:
Attitude; breathing;
stance; balance; kiai

Demonstrate:
Each individual technique:
tempo; power fluctuation

SPARRING
Semifree one-time attack

Emphasize:
Maintainance of correct distance
between opponents

SPECIAL EXERCISES
Free-style sparring

Closing Calisthenics

Eighth Month

Opening Calisthenics

BASIC TRAINING
  Review
  Hand attacks
    Multiple punching
  Foot attacks
    Combination kick: front kick,
    side-thrust kick

Emphasize:
  Consistently high level of power

FORMS
  Review

Emphasize:
  The practice of forms outside the class session

SPARRING
  Holding techniques; methods of
    escape and counterattack
  Special techniques for close combat

Emphasize:
  Reaction speed

SPECIAL EXERCISES
  Free-style sparring

Closing Calisthenics

Ninth Month

Opening Calisthenics

BASIC TRAINING
  Review
  Foot attacks
    Basic; combination

Emphasize:
  Front kick—front kick
  Front kick—side-thrust kick
  Front kick—round kick

FORMS
  Review

Emphasize:
  Concentrate upon each individual technique
  within a form

SPARRING
  Three-time attack
  Free one-time attack

SPECIAL EXERCISES
  Free-style sparring

Emphasize:
  Study opponent; attack at most advantageous
  moment

Closing Calisthenics

Tenth Month

Opening Calisthenics

BASIC TRAINING
  Review
  Hand attacks
    Reverse punch
    Multiple punching—forward
      stance, straddle-leg stance

Emphasize:
  Breath control; speed;
  power

FORMS
  Review

Emphasize:
  Concentrate upon each individual technique
  within a form

SPARRING
    Free one-time attack

Emphasize:
    Study opponent and attack at the most
    advantageous moment

SPECIAL EXERCISES
    Free-style sparring

Closing Calisthenics

Eleventh Month

Opening Calisthenics

BASIC TRAINING
    Review
    Hand attacks
        Reverse punch; lunge punch
    Foot attacks
        Front kick—side-thrust kick

Emphasize:
    Basic stance; slide-step

FORMS
    Review

Emphasize:
    Concentrate upon each individual technique
    within a form

SPARRING
    Basic one-time attack, inward block,
        assuming straddle-leg stance

Emphasize:
    Slide-shift forward and with a strong hip
    swiveling motion adopt the straddle-leg stance

SPECIAL EXERCISES
    Free-style sparring

Closing Calisthenics

Twelfth Month

Opening Calisthenics

BASIC TRAINING
    Review
    Foot attacks
        Various combinations

Emphasize:
    "Helpful Hints"

FORMS
    Review

Emphasize:
    Concentrate upon each individual technique
    within a form

SPARRING
    Continuous attacks: foot, hand
        combinations
    Blocking continuous attacks

Emphasize:
    Consistent low stance;
    Speed; power

SPECIAL EXERCISES
    Free-style sparring

Closing Calisthenics

End of Twelfth Month: EXAMINATION AND CRITIQUE

Thirteenth Month

Opening Calisthenics

(Thirteenth month cont'd)
BASIC TRAINING
    Review
    Combination hand and foot attacks
        Lunge punch—front kick
        Front kick—lunge punch
        Reverse punch—front kick
        Front kick—reverse punch

Emphasize:
    Low stance; speed; power

FORMS
    Review

Emphasize:
    Concentrate upon each individual technique
    within a form

SPARRING
    Free style

Emphasize:
    Controlled attack and counterattack

EXERCISES
    Punching, kicking, blocking

Closing Calisthenics

Fourteenth Month

Opening Calisthenics

BASIC TRAINING
    Review
    Combination foot attacks
        Front kick—side-thrust kick
        Front kick—round kick
        Front kick—rear kick

Emphasize:
    Flexible kicking knee;
    strong supporting leg

FORMS
    Review

Emphasize:
    Visualize actual opponents

SPARRING
    Free style

Emphasize:
    Control; feeling of realism; calmness

EXERCISES
    Punching, kicking, blocking

Closing Calisthenics

Fifteenth Month

Opening Calisthenics

BASIC TRAINING
    Review
    Open-leg stance
      Attacker: a) Right slide-steps forward delivering a
                  right reverse punch, lower level
              b) Right slide-steps forward delivering a
                   right reverse punch, upper level
      Defender: Right or left slide-steps backward executing
                the appropriate block and counterattack
    Forward stance
      Attacker: Substituting a lunge punch, repeat open-leg
                stance exercise above
    Open-leg stance
      Defender: Repeat open-leg stance exercise above

Emphasize:
    Gauging correct moment
    for attack[1]

    [1] Within each student there is a rhythmical rise and fall in the level of power. The attacker must gauge the precise moment when his opponent is weakest and launch his attack swiftly, precisely then.

FORMS
  Review
  Heian 1

Emphasize:
  Each individual technique

SPARRING
  Basic one-time attack
  Free style

Emphasize:
  Controlled attack and counterattack

SPECIAL EXERCISES
  Endurance

Closing Calisthenics

Sixteenth Month

Opening Calisthenics

BASIC TRAINING
  Review
  Combinations of continuous hand
    and foot attacks

Emphasize:
  Each attack combination to be performed
  during a single controlled exhalation of air

FORMS
  Review

Emphasize:
  Each student should stress his favorite form
  (under instructor's guidance and on his own)

SPARRING
  Free-style one-time attack

Emphasize:
  A penetrating attack with the feeling of
  "going through" opponent

  Free style

Emphasize:
  Control; avoidance of contact

CREATING AN OPENING

Closing Calisthenics

Seventeenth Month

Opening Calisthenics

BASIC TRAINING
  Review
  Combinations of continuous hand
    and foot attacks

Emphasize:
  A consistent level of power

FORMS
  Review
  Heian 2
  Tekki 1

Emphasize:
  Class performance in unison

SPARRING
  Basic one-time attack
  Free style

Emphasize:
  Clear, calm mind;
  etiquette and a strong attitude

SPECIAL EXERCISES
  Leg stretching; blocking power

Closing Calisthenics

■ Summer Training Schedule

Requirements for Participation:
1. Participants should be conditioned by a minimum of six months prior training.[1]
2. Participants should know all Heian and Tekki forms, plus the independent forms indicated in the schedule.[2]
3. Participants should have either personal or group medical insurance plans.

First day

5:45 A.M.	Rise Drink supplement of honey-lemon juice
6:00–8:00 A.M.	Run 2 miles Basic training
8:00–9:00 A.M.	Punching board
9:00–9:45 A.M.	Breakfast
10:00 A.M.–2:00 P.M.	Rest—lunch—rest

2:00–4:00 P.M.	Basic training:
	  Heian 1—5 times
	  Heian 2—5 times
	  Heian 3—5 times
	  Heian 4—5 times
	  Heian 5—5 times
	  Tekki 1—5 times
	  Sambon kumite—repeat 3 times[3]

4:00–6:00 P.M.	Rest
6:15–7:00 P.M.	Dinner
7:00–8:00 P.M.	Group discussion
8:15 P.M.–5:45 A.M.	Sleep

[1] Students should prepare themselves to perform such basic feats as are described in the schedule.

[2] A separate group of those who have not learned the independent forms will occupy themselves with the practice of known forms.

Second Day

5:45 A.M.	Rise Drink supplement of honey-lemon juice
6:00–9:00 A.M.	Run 2 miles Basic training Hold straddle-leg stance 1 hour
9:00–9:45 A.M.	Breakfast
10:00 A.M.–2:00 P.M.	Rest—lunch—rest
2:00–4:00 P.M.	Basic training Bassai—30 times Kihon ippon kumite—repeat 3 times[3]
4:00–6:00 P.M.	Rest
6:15–7:00 P.M.	Dinner
7:00–8:00 P.M.	Group discussion
8:15 P.M.–5:45 A.M.	Sleep

Third Day

5:45 A.M.	Rise Drink supplement of honey-lemon juice
6:00–8:00 A.M.	Run 2 miles Basic training Hold back stance 30 minutes on left and then right side
8:00–9:00 A.M.	Punching board
9:00–9:45 A.M.	Breakfast
10:00 A.M.–2:00 P.M.	Rest—lunch—rest
2:00–4:00 P.M.	Basic training Kanku—30 times Jiyu ippon kumite—repeat 3 times[3]
4:00–6:00 P.M.	Rest
6:15–7:00 P.M.	Dinner
7:00–8:00 P.M.	Lecture by instructor
8:00–8:45 P.M.	Group discussion
9:00–11:45 P.M.	Sleep
12:00–1:00 A.M.	Night training: sanbon kumite and forms
1:15–8:45 A.M.	Sleep

[3] Partners are then changed until each individual has faced every other student.

Fourth Day

8:45 A.M.	Rise
9:00–9:45 A.M.	Breakfast
9:45–12:00 P.M.	Free time
12:00–3:00 P.M.	Run 2 miles Heian 1—5 times Heian 2—5 times Heian 3—5 times Heian 4—5 times Heian 5—5 times Tekki 1—5 times Bassai—10 times Kanku—10 times Jiyu kumite—repeat 3 times[3]
3:00–4:00 P.M.	Rest
4:00–6:00 P.M.	Dinner party celebrating end of special summer training

There should be no rest breaks during actual training sessions except for the normal pause between exercises. When the special summer training schedule is limited to a minimum of three days, then a total of eight workouts will be performed.

When performing fifty continuous repetitions of forms students should strive to execute each succeeding one with more precision than the last. Their attitude should be that the forty-ninth repetition is only the halfway mark.

In all humility each student's attitude while sparring must be one of neither inferiority nor superiority to his opponent, regardless of rank.

To the uninformed, summer training appears to be simply a crash program designed to build the student's physical endurance and raise his technical level. Actually the paramount reason for this undertaking is to provide for those who persevere a step forward toward the forging of an indomitable will.

■ PART 2
TRAINING

▪ Vital Areas and Natural Weapons

Visually divide the opponent's anatomy as follows: draw an imaginary vertical line straight down the middle of his body and another horizontally around the body crossing the elbows. An attack along either the vertical or horizontal line will strike many vulnerable points, as indicated in the following:

DIRECTION	VULNERABLE POINTS
Vertical *(below left)*	Nose, chin, throat, sternum, solar plexus, abdomen, groin; base of skull, spinal column, and coccyx
Horizontal *(below right)*	Short ribs, solar plexus, liver, spine and kidneys

 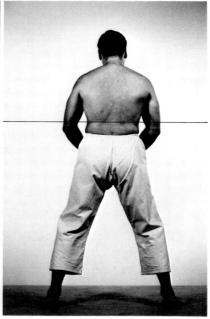

Due to the potential for damage inherent in these techniques those marked with an asterisk (*) are not to be used except against an assailant with deadly intent. The student must remember that each of the techniques, in itself, can seriously injure a fellow student; therefore, extreme caution should be exercised in their use.

The more vulnerable and unprotected areas of the body (eyes, throat, solar plexus, etc.) indicate the use of penetrating effects created by the index finger, knuckle-fist, spear-hand, and similar natural weapons; on the other hand, the fore-fist, back-fist, forearm, knee, and like natural weapons will be more successfully used against areas reinforced by bone and muscle.

WEAPON USED	AREA ATTACKED	COMMENT
1. Index finger*	Eyes	*Never* to be used. Practice only with an imaginary opponent
2. Pair middle with index finger; then ring with little finger, separating pairs*	Eyes	*Never* to be used. Practice only with an imaginary opponent
3. Separate index and ring fingers*	Eyes	*Never* to be used. Practice only with an imaginary opponent
4. Thumbs*	Eyes	*Never* to be used. Practice only with an imaginary opponent
5. Knuckle Fist*	Throat	Avoid usage during free-style sparring
6. Index-knuckle fist*	Eye	Avoid usage during free-style sparring
7. Middle-knuckle fist*	Temple	Avoid usage during free-style sparring
8. Fore-fist	Any part of the anatomy, especially the face, solar plexus, ribs, and lower abdomen	Do not bend the wrist. Striking surface consists of the index and middle fingers
9. Back-fist	Any part of the anatomy, especially the face, solar plexus, ribs, and lower abdomen	Best used when attacking to the side
10. Bottom-fist	Any part of the anatomy, especially the face, solar plexus, ribs, and lower abdomen	Best used when attacking downward or to the side Presents little danger of injury to the hand
11. Knife-hand	Temple, neck, and collarbone	In positions 11, 12, and 13, the middle finger is retracted so that the tips of the index, middle, and ring fingers are squared
12. Ridge-hand	Temple and face	
13. Spear-hand	Eyes, throat, ribs, and solar plexus	*Never* to be used. Substitute the palm-heel during sparring. Practice only with an imaginary opponent
14. Palm-heel	Face, ribs, and solar plexus	Can also be used as a block

WEAPON USED	AREA ATTACKED	COMMENT
15. Elbow	Very effective against any part of the anatomy	Flex the elbow completely. Provides exceptional concentration of power
16. Forearm	Very effective against any part of the anatomy	Flex the elbow halfway. An extremely powerful attack
17. Forehead*	Face and sternum	Avoid usage during free-style sparring
18. Knee	Any part of the anatomy, especially the face, solar plexus, and lower abdomen	An extremely powerful attack. Most effective when at close quarters
19. Ball of foot	Any part of the anatomy, especially the solar plexus, lower abdomen, groin, and kneecap	Used in front and round kicks. Flex the toes strongly upward.
20. Foot-edge	Any part of the anatomy, especially the solar plexus, ribs, lower abdomen, and kneecap	Used in side-thrust, side-snap, and stamping kicks. Flex the toes strongly upward

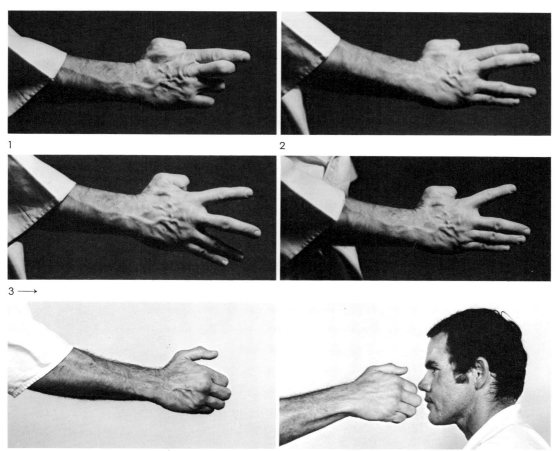

1

2

3 $\longrightarrow$

4 $\longrightarrow$

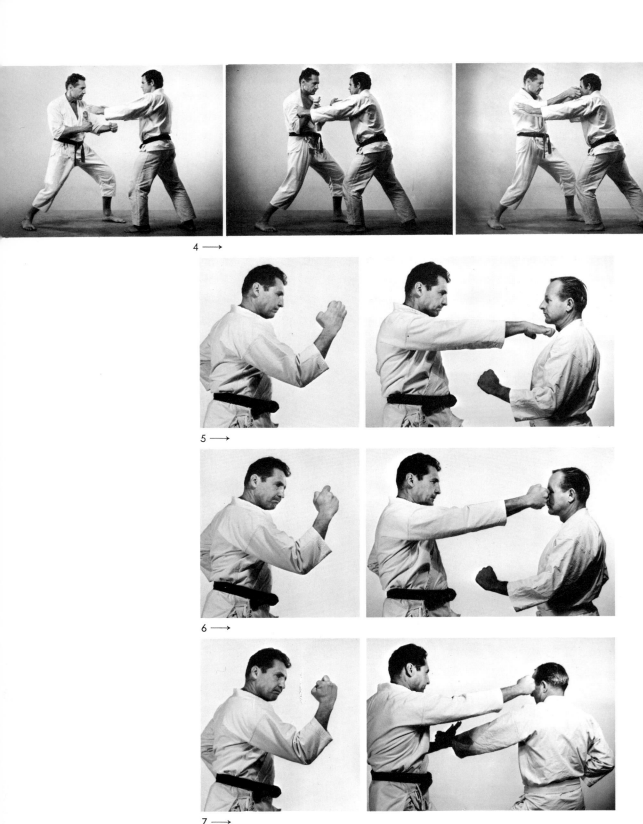

4 ⟶

5 ⟶

6 ⟶

7 ⟶

8

9

10

11

12

13

14

15

16

17

18

19

20

◼ The Kiai

This vocal expulsion of air should be coordinated with both attack and defense techniques. The elementary understanding of the physical and psychological effects of the kiai is as follows:

1. Its piercing shriek can destroy an opponent's composure, creating momentary vulnerability. However, its value is limited.[1]
2. The portion of air forced downward tightens the lower abdominal muscles. This produces additional power when required.
3. If an attack to the midsection is sustained, the tense condition of the lower abdominal region due to the kiai will minimize any damaging effect.

For the advanced student there is a more profound significance associated with the kiai. Imagine, if you will, that in the act of forcing air into the lower abdomen the student is also compressing his entire physical and mental being downward into a smaller and smaller area until this inevitably bursts outward with explosive force. This dynamic power, rather than dissipating itself, is concentrated by being channeled through the attacking arm or leg. The kiai should be coordinated precisely with the technique it accompanies.

---

[1] The advanced student will utilize a different strategy. His kiai, emanating from the depths of the abdomen, will sound like a fierce brief grunt much lower pitched. It will enable him to employ that total power which the novice unwittingly dissipates in order to produce the loudest kiai.

■ Body Positions

1. Unless otherwise indicated, when the forward stance is assumed, the left foot is placed to the front. The right arm and leg are then in a position to deliver the most powerful attack. This does not preclude an attack with the left hand or foot, which will of course be weaker. When left forward stance is specified the right foot will then be placed to the front.
2. Unless otherwise indicated, begin all exercises in forward stance.
3. To eliminate unnecessary repetition, it should be understood that, unless otherwise indicated, in all blocking and attacking techniques using either hand the opposite hand will be quickly withdrawn to a position above the corresponding hip.
4. The terms "upper level" and "lower level" refer to head and midsection, respectively.
5. Unless otherwise indicated, all hand attacks will be upper level.
6. Unless otherwise indicated, all foot and hand attacks will be forward.[1]
7. Unless otherwise indicated, all forward-foot attacks will terminate with the kicking foot being lowered forward to the floor.
8. Practice all techniques by alternating left and right sides.
9. Unless otherwise indicated, when the end of the training hall has been reached, all blocking or attacking techniques are repeated while moving backward.
10. In all exercises performed with a partner, when the attacker has completed specified techniques, the roles are reversed; that is, defender then becomes attacker. This pattern should be repeated until each student has performed each role at least three times. Partners are then changed until each individual has faced every other student.

NOTE: Special material throughout the book (indicated by NOTE) is not intended to be read once and put aside. It should serve as a constant guide toward the improvement of technique. The student should formulate a system of review whereby he may check his current level of performance against the standards gleaned from the notes.

[1] The rear kick is the sole exception.

■ Calisthenics

Complete abstinence from food for a period of two hours preceding a workout is necessary to prevent unpleasant aftereffects. The consumption of liquids during the workout can also have adverse consequences and is likewise frowned upon.

To insure against ligament or muscular strain it is mandatory to commence each training session with a warm-up. A careless disregard of this principle could result in an injury that would cause the student to remain inactive for some time. It should be noted that the opening calisthenics are designed to limber up the entire body.

One's personal objective should be a loose, supple, and agile physique; therefore, any activity that produces muscular tension must be followed by a loosening-up exercise.

When performing calisthenics it is important to keep in mind that we do not limit our movements simply to the point to which we believe we are capable; rather, we should extend the body beyond its limit in each exercise to realize the full benefit of that particular drill. With this approach it will be noted that resistance soon becomes less intense, enabling us to stretch our limbs farther than we had previously thought possible. The result will be more return for less effort, thus providing the student with greater physical and mental economy. Experience has shown that this benefit plus that of increased self-reliance can be the reward of the serious karate student under proper supervision, usually within six months of training.

OPENING CALISTHENICS

Open-Leg Stance: stand erect with feet a shoulder's width apart and parallel, knees slightly bent, and toes pointed forward. Clench fists in front of lower abdomen.
1. Neck Limbering
   (a) Turn head from left to right.
   (b) Raise and then lower head.
   (c) Twist head in a circle; then reverse direction.
   (d) Tip head straight sideways down toward one shoulder, then the other.

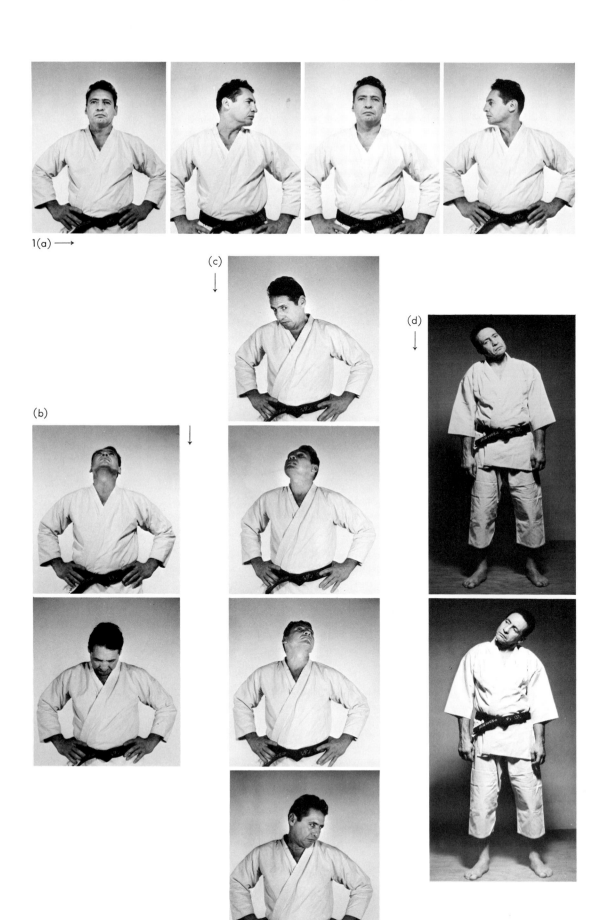

1(a) ⟶

(b)

(c)

(d)

2 ⟶

3 ⟶

4

2. Relax while swiftly rotating arms in a circular motion. Reverse direction and repeat.
3. Without moving feet twist the body from side to side.
4. Bend straight to one side slowly, then the other, reaching down as far as possible.
5. Bend forward and backward slowly as far as possible; then rotate body in a circular motion; then reverse direction.

5

6 ⟶

7 ⟶

8 ⟶

9 ⟶

6. Alternately swing legs to the front and then to the sides.
7. Standing on one leg, grasp other leg above ankle and, bending forward, pull the foot back as far as possible.
8. Alternately raise knees to chest without bending forward.
9. Alternately stretch legs out to the side, and with hand apply pressure downward at the knee.

10

11 →

12

13 →

10. Stand with feet wide apart, alternately twisting trunk to each side, applying pressure horizontally with hands at hips.
11. Side-straddle hop.
12. Relax entire body, loosely shaking wrists and ankles.
13. Student lies on floor on his back, completely relaxed. Partner, straddling supine student, grasps his belt with both hands and slowly lifts it, pulling the inert body up until student's head just grazes the floor.

14(a) $\longrightarrow$

14(b) $\longrightarrow$

14. (a) Breathing slowly through slightly opened mouth, inhale deeply, feeling as if you were filling the lower abdomen with air. Be sure to keep lower abdomen and buttocks firmly tensed. Concentrating on expelling all air, exhale in the same manner, relaxing completely.

(b) Sit on floor with feet spread apart and hands extended to the rear on floor. Inhale as in preceding exercise while raising body, and exhale while lowering body.

NOTE: Do not raise chest while inhaling. The instructor should test the state of tenseness of each student's lower abdomen and buttocks during inhalation. Be sure to relax the abdomen and buttocks while exhaling.

1

1(a)

1(b) ⟶

2

CLOSING CALISTHENICS

1. Students stand back to back with interlocked arms.
   (a) One student bends forward supporting partner's weight on his back, then gently rocks up and down before resuming original position.
   (b) Both students slide down into a sitting position keeping arms interlocked. One student alternately shifts feet backward, slowly forcing his upper body onto partner's back. His partner will allow himself to bend forward as far as he can before resisting.
2. Students sit facing each other with outstretched legs.
   One student places feet at ankles of partner's outstretched legs. Grasping each other's wrists, they rock to and fro, locking the knees and keeping buttocks on floor.

3(a)

3(b) —→

4

3. One student lies face down with partner standing on his thighs.
   (a) Partner slowly walks up and down back of thighs.
   (b) Grasping prone partner's ankles and facing in opposite direction, standing partner squats and pushes his legs downward on the outside, then inside.
4. Deep knee bend, raising heels. Knife-hand lightly strikes insides of thighs.
5. Breathing slowly through slightly opened mouth, inhale deeply, feeling as if you were filling the lower abdomen with air. Be sure to keep lower abdomen and buttocks firmly tensed. When lungs are half filled, push shoulders back and shift emphasis to upper torso, filling lungs completely. Concentrating on expelling all air, exhale with the same deliberate control, relaxing completely. Increasing the tempo, swing both arms straight outward to shoulder level, filling lungs completely; then bring arms down, simultaneously exhaling. Repeat sequence five times.
   NOTE: The closing calisthenics provide excellent stretching and massaging action. Use of these exercises will encourage cooperative attitudes.

■ Stance

1

2

1. Close-Leg Stance

Stand erect with feet together, toes pointed forward, allowing arms to hang at the side with hands relaxed.

2. Open-Leg Stance

Stand erect with feet a shoulder's width apart and parallel, knees slightly bent and toes pointed forward. Clench fists in front of lower abdomen.

NOTE: These are basic stances, ones from which the student can readily shift into any other stance.

3 ⟶

3. Forward Stance

From the open-leg stance slide left foot smoothly inward toward right foot (momentarily shifting most of the body weight to right foot) then outward in a forward arc to a position double shoulder's width apart to the front and rear. Both feet should be no wider than a shoulder's width apart to either side. The moving foot is slightly raised so it barely grazes the floor; toes are curled upward to avoid stubbing and to prevent the heel from rising. The supporting leg should push against the floor, propelling the body strongly forward. This movement will henceforth be referred to as a slide-step since the foot in motion remains in contact with the floor. At the termination of the slide-step the position in which the student now finds himself will be termed the forward stance.

NOTE: The slide-step is an important basic movement and must be thoroughly assimilated. The slide-step requires speed and proficiency coupled with positive equilibrium. It is basic to karate since it is utilized so frequently within various movements.

For a strong forward stance the following factors should be stressed:

(a) The lower abdomen and buttocks are firmly tensed.
   NOTE: This should be considered a requirement for the proper execution of every exercise.
(b) The body is carried erect with chest held high and shoulders in a relaxed state.
(c) The front foot points straight forward or slightly inward.
(d) With center of gravity considerably lowered the knee of the forward leg should be bent until it is directly over the toes.
(e) The weight distribution should be 60/40 with the greater stress falling on the front foot.

4

$\longrightarrow$

(f) The knee of the supporting rear foot, although firm, is not locked but slightly bent and bowed out with toes pointing outward at a forty-five-degree angle. Any greater angulation will merely weaken the stance by not utilizing fully the supporting strengths of heel and knee. In addition the rear foot is better aligned for a rapid forward step or kick. If the rear foot toes out at a right angle (a common error among beginners) or is in too direct an alignment with the front one or a combination of the two, a following front kick will be drawn off course to a right oblique. On the other hand if the feet are separated on the right and left by more than one shoulder's width the student will be too far off-balance in the performance of any forward movement of the rear leg since the supporting knee will tend to buckle.

(g) There should be very noticeable pressure on the outside edge of the foot. This should be coupled with a concerted gripping action by toes of both feet.

(h) The left arm is extended forward with elbow slightly bent and fist turned down. Right fist, facing up, should be withdrawn to a point just above right hip.

(i) A good indication of the proper stance is its feeling of stability.

(j) In executing the slide-step the hips are to be propelled forward while the driving force comes from the inner thighs and the supporting leg.

4. Half-Front-Facing Stance

From the open-leg stance, left slide-step forward into the forward stance, twisting only the trunk clockwise.

NOTE: This position is an important variation of the forward stance.

5 →

6 →

7 $\longrightarrow$

5. Straddle-Leg Stance

From the open-leg stance, right slide-step smoothly to the right in a straight line until both feet are double shoulder's width apart.

6. Back Stance

From the open-leg stance, half left slide-step forward or half left slide-step backward, simultaneously bowing right knee outward. Most of the body weight rests on rear leg and can be readily shifted forward when occasion demands. The student should be able to lift the forward leg off the floor without losing balance.

7. Cat Stance

From back stance, left slide-step back to a point just ahead and to the left of right foot. Force both knees slightly inward, resting body weight entirely on right leg and keeping body erect. In this stance as well the student should be able to lift the forward leg off the floor without losing balance.

NOTE: It is imperative that the student master 1 through 7 inclusive since a strong stance provides the foundation for everything that follows.

■ Balance

1 ⟶

2

3

1 ⟶

2 ⟶

(Open-Leg Stance) (See facing page.)
1. Jump clockwise one-fourth of a complete circle; land firmly upright in open-leg stance.
2. In the preceding manner progress to a jump comprising one-half of a circle.
3. Finally, leap into the air, twisting body in a full turn and land in original position.
4. Repeat this pattern, jumping in a counterclockwise direction.

(Left Forward Stance)
1. Leap straight ahead, landing on left foot, simultaneously pivoting clockwise and facing to the rear in left forward stance.
2. Leap straight ahead, simultaneously pivoting clockwise in mid-air, landing in left forward stance.
3. Repeat 1 and 2, pivoting counterclockwise.
4. Repeat 1–3 in right forward stance.

■ Slide-Step

1

2 ⟶

—A—

(Forward Stance)

1. Place both hands (palm down) on buttocks, forcing them ahead; alternating right and left slide-steps, move across training hall. Repeat moving backward, keeping both heels in contact with floor. The very first thing that should move is the front leg.

    NOTE: This will help correct the tendency to lean forward, a posture which seriously weakens the stance.

2. Alternate slide-steps across training hall; repeat moving backward.

3. Alternate slide-steps in various directions, confining action to small area.

4. Alternate right and left forward slide-steps; repeat moving backward.

5. Alternate right, left, and right forward slide-steps; repeat moving backward.

6. Gradually increase the number and tempo of slide-steps taken.

7. Repeat 4 and 5 moving about in alternate directions.

    NOTE: Remain low with lower abdomen and buttocks firmly tensed. Major emphasis of body weight should remain on front leg. However students should be able to lift the forward leg off the floor by rapidly shifting body weight to rear leg without impairing balance. Make certain, also, that each forward movement is accompanied by a shift forward of the leading knee. If this is not done, the body tends to rise and weaken the stance.

6 ⟶

7 ⟶

—B—

1. Half left slide-step forward; repeat with right foot. Half right slide-step backward; repeat with left foot.
2. Half right slide-step backward; repeat with left foot. Half left slide-step forward; repeat with right foot.
3. Half right slide-step backward, obliquely to the right rear; repeat with left foot. Half left slide-step forward along the same diagonal; repeat with right foot.
4. Half right slide-step backward to the left rear; repeat with left foot. Half left slide-step forward along the same diagonal; repeat with right foot.
5. Slide left foot backward to the left oblique, describing a semicircle with that foot; half right slide-step backward to the left oblique. Half right slide-step forward along the same diagonal; repeat with left foot.
6. Half left slide-step backward to the left oblique, describing a semicircle with that foot; right slide-step forward.
7. Left slide-step forward; then slide right foot up to resume normal interval for forward stance.
   NOTE: The stance remains low with the lower abdomen and buttocks vigorously tensed.

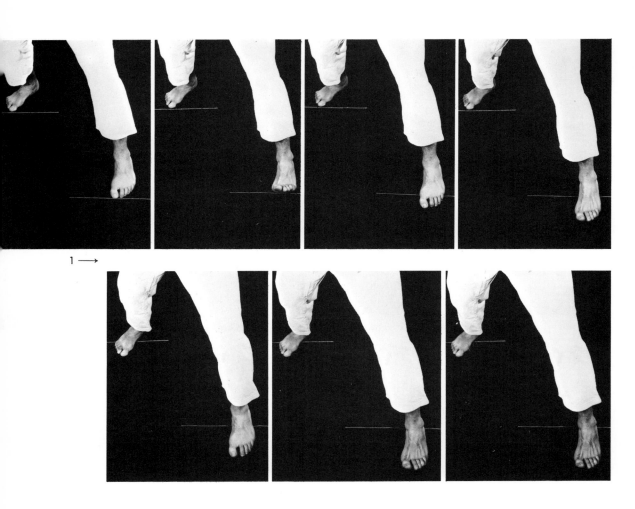

1 ⟶

3(a) ⟶

4 ⟶

—C—

1. With rigidly controlled deliberateness, left slide-step forward several inches; then immediately slide right foot forward resuming same relative distance. Student's balance should remain strongly distributed over both legs.

   NOTE: This subtle forward movement often proves disarming to many students, who as a result allow an opponent to get too close before becoming aware of the inherent danger.

2. Right and then quickly left slide-step forward; repeat backward.

3. (a) Move forward by first shifting right foot to a point just ahead of the left; half left slide-step forward recovering the original stance.

   (b) Repeat (a), adding a right slide-step.

4. Move forward by first shifting right foot to a point immediately to the rear of the left foot; half left slide step forward recovering the original stance.

5. Repeat 3 and 4 backward.

   NOTE: This variation of the slide-step enables the student to cover ground quickly. When this is done smoothly and with the upper body erect, the element of surprise is added.

—D—

1. On instructor's command of execution students will slide the left foot, then the right foot, approximately six inches forward; on the next command of execution slide the right foot and then the left foot backward, regaining original position.

2. Alternately repeat 1 to the right and left diagonal.

3. Alternately repeat 1 and 2 with only one command of execution.

SLIDE-STEP **91**

■ Hand Techniques

BLOCKING

As the student assimilates the following blocks, he will be learning defensive movements in reaction to his opponent's aggression. There is a point involved here that is well worth considering: a block executed with the utmost skill and power could very properly be called a counterattack. Its effect at the very least will be to put the startled opponent on the defensive.

1. Rising Block (Open-Leg Stance)
 1. Cross wrists with clenched fists at face level, left fist on the outside. Keep feet in place and, twisting clockwise, simultaneously bring right fist back to a position above right hip, while left fist (thumb down) moves upward to a point three inches in front of forehead with forearm tilted downward.
 2. Repeat 1 on opposite side, beginning with right fist on the outside.
 3. The blocking fist can effectively function from forehead level (as stated above) to a point several inches higher, but no more. This is of secondary importance in relation to proper muscular tension. The inclination will be to tense both arm and shoulder. The student must attempt to relax the muscles in these two areas; he should, instead, vigorously tighten the latissimus dorsi.[1]
 NOTE: To insure maximum power, the blocking forearm should be held squarely to the front. The elbow should not be allowed to move outward.

2. Outward Block (Open-Leg Stance)
 1. Cross fists in front of abdomen, with left one beneath. Move left fist adjacent to right armpit. Simultaneously, swing left forearm forward and twist body clockwise as far as possible, keeping both feet in place and knees steady.
 2. Repeat on opposite side, beginning with right hand crossing beneath left hand.
 NOTE: Do not swing forearm outward beyond edge of body.

[1] Experimentation with a partner in both right and wrong muscular control will soon demonstrate the efficacy of these instructions.

1 : 1 →

2 : 1 →

3 : 1 →

3 : 2

3. **Inward Block** (Open-Leg Stance)

1. Keeping left hand in place, lift right fist to right ear. Simultaneously, swing right forearm downward and to the front, twisting counterclockwise and keeping both feet in place.
   NOTE: Swing forearm inward to edge of body.
2. When executing the inward or outward block, the blocking arm should form a right angle with the fist normally held at shoulder level.
3. The inward or outward block should strike at a point midway between the opponent's wrist and elbow.
   NOTE: The higher above the wrist that the blocking hand strikes, the more momentum the attacking hand has gained.

4. Downward Block (Open-Leg Stance)

    1. With clenched fists, cross hands in front of body with right hand underneath, swinging left fist up to right ear. Simultaneously, thrust left fist downward to left, twisting clockwise and keeping both feet in place and knees steady.

    2. Repeat 1 on opposite side, beginning with left hand crossing beneath right hand.

    NOTE: Do not swing forearm outward beyond edge of body. To increase the power of a block, sharply twist the forearm during its execution so that the palm is downward. The termination of any block should find the student in a position from which to launch an effective counterattack.

5. Knife-Hand Block (Straddle-Leg Stance, Front Facing)

    1. Crossing both hands in front of body with right hand underneath, fingers outstretched and palm up, swing open left hand to right ear. Thrust left hand downward and to the front but not beyond edge of body; simultaneously shifting left leg counterclockwise to the side, bring open right hand to a position guarding solar plexus. Student should now be in the backward stance and half-front-facing position.

(Open-Leg Stance)

    2. Crossing both hands in front of body with right hand underneath, swing open left hand to right ear. Thrust left hand downward and to the front, simultaneously twisting clockwise; keeping both feet in place, bring open right hand to a position guarding solar plexus.

    3. Repeat 2 on opposite side, beginning with left hand crossing beneath right hand.

    4. Right slide-step sideways into straddle-leg stance. Left slide-step to rear, pivoting on ball of right foot (at this point student should be in the back stance, facing to the left side), and simultaneously execute left knife-hand block. Alternately repeat on both sides.

    5. Keeping left foot in place, pivot one quarter-turn to the right (assuming back stance), simultaneously executing right knife-hand block; pivoting one half-turn counterclockwise on ball of right foot assume back stance, simultaneously executing left knife-hand block; pivoting one quarter-turn to the left on ball of right foot resume back stance, simultaneously executing left knife-hand block; pivoting one half-turn clockwise on ball of left foot resume back stance, simultaneously executing right knife-hand block.

    NOTE: Keeping elbow of blocking hand in close to body, use the latissimus dorsi to provide power (rather than the shoulder, which should not be raised). These basic exercises will acquaint the student with the mechanics of the illustrated blocks.

6. Twisting in place, execute a left and then right knife-hand block to each side. Left slide-step backward, executing right knife-hand block to the front. Left slide-step forward, resuming open-leg stance. Continue, repeating to other side.

NOTE: This exercise can be performed in a limited area since space for only one slide-step per pupil is required.

(Forward Stance)

7. Right slide-step forward, simultaneously executing right knife-hand block. Right slide-step backward, simultaneously executing left knife-hand block.

NOTE: Left foot twists in place throughout this exercise.

6. Block and Slide-Step (Open-Leg Stance)

1. Left slide-step forward, simultaneously raising open right hand on the diagonal above head, with left fist drawn back above corresponding hip; start left hand up toward blocking position keeping close to body, simultaneously withdrawing right fist to position above right hip. During the second phase of this exercise the arms should cross at eye level employing a rapid whiplike motion. Exercise terminates in a half-front-facing stance.

2. Right slide-step backward, simultaneously executing left rising block.

3. Left slide-step forward, simultaneously executing left rising block, and then right slide-step forward, executing right rising block. When end of training hall is reached, slide-step backward with foot opposite to blocking hand (simultaneously right slide-step back with left rising block or left slide-step back with right rising block).

NOTE: With the class moving in either direction, the instructor should shift about stopping in front of each student to deliver a lunge punch just short of contact. With the instructor exerting moderate pressure, any blocking arm that yields will thereby indicate to the student that his block did not terminate with maximum body tension. Each of the various blocks should be similarly tested.

4. Execute the outward, inward, downward, and knife-hand blocks in the same manner as in 3.

NOTE: When executing the knife-hand block in the forward stance the body weight shifts back, resting on the rear foot. This technique must be so diligently practiced that it will be swiftly accomplished. The power for this block is produced by the latissimus dorsi. The body should remain low, ending in a half-front-facing stance.

5 : 7 →

6 : 1 →

6 : 2 →

6 : 3 →

7 ⟶

7. Pressing Block (Forward Stance)

Move left forearm forward and down against attacking arm while it is still in its weak starting phase.

NOTE: Merely pushing against the attacking arm will prove ineffective. The blocking forearm should be thrust down with maximum power.

8. Cross-Arm Block (Open-Leg Stance)

1. Upward. Cross hands at wrists, with fists clenched for added power and avoidance of injury to fingers. To facilitate effective grasping action, the hand corresponding to the attacker's fist should be placed on the outside. Slide-step forward on foot opposite attacking fist, thrusting both hands forward and upward, keeping elbows within shoulder width and the body erect.
2. Downward. Cross hands as in preceding exercise. Move hands sideways to just above the right hip; left slide-stepping forward, simultaneously thrust both hands slightly forward and downward directly to the front.

9. Palm-Heel Block (Forward Stance)

1. Upward. Bending right hand back, thrust palm up and forward.
2. Forward. Bend left hand back moving it to left rear. Pivoting clockwise on ball of left foot, simultaneously shift right foot to the left; quickly thrust palm forward and to the right.

NOTE: When blocks are performed while moving backward it is essential that the weight stress shall have shifted to the rear leg. On the other hand, when performing blocks while moving forward the weight stress is to be on the front leg. [2]

[2] The single exception to this is the knife-hand block, which requires that the major portion of body weight be on the rear leg.

8 : 1

8 : 2 ⟶

9 : 1 ⟶

9 : 2 ⟶

ATTACKING

1. Close Punch (Open-Leg Stance)

Starting with left hand outstretched and right fist above right hip, thrust right hand forward, stopping when elbow is just past hip. Remember to withdraw extended arm when executing the punch.

2. Vertical Punch (Open-Leg Stance)

Repeat preceding exercise ending by making one quarter-turn counterclockwise with right fist.

3. Straight Punch (Open-Leg Stance)

1. Repeat preceding exercise, ending with the right arm fully extended and the fist making one half-turn counterclockwise.

   NOTE: When punching, be sure to tighten the body, concentrating on lower abdomen, buttocks, and muscles of the chest (pectoral) and under the arm (latissimus dorsi). The shoulders are never to be elevated when executing a punch. It is important also that the shoulders be squared at the termination of this punch. The punching arm should be thrust forward (perhaps only an inch) without breaking this alignment so that the shoulder blade ceases to protrude. The above techniques are not only highly effective when fighting at close range, but also aid in development of the lunge punch.

2. Stand facing partner so that fingertips of outstretched hands just barely touch his chest. Lower right fist to right hip and, aiming directly at his chest, alternately execute right and left straight punches.

   NOTE: In this self-corrective exercise a partner acts as a constant reminder that the termination of each punch should find shoulders squared. Students will find that facing a wall instead of a partner will be more than adequate.

4. Reverse Punch Preparation (Half-Front Facing)

To assume this stance, shift torso forty-five degrees to the right, keeping feet and knees firmly in place. Placing fists on hips with back held straight, twist trunk vigorously forward with increasing speed. As torso rotates, push forward from the right leg, forcing left knee forward. This resulting momentum will increase forward thrust and penetration.

NOTE: This exercise is an essential prelude to the powerful application of the reverse punch. The effectiveness of the reverse punch is largely determined by the proper execution of this motion.

5. Reverse Punch

Strongly twisting hips counterclockwise and forward, deliver the right straight punch. When executed in above manner, this shall be referred to as a reverse punch.

1 —→

2

3 : 2 —→

3 : 1

4

—→

5

NOTE: The attacking arm should never be fully tensed at the commencement of any punching attack. This condition would only serve to restrict student's speed and therefore impair striking power. The desirable procedure is to concentrate extreme effort on vigorous withdrawal of the opposite arm during its backward movement. At the instant of impact the entire body must be rigorously tensed without raising the shoulders. Keep in mind that the forearms should brush the sides of the body simultaneously when executing the punch. At this point the fists make one half-turn. Execute exercise slowly and deliberately at first, progressing toward a pistonlike movement. The strongest attack is one delivered front and center. This allows the pectoral and latissimus dorsi to exert their maximum potential. Maintain a strong forward thrust in the leading knee and hip throughout this movement.

6. **Lunge Punch Preparation** (Open-Leg Stance)
   1. Half left slide-step forward, holding open right hand straight in front at shoulder level; bring left fist back to a position above left hip. Complete slide-step, executing a left straight punch.
      (a) Right slide-step forward, executing right straight punch, simultaneously thrusting left fist to a point six inches behind the right fist.
      (b) Right slide-step forward, executing a right straight punch and bringing the left fist back to a position above the left hip in a single synchronized movement.
   (Forward Stance)
   2. Right slide-step forward, stopping when both feet are parallel and nearly together. At this point the elbows should be touching the sides and left fist should be drawn back above hip. Proceed smoothly with the following:
      (a) Right slide-step forward, simultaneously executing right straight punch; then immediately left slide-step forward into close-leg stance.
      (b) Repeat (a), but instead of terminating in close-leg stance progress smoothly into a left straight punch coupled with a left slide-step.
      NOTE: (a) and (b) are designed to promote rapid forward-foot shifting in multiple attack situations. Here again speed and fluidity are vital to the success of the maneuver. The student should practice the above whenever possible, while improvising kicking and blocking exercises later on.

6 : 1 ⟶

6 : 1(a) ⟶

6 : 1(b)

6 : 2 ⟶

6 : 2(b)

6 : 2(a)

7. Lunge Punch (Forward Stance)

Right slide-step forward, simultaneously executing right straight punch. (This combination shall be referred to as a lunge punch). With left heel firmly on floor and knee tense but not locked, leg functions as shock absorber at moment of impact. The rapidity and smoothness of the initial movement are all-important. The student must consider the punching arm as an extension of the supporting heel. There should be a determined effort, as well, directed toward pushing off from the foot to the rear (right foot). As this foot approaches and then passes opposite foot, the roles are reversed. Maintain a strong forward thrust in the left knee and hip throughout this movement.

8. Lunge Punch Development (Left Forward Stance)
1. Holding right hand outstretched at shoulder level, slide right foot forward, simultaneously bending the hand back at the wrist and tensing latissimus dorsi, pectoral, and lower abdominal muscles. This corresponds to the final movement of the lunge punch and when done properly (i.e., with buttocks firmly tensed, hips low and tucked forward), provides an excellent lunge-punch development exercise.
2. Slide-stepping across training hall, push both hands (palm-heel) forward with studied slowness. Shoulders should be squared with hand corresponding to leading foot, several inches ahead of the other.
   NOTE: For maximum benefit be sure to keep the elbows close to the body. The instructor, lower abdomen and buttocks tensed, from a position in front of each student in turn, drives his midsection forward toward student's hands. Student simultaneously thrusts hands forward to resist instructor's momentum.
3. Slide-stepping forward, alternately deliver left and then right upward palm-heel block with studied slowness to the count of ten.
   NOTE: Tense muscles as indicated in 1.

(Forward Stance)
4. Students form facing parallel lines. Students in one line grasp with left hand ends of belt worn by partner opposite. Partner slowly executes alternate lunge punches across training hall. Assisting student, slide-stepping backward in unison, exerts a continuous, strong pull on belt. When end of training hall has been reached, reverse roles and reverse steps.
   NOTE: The tug on the belt represents a constant reminder that the hips must lead. This "exaggeration for effect" will produce the tight, erect body alignment required for a powerful performance.

7 →

8 : 1 →

8 : 2

8 : 3 →

8 : 4

5. Slide-step forward, alternately executing right, and then left lunge punches, one per step. When end of training hall is reached, slide-step backward, simultaneously delivering the lunge punch, using opposite hand and foot.

   NOTE: As the class performs in unison the instructor should move about, stopping in front of each student to deliver a forward palm-heel attack to the extended fist. The student's attack has not terminated with maximum body tension if his upper body yields under the pressure exerted by the instructor. Each of the various hand attacks should be similarly tested.

6. Repeat 5, facing an opposing student who is resisting with palm-heel of each hand pressing against your fists and providing constant tension.

7. Execute right lunge punch quickly followed by left reverse punch. Withdraw left fist to point above hip and repeat.

8. To prevent an inflexible and limited attack repeat exercise 5, this time following each lunge punch with two alternate reverse punches. After intensive drill one lunge punch followed by four alternate reverse punches should be substituted.

9. Execute right lunge punch quickly followed by alternate left and right lunge punches.

   NOTE: It is imperative that each segment of this exercise be pursued with a consistently high level of power and at an even tempo.

10. Students form facing parallel lines an arm's length apart, with attackers in forward stance and defenders in open-leg stance. One line assumes reverse-punch stance with one fist at opponent's abdomen, elbow slightly flexed, and other fist held approximately four inches in front of corresponding hip. On command, students execute the final movement of the reverse punch. Opposing students check latissimus dorsi tension and advise as to relative punching power.

11. One line of students assumes lunge-punch position, and preceding exercise is repeated.

12. Students form facing parallel lines an arm's length apart. One line of students assumes reverse punch position with fists against opposing students' abdomens. Remembering to stress the tightening of latissimus dorsi in addition to normal body tension, opposing students attempt to press forward and force partners backward. Students who are forced back need to concentrate further on the correct muscular tension.

13. One line of students assumes lunge-punch position with fists against opposing students' abdomens, and preceding exercise is repeated.

8 : 5 →

8 : 6

8 : 10 →

8 : 12

8 : 14 $\longrightarrow$

14. Students form facing parallel lines an arm's length apart. First line (the attackers) commences the right lunge punch with studied slowness. Second line (the defenders) slides left and then right foot several inches forward as soon as attackers begin, simultaneously executing a double forward palm-heel attack against opponent's flexed arms directly above the elbows. Pressure is applied and maintained by both sides for several seconds. (Open-Leg Stance)

15. Hold left arm out to side and right fist above corresponding hip; pivot counterclockwise on ball of left foot executing right lunge punch; right slide-step backward to original position, simultaneously executing a left straight punch to the left side.

9. Lunge Punch Variation (Forward Stance)

Extend right hand forward at shoulder level and hold left fist above left hip; simultaneously left lunge punch and right slide-step forward. When end of training hall is reached, repeat backward, keeping the attacking hand and slide-stepping foot on same side.

10. Rising Punch (Forward Stance)

Beginning with a close punch, quickly shift into the vertical and then straight punch, in a steadily rising action involving one smooth continuous attack.

11. Hook Punch (Straddle-Leg Stance)

Hold left fist above left hip and right hand high and to the side, palm facing in; execute left close punch, twisting left fist downward; as the elbow passes the hip, continue on the diagonal, striking the right palm.

NOTE: Keep elbow close to the side while punching forward. The power of this attack is generated by the dynamic rising thrust of the upper arm to a point paralleling the floor at the moment of impact. Students should stress the development of this powerful punch.

8 : 15 ⟶

9 ⟶

10 ⟶

11

12 : 1 ⟶

12 : 2 ⟶

12 : 3 ⟶

13 ⟶

12. Back-Fist Strike (Forward Stance)

1. Raise left fist turned inward to right ear. Deliver left back-fist strike to the front.
2. Deliver left back-fist strike to the upper level, quickly followed by a right reverse punch, lower level.
3. Deliver simultaneous left back-fist strike and right reverse punch to the upper and lower levels respectively.

13. Bottom-Fist Strike (Forward Stance)

Right slide-step forward, simultaneously raising right fist turned inward to left ear; execute right bottom-fist strike to the front.

NOTE: In the back- or bottom-fist strike utilize the springlike action of the elbow.

14 : 1 ⟶

14 : 2 ⟶

14 : 3 ⟶

15 : 1

15 : 2 ⟶

14. **Double Close Punch** (Open-Leg Stance)
1. Starting with both fists turned upward resting above hips, deliver a double close punch to the front.
2. Right or left slide-stepping forward, deliver double close punch to the front.

(Forward Stance)
3. Bringing left fist back to left hip, right slide-step forward and deliver the double close punch to the front.

15. **Double Straight Punch** (Open-Leg Stance)
1. Standing in place, deliver double straight punch forward.
2. Right or left slide-stepping forward, simultaneously deliver double straight punch to the front.

16. Double Reverse Punch (Forward Stance)

1. Half left slide-stepping forward, simultaneously deliver double reverse punch to the solar plexus and face.
   NOTE: Both fists should strike in a vertical line while remaining parallel to each other. This attack can be preceded by a front or side-snap kick to further insure its success. When practiced from the left forward stance, merely reverse the position of the hands.
2. Right slide-stepping forward, simultaneously deliver double reverse punch to the solar plexus and face.

17. Combinations (Forward Stance)

1. Right slide-step forward, simultaneously executing right lunge punch to the upper level. Standing in place, quickly deliver a left and then right reverse punch to the lower level.
2. Right slide-step forward, simultaneously executing right lunge punch to the upper level. Standing in place, quickly deliver a left reverse punch, lower level, and a right reverse punch, upper level.
3. Right slide-step forward, simultaneously executing right lunge punch to the lower level. Standing in place, quickly deliver a left and then right reverse punch to the upper level.
4. Right slide-step forward, simultaneously executing right lunge punch to the upper level. Standing in place, quickly deliver a left reverse punch, upper level, and a right reverse punch, lower level.
5. Right slide-step forward, simultaneously executing right lunge punch to the upper level; standing in place quickly execute a left and then right reverse punch to the lower level; left slide-step forward, simultaneously executing left lunge punch to the upper level. Standing in place, quickly execute a right and then left reverse punch to the lower level.
6. Deliver right reverse punch to the upper level. Standing in place, quickly bring right fist back to position above right hip and immediately deliver right reverse punch to the lower level.
7. Repeat 6, transposing the order of the reverse punches.
8. Repeat 6, directing both reverse punches to the upper level.
9. Repeat 6, directing both reverse punches to the lower level.
   NOTE: Between reverse punches, the left fist should be used as a feint or in a pushing movement at opponent's face rather than as a punch.
10. Right reverse punch, lower level; left reverse punch, upper level.

16 : 1 ⟶

16 : 2 ⟶

17 : 1 ⟶

17 : 6 ⟶

18 : 1 ⟶

18 : 2 ⟶

18. Jab

1. With a snapping motion thrust the left fist forward at shoulder level, simultaneously twisting the torso into the half-front-facing position.
2. Repeat 1, adding a left back-fist strike, upper level.

   NOTE: Do not withdraw left leading hand before commencing attack. Legs remain in original stance throughout.
3. Repeat 1, adding a right reverse punch, lower level.
4. Repeat 1, adding a right and then left reverse punch to the lower level.
5. Repeat 3 and 4, adding a left back-fist strike, upper level.
6. Repeat 1, adding a right lunge punch, upper level, then left reverse punch, lower level.
7. Left jab, upper level; quickly half right and then half left slide-step forward, executing a right and then left reverse punch to the upper and lower levels respectively.
8. Half left and then quickly half right slide-step forward and slightly to the left oblique; execute left jab to upper level, simultaneously shifting into right straddle-leg stance; quickly deliver right reverse punch while shifting back into forward stance.

   NOTE: In the initial movement the right foot swings sharply enough to the left so that the student now faces his opponent from the oblique and in a forward stance.

18 : 3

→

18 : 4 →

18 : 8 →

19. Lunge Jab

1. Left half slide-step forward, simultaneously executing the left jab.

   NOTE: This technique will henceforth be designated the lunge jab.

   (a) Repeat Jab 1–6 inclusive (p. 114), substituting the lunge jab.

   (b) Left lunge jab; keeping left hand extended, snap right foot forward to a position just ahead of the left foot; slide the right foot back to original position, simultaneously executing the right reverse punch.

   (c) Left lunge jab; keeping left hand extended, snap right foot forward to a position just ahead of the left foot; half left slide-step forward, simultaneously executing the right reverse punch.

2. Simultaneously left jab and half right slide-step forward.

   NOTE: This prepares the student for the performance of a left jab quickly followed by a right lunge punch.

3. Repeat 2 and, at this point, either right slide-step backward into original forward stance or left slide-step backward, simultaneously delivering right reverse punch.

4. Repeat 2 and, at this point, left slide-step forward and deliver right reverse punch or right slide-step forward and deliver right lunge punch.

   NOTE: The serious student, in order to take advantage of a constantly changing situation during sparring, must be prepared to shift adroitly into new patterns of attack and defense.

19 : 1(c)

19 : 2

19 : 3

4

20. Extended Reverse Punch

Deliver right reverse punch, upper level, quickly followed by left and right extended reverse punches to the upper level.

NOTE: The initial punch is strongly executed with the shoulders squared. On the next attack, sharply twist the body clockwise, thereby extending the punching range. As proficiency is attained, add the third reverse punch to this exercise by twisting body counterclockwise. Beginning on the instructor's command, this exercise shall be performed in three unequal counts with 3 following rapidly after 2.

21. Extended Lunge Punch

1. Deliver right extended lunge punch to the upper level, simultaneously twisting body counterclockwise.
2. Deliver right extended lunge punch to the upper level, simultaneously twisting body counterclockwise and ending in straddle-leg stance.

NOTE: The element of surprise should be cultivated as a distinctive technique which may often be critical to success or failure. When opponents are momentarily farther apart than normal, the extended lunge punch may be made the basis of a successful attack. In all punching exercises the attacking fist should be directed to a point which is straight out both vertically and horizontally from the center of the body. When the attacking hand is off-center, the student finds himself in a weakened stance and in addition exposes too much of his body to a possible counterattack.

22. Elbow (Forward Stance)

1. Basic Forward Attack. Extend right hand forward till elbow rests above hip. Strike forward with elbow, simultaneously twisting right fist sharply in a half-circle counterclockwise so that the maneuver terminates with fist turned down beneath chin with attacking arm parallel to floor.
2. Basic Upward Attack. Extend right fist forward until elbow is poised above hip. Strike upward with elbow, simultaneously twisting right fist sharply in a quarter-circle counterclockwise so that the maneuver terminates with fist turned inward next to right ear and with attacking upper arm parallel to the floor.

   Repeat 1 and 2, beginning with right fist drawn back to a position above right hip.
3. (a) Advanced Forward and Upward Elbow Attacks. Slide-stepping across the training hall, deliver alternate left and right forward elbow attacks.
   (b) Repeat, substituting upward elbow attack.
       In preceding manner, deliver upward elbow attack:
   (c) Standing in place, deliver a right and then left forward elbow attack, and a right and then left upward elbow attack.
   (d) Standing in place, deliver a right upward and then left forward elbow attack.

20 —→

21
↓

22 : 1-2
↓

22 : 3(b)

→

(e) Standing in place, deliver a right forward and then left up-ward elbow attack.

(f) Repeat (c)–(e) in lunge form.

(g) Deliver right reverse punch to the upper level. Standing in place, quickly bring right fist back to position above right hip and immediately execute right forward elbow attack, lower level, followed by left upward elbow attack, upper level.

NOTE: Between the first two attacks the left fist should be used as a feint or in a pushing movement at opponent's face rather than as a punch.

(h) Deliver right lunge punch to the upper level and, standing in place, execute left forward and then right upward elbow attack.

4. Downward Elbow Attack. (Straddle-Leg Stance)

(a) Raise right fist turned inward above head and withdraw left fist to a position above left hip. Execute a downward elbow attack, being careful not to lean forward.

(Forward Stance)

(b) Slide-stepping across the training hall, deliver alternate left and right downward elbow attacks.

5. Backward Elbow Attack. (Straddle-Leg Stance)

(a) Deliver left backward elbow attack and simultaneous right spear-hand attack over left shoulder.

(Forward Stance)

(b) Slide-step forward across training hall, simultaneously delivering backward elbow and backward spear-hand attacks.

(Open-Leg Stance)

(c) Pivot one quarter-turn counterclockwise on left foot into straddle-leg stance and then execute the right backward elbow attack and left forward straight punch together.

NOTE: Elbow and forearm attacks are extremely powerful. In execution, do not swing elbow outward to the side or attack with elbow any higher than shoulder level. These errors reduce attacking power and needlessly expose too much body surface. For greater accuracy and speed make certain the elbow moves in on a straight line to the target.

22 : 3(g) ⟶

3(h) ↓

4(a) ↓

5(a) ↓

22 : 5(b)

22 : 5(c) ⟶

23

$\longrightarrow$

23. Forearm Attack

This technique is executed in a manner similar to the forward and upward elbow attacks, the one difference being that the striking area is now the outer forearm.

24. Knife-Hand Strike (Open-Leg Stance)

1. Raise open right hand, palm outward, with fingertips touching right ear. Simultaneously, execute right knife-hand strike forward, moving left fist to a position above the corresponding hip.
2. Raise open right hand across body, palm inward, with fingertips touching left ear. Simultaneously, execute right knife-hand strike forward, moving left fist to a position above the corresponding hip.
3. Combine 1 and 2 in one exercise.

(Forward Stance)

4. Alternate left and right slide-steps across training hall, delivering the combined knife-hand strike.
5. Using same hand, combine the inward or outward knife-hand strike with an upward elbow attack.

25. Palm-Heel Attack (Open-Leg Stance)

1. Upward. Bending right hand back, thrust palm up and forward.
2. Forward. Bend right hand back, simultaneously moving it to right rear. Using a snapping motion, thrust palm forward.

(Forward Stance)

3. Slide-step across training hall, delivering alternate upward palm-heel attacks.
4. Repeat 3 with forward palm-heel attack.

    NOTE: The palm-heel can also be used as a blocking technique. In either event it is imperative that the shoulders remain relaxed with the latissimus dorsi fully tensed.

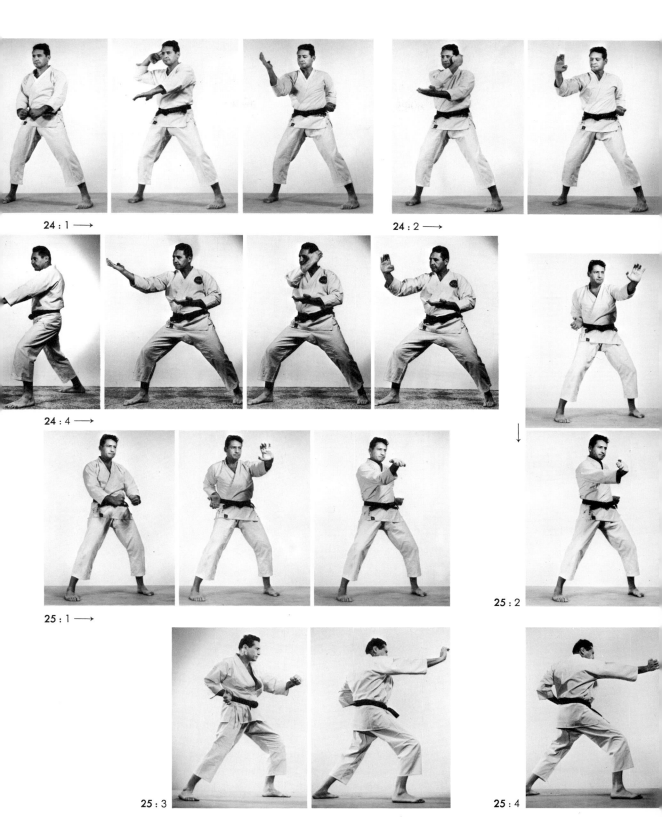

24 : 1 ⟶

24 : 2 ⟶

24 : 4 ⟶

25 : 1 ⟶

25 : 2

25 : 3

25 : 4

26 : 1 ⟶

26 : 3 ⟶

26. Ridge-Hand Strike (Forward Stance)

1. Swinging the right hand in an arc from the outside, deliver ridge-hand strike forward.
2. Slide-step across training hall, delivering alternate ridge-hand strikes.
3. Combine palm-heel attack and ridge-hand strike in one exercise.
   NOTE: In executing any multiple hand attacks the advanced student will learn to compensate for an opponent's retreat as well as for his own possibly diminishing power by utilizing body momentum to extend his forward movement six inches or more toward an opponent. This technique transforms the termination of a basic slide-step and hand attack into a far more potent device.

1:1 ⟶

1:2 ⟶

COMBINATION BLOCKING AND ATTACKING

1. Basic (Open-Leg Stance)

1. Left slide-step forward, executing left rising block, quickly followed by right reverse punch. Moving left hand to the front, right slide-step forward, simultaneously retracting right fist to corresponding hip. Execute right rising block, simultaneously retracting left fist to corresponding hip, and then execute an immediate left reverse punch.

   NOTE: Slide-stepping across training hall, alternately execute this important exercise, striving for swift, continuous movements.

2. On instructor's command of execution, right slide-step backward, simultaneously executing left rising block, quickly followed by right reverse punch. Recover original stance. Repeat fifty times, alternating left with right foot. Each of the last ten movements should be accompanied by a kiai.

   NOTE: With even a large group this exercise can be performed in in a limited area since space for only one slide-step per pupil is required.

1 : 3 ⟶

1 : 4 ⟶

1 : 5 ⟶   1 : 6 ⟶

1 : 9 ⟶

1 : 10 ⟶

3. Outward block followed by reverse punch. Repeat as in 1 and 2.
4. Inward block, followed by reverse punch. Repeat as in 1 and 2.
5. Knife-hand block followed by spear-hand attack. Repeat as in 1 and 2.
6. Downward block, followed by reverse punch. Repeat as in 1 and 2.
7. Repeat each block; then execute forward elbow attack.
8. Repeat each block; then execute upward elbow attack.
9. Execute left downward and then left rising block, followed by right reverse punch. Repeat as in 1 and 2.
10. Left downward block; right reverse punch, lower level; left rising block; right reverse punch, upper level. Repeat as in 1 and 2.
11. (a) Left outward block; right reverse punch, upper level; left downward block; right reverse punch, lower level.
    (b) Left inward block; right reverse punch, lower level; left downward block; right reverse punch, upper level.
    (c) Repeat, substituting a variety of blocks and counterattacks.

1 : 15 →

1 : 16 →

1 : 14

(Forward Stance)

12. Right reverse punch; left downward block, simultaneously retracting right fist to corresponding hip.

13. Repeat reverse punch, adding in turn:
    (a) left outward block
    (b) left inward block
    (c) left knife-hand block
    (d) left rising block

14. After right reverse punch, quickly right slide-step forward, executing right downward block.

15. Right lunge punch; then, standing in place, execute right downward block.

16. Right lunge punch; then, standing in place, execute left downward block to the left side.

2 : 1 ⟶
2 : 2 ⟶

⟶

2. Advanced (Open-Leg Stance)

1. Left slide-step forward, executing left rising block and then right reverse punch. Without moving forward, execute left inward block and then right reverse punch.

2. Right slide-step forward, executing right inward block and then left reverse punch. Left slide-step forward, executing left outward block and then right reverse punch. Without moving forward, execute right and then left rising block and then right reverse punch.

2:3

2:8 ⟶

4

5

6

3. Left slide-step forward, executing simultaneous left rising block and right reverse punch.
4. Left slide-step forward, executing simultaneous left outward block and right reverse punch.
5. Left slide-step forward, executing simultaneous left inward block and right reverse punch.
6. Left slide-step forward, executing simultaneous left downward block and right reverse punch.
7. Right slide-step backward repeating 3–6.
8. Right slide-step forward and, standing in place, execute right and then left rising block, quickly followed by right reverse punch, upper level, and then left reverse punch, lower level.

3. Reversing Direction (Forward Stance)
1. On command to reverse direction, slide right foot sideways to the left, pivoting clockwise on balls of both feet simultaneously. Right foot must slide far enough to the side so that there is ample space for left foot to advance without touching it.
2. Execute right lunge punch; reverse direction keeping right arm extended, then execute left reverse punch.

(Left Forward Stance)
3. Execute left lunge punch; then, momentarily keeping left arm raised to the front, reverse direction and execute the right upward elbow attack.

(Forward Stance)
4. Alternate left and right slide-steps across training hall, executing lunge punch. At end of training hall (in this case student will have completed right lunge punch) and on instructor's command, student quickly reverses direction, executing left downward block, and then right reverse punch and simultaneous kiai. Recover forward stance and continue this pattern.

3 : 1 ⟶

3 : 2

3 : 3 ⟶   ⟶

3 : 4 ⟶

4 : 1

4 : 2

3

4 : 4 →

4 : 5

4 : 6 →

4 : 7

5:1 →

→

4. Body Shifting: Basic (Forward Stance)

1. Pivot counterclockwise on ball of right foot, turning one quarter-turn to the left; simultaneously slide left foot in a modified outward arc to the left. This will find the student resuming the forward stance. Quickly execute the left rising block; then, immediately pivot clockwise one half-turn (to face in opposite direction) and execute right rising block.
2. Substituting outward block, repeat 1.
3. Substituting knife-hand block, repeat 1.
4. Substituting downward block, repeat 1.
5. Adding a reverse punch to each block, repeat 1–4.
6. Substituting a left back-fist strike, upper level, repeat 1.
7. Adding a reverse punch, lower level, to the back-fist strike, repeat 6.

5. Body Shifting: Advanced (Forward Stance)

1. Repeat Body Shifting: basic 1–7, replacing sliding motion with a low forward hop when changing direction.
2. Repeat 1, varying degree of turn slightly until one full circle is completed clockwise and then counterclockwise.

6 : 1 ⟶

6 : 2 ⟶

6. Body Shifting: Variations (Open-Leg Stance)

1. Left slide-step forward, executing left knife-hand block. Standing in place, execute right knife-hand downward block to the right side.

(Forward Stance)

2. Half right slide-step forward into open-leg stance, executing right bottom-fist strike to the side. Right slide-step forward, executing right bottom-fist strike to the front.
3. Right reverse punch; then half right slide-step forward into open-leg stance, executing right bottom-fist strike to the side.
4. Deliver left back-fist strike to the upper level. Quickly right slide-step forward, executing the right bottom-fist strike to the front.
   NOTE: The bottom-fist strike is relatively powerful, involving little or no danger of injury to the attacking hand.
5. Alternately right and left slide-step forward across training hall, swiveling body into slide straddle-leg stance with each step.
6. Repeat 5 moving backward.
7. Repeat 5 and 6, adding a lunge punch with hand corresponding to forward leg.
   NOTE: Remain low throughout with shoulders relaxed. Movements forward or backward are best accomplished by a vigorous hip-swiveling motion. The rear leg acts as support for the punching hand.

6:3 →

6:4 →

6:5 ↓

→

6:7 →

1 ⟶

(Open-Leg Stance)

1. *Attacker:* Right slide-steps forward reaching for throat or lapel with both hands.

   Defender: Right slide-steps backward. Holding arms to form an inverted **V** and with fists clenched, simultaneously thrusts upward and outward against attacker's forearms; half left slide-steps forward delivering double bottom-fist strike to attacker's sides.

   NOTE: This technique will adapt to movements in any direction.

(Forward Stance)

2. *Attacker:* Right slide-steps forward reaching for throat or lapel with both hands.

   Defender: Executes simultaneous left rising block and right lunge punch; or

   Defender: Executes double hook punch to attacker's temples; or

   Defender: Executes double reverse punch to attacker's abdomen.

3. *Attacker:* Delivers right lunge punch.

   Defender: Left slide-steps forward, executing upward cross-arm block. Quickly opens right fist and grasps sleeve or wrist of attacking hand, pulling down to the side.

   NOTE: This action will simultaneously break attacker's balance and also prevent an attack from his other hand. Quickly counterattack with:

   1. left reverse punch
   2. left spear-hand attack
   3. right front kick

   NOTE: Above 1–3 are to be practiced singly, with several repetitions of each.

4. *Attacker:* Delivers left jab to the upper level.

   Defender: With left hand grasps attacking arm, pulling forward and down to the left; then right slide-steps forward, counterattacking with right downward elbow attack.

2 ⟶   LEFT RISING BLOCK

DOUBLE HOOK PUNCH

DOUBLE REVERSE PUNCH

3 ⟶   UPWARD CROSS-ARM BLOCK   LEFT REVERSE PUNCH

4 ⟶

5 ⟶

6 ⟶

5. *Attacker:* Delivers right lunge punch to the upper level.
   Defender: Executes left rising block and, shifting right foot forward and slightly to the right, counterattacks with right close punch, upper level.

6. *Attacker:* Delivers right lunge punch to the upper level.
   Defender: Left slide-steps backward, executing right outward block; then continues smoothly with a right close-punch counterattack.

7. *Attacker:* Delivers right lunge punch to the lower level.
   Defender: Shifting left and then right foot forward and slightly to the left, executes left palm-heel block, quickly counterattacking with left upward and then right forward palm-heel attack.

8. *Attacker:* Delivers right lunge punch to the upper level.
   Defender: Shifting left and then right foot forward and slightly to the left, executes left palm-heel block, sweeping attacking hand across his chest; then counterattacks with right forward palm-heel attack.

9. *Attacker:* Delivers right lunge punch to the upper level.
   Defender: Shifting left and then right foot forward and slightly to the left, executes left forward palm-heel block, sweeping attacking hand across his chest; then counterattacks with double bottom-fist strike to the back and stomach.
   Repeat 9 substituting double hook-punch counterattack.
   NOTE: Avoid contact as this counterattack can be extremely painful.

7 $\longrightarrow$

8 $\longrightarrow$ 9 $\longrightarrow$

DOUBLE HOOK PUNCH

10 ⟶

10. *Attacker:* Delivers right lunge punch to the upper level.
    Defender: Shifting left and then right foot diagonally forward to the left, executes left forward palm-heel block, sweeping attacking hand across his chest; then counterattacks with right ridgehand strike to opponent's temple.
    NOTE: Swiftly twist counterattacking hand over in a small arc immediately prior to contact.
    Repeat 10, with defender substituting left inward block for left forward palm-heel block.

11.(a)*Attacker:* Delivers right lunge punch to the upper level.
    Defender: Half left slide-steps forward, executing simultaneous blocking left lunge jab or palm-heel attack, upper level, and right reverse punch, lower level.

    (b)*Attacker:* Delivers right lunge punch to the upper level.
    Defender: Shifting left and then right foot forward and to the left to a position effecting a forty-five degree angle with attacker, executes simultaneous left and right reverse punches to the upper and lower levels respectively.

    (c)*Attacker:* Delivers right lunge punch to the upper level.
    Defender: Half left slide-steps forward, stopping attack with left upward palm-heel block to upper right side of chest; then quickly counterattacks with left upward palm-heel attack and right reverse punch to the lower level.
    (*1*) Repeat (c). After executing left upward palm-heel block, grasp attacker's training uniform with left hand, pulling him forward and to his right. Execute right upward elbow attack.
    (*2*) Repeat (c). After executing left upward palm-heel block, slide left and then right foot forward, clasping both hands (intertwining fingers) back of attacker's neck. Pulling downward strongly, execute right knee kick.
    (*3*) Repeat (*2*), substituting forehead attack.
    NOTE: Use extreme caution in avoiding contact.

PART 2 : TRAINING **140**

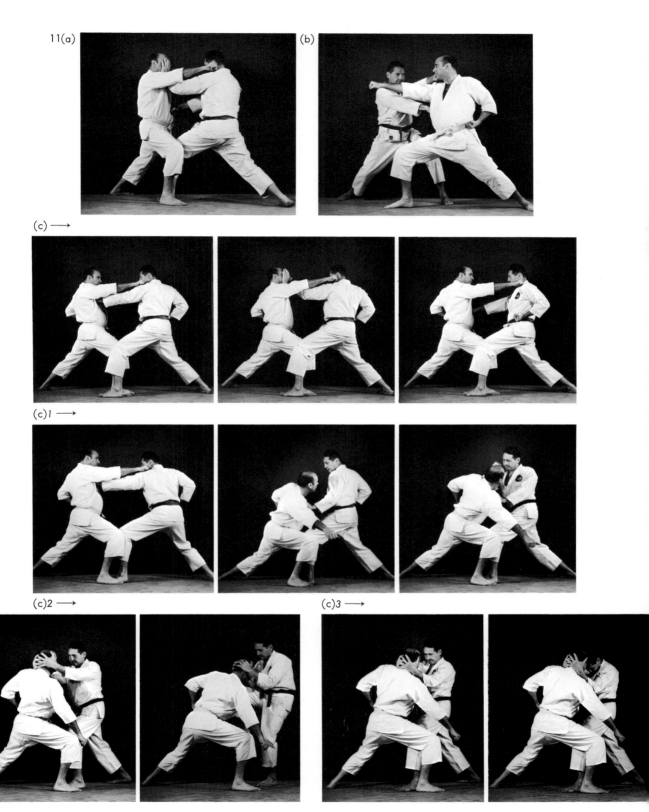

11(a)

(b)

(c) ⟶

(c)1 ⟶

(c)2 ⟶

(c)3 ⟶

12 ⟶

12. *Attacker:* Delivers right lunge punch to the upper level.
    Defender: Left and then quickly right slide-steps forward, executing a left upward palm-heel thrust to right side of attacker's chest followed by right reverse punch, lower level.

13. *Attacker:* Delivers right lunge punch to the upper level.
    Defender: Slides left foot slightly forward to the left oblique; then shifts right foot backward to the left, assuming a side straddle-leg stance and simultaneously delivering a left reverse punch, lower level.
    Attacker: Delivers right lunge punch to the upper level.
    (Left Forward Stance)
    Defender: Slides right foot slightly forward and to the right oblique; then shifts left foot backward to the right, assuming a side straddle-leg stance and simultaneously delivering a right reverse punch, lower level.

14. *Attacker:* Delivers right lunge punch to the upper level.
    Defender: Half left slide-steps forward, stopping attack with right upward palm-heel block to upper right side of chest, counterattacking with left and then right reverse punches to the lower level.

15. *Attacker:* Delivers right lunge punch to the upper level.
    Defender: Executes left outward block and, grasping the wrist, slide-steps forward, counterattacking with right downward bottom-fist strike.
    NOTE: Attacking the biceps in this manner is designed to temporarily immobilize an opponent's arm.

16. *Attacker:* Delivers right lunge punch to the upper level.
    Defender: Shifting left and then right foot straight forward, executes left rising block. The blocking forearm strikes attacker's right armpit, breaking his balance. Quickly counterattack with right forward elbow attack.

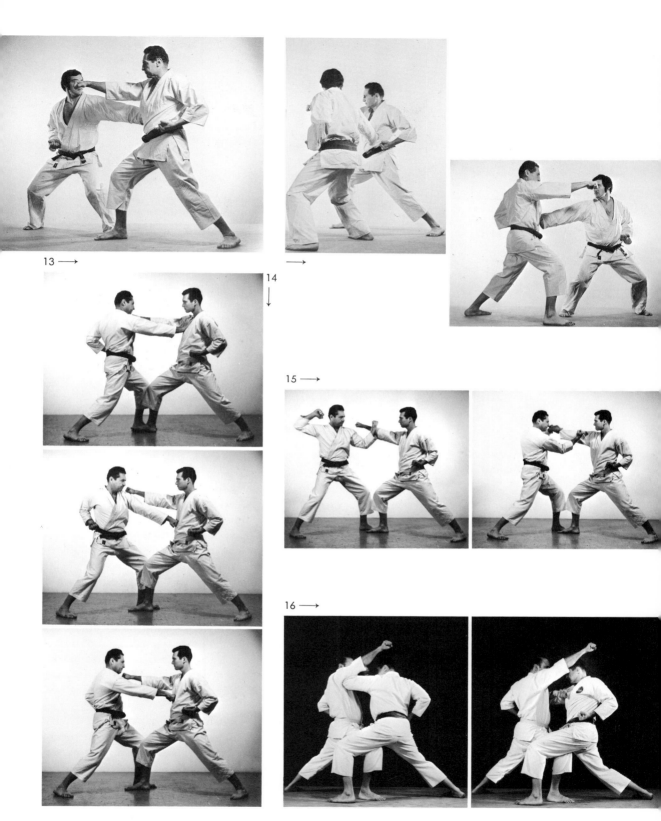

13 →

→

14
↓

15 →

16 →

17. *Attacker:*   Delivers right lunge punch to the upper level.
    Defender: Slides left and then right foot slightly to the left, simultaneously executing the right and left inward blocks to attacker's forearm and upper arm respectively.
    NOTE: Use extreme caution as severe damage to the elbow can result from use of excessive force.

18. *Attacker:*   Delivers right lunge punch to the upper level.
    (Open-Leg Stance)
    Defender: Right slide-steps forward, simultaneously executing right inward block and quickly shifting into side straddle-leg stance; sliding right and then left foot sideways toward attacker, delivers sideward elbow attack augmented by left palm-heel, followed by right back-fist strike to opponent's face.

19. *Attacker:*   Delivers alternate right and left multiple reverse punches to the lower level.
    Defender: With both hands held open and palms facing inward, vigorously thrusts both arms down and to their respective sides, simultaneously twisting palms strongly outward to block the attack. Holding left hand rigid, quickly executes right upward palm-heel attack, upper level.

20. *Attacker:*   Delivers right lunge punch to the upper level.
    Defender: Keeping left foot in place, drops to right knee, counterattacking with right reverse punch.
    NOTE: Combinations of blocks and attacks offer a wide variety from which the alert student can readily improvise. It should be kept in mind that each individual technique within any combination must be strongly executed, with the student remaining well balanced throughout. Skillful execution of various combinations of blocks and attacks is mandatory to a successful performance during sparring, especially when dealing with multiple opponents.

    While sparring the student may adapt the prescribed manner of executing a block to the needs of the moment. Thus, to produce a speedy reaction to a given attack, the student may eliminate the initial wide sweep of the arm, going directly into the appropriate block while thrusting the shoulder sharply forward.

17

18 →

19 →

20 →

■ Foot Techniques

1. Front Kick (Close-Leg Stance)

  1. Bend knees slightly, holding both arms to the side. Flexing toes strongly upward raise right foot beside left knee, holding parallel to floor. Using knee as fulcrum, kick to the front with toes remaining tightly flexed upward but ankle rotated forward. Snap foot back beside left knee, holding parallel to floor before lowering. This is a four-count exercise.

  2. Repeat 1 in only two counts (of two movements each), then one count.

  3. Repeat 2, combining right, then left front kick in one count.

  4. Repeat 3, beginning with the left front kick.

    Striking area—ball of foot.

    NOTE: The supporting leg, although slightly bent, is fully tensed as are the lower abdomen, buttocks, and latissimus dorsi. This holds true for every kick covered throughout the book.

(Forward Stance)

  5. Swiftly raise right foot beside opposite knee. Then return to original position. This is a two-count exercise.

    NOTE: Since this preliminary movement is essential to the success of the front kick, the student should strive for maximum speed. Flex toes vigorously upward the instant the movement is started. This causes toes and heel to launch simultaneously off the floor into the kick. Otherwise the student will find himself pushing onto the ball of the foot before raising it to knee, with subsequent loss of vital time.

  6. Executing right front kick, return to forward stance on fourth count. This is a four-count exercise.

    NOTE: At the outset (forward stance) body weight should be distributed between front and back foot with slight stress falling on the forward foot. If the student chooses to commence with more weight on the rear foot, he will find that he must then shift noticeably forward before raising the kicking foot. An alert opponent would react accordingly to this indication of an imminent attack. The recommended weight distribution facilitates lightning-swift action. With this, as with every offense, the attacking limb must pursue a straight line to insure maximum potential. Maintain a strong forward thrust in the left knee and hip throughout this movement.

1 : 1

1 : 5

1 : 6

1 : 7 →

7. Execute right front kick, snapping kicking foot back to opposite knee before lowering forward to the floor.[1] Maintain a feeling of forward thrust in the supporting knee and hip throughout this movement. Remaining in left forward stance, slide-step back to starting point. Repeat exercise fifty times, alternating sides, with each of the last ten movements accompanied by kiai.

8. Snap left foot rapidly back beside right knee. Flexing toes upward and using knee as fulcrum, kick to the front. Bring the kicking foot back beside opposite knee before lowering it forward to the floor.

NOTE: Body weight should shift firmly forward beyond supporting foot.

9. Executing right front kick, lower kicking foot forward to floor, ending on the fourth count in left forward stance. Alternately repeat this exercise across training hall. When end of training hall has been reached and on instructor's command, reverse direction, simultaneously executing front kick and kiai.

NOTE: The kick will be stronger if the supporting foot is not permitted to twist outward until the kicking foot is lowered to the floor.

[1] When kicking foot is not withdrawn before lowering to floor, the resulting stance will be higher, weakening any subsequent kick.

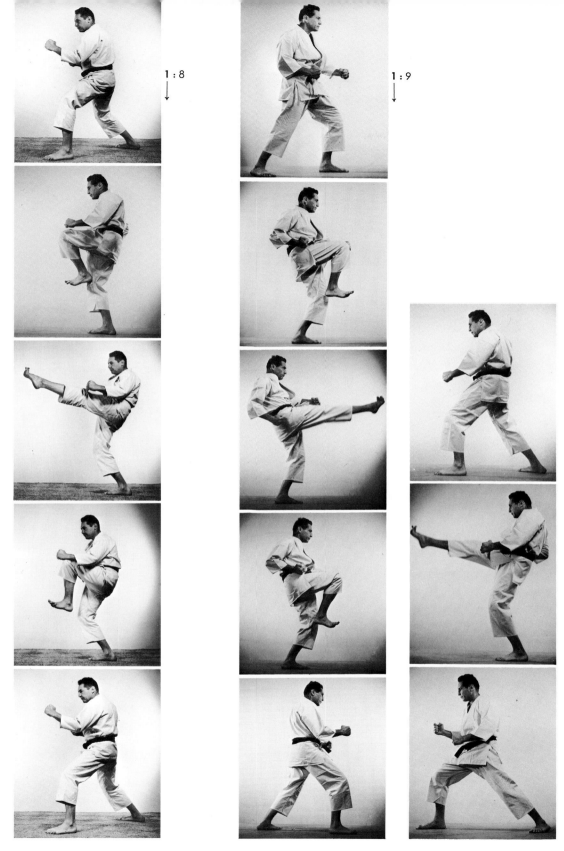

1 : 10 $\longrightarrow$

10. Begin as in 9. When end of training hall has been reached and, for example, student is in the forward stance, he will execute the front kick with the leading (left) foot, setting it down to the rear on the fourth count.

11. Begin as in 9. When end of training hall has been reached and, for example, student is in the forward stance, he will perform the following: left slide-step backward; left front kick, lowering kicking foot to the rear; right slide-step backward; right front kick, lowering kicking foot to the rear.

    NOTE: This exercise develops mobility through the need to shift quickly from the retreat to a strong forward attack, and is a unique strategy forming an integral part of all martial arts. Do not underestimate its value; through its practice, the student's mental attitude can be vastly strengthened. In circumstances where retreat is the only logical move for the moment, the student may still apply this exercise to advantage. He must continue to perform with precision and power, all the while awaiting an opening. Contrastingly, from a posture of impending defeat, conveying weakness to an opponent, the alert student can lead the aggressor into the very vulnerable state of overconfidence and then deliver the final blow. There are profound philosophical lessons beyond the scope of this book to be learned from these maneuvers. The mental capacity to extract the good from any situation, no matter how desperate, constitutes invaluable wisdom.

1 : 11 ⟶

1 : 12(a) ⟶

12. (a) Execute right front kick; returning kicking foot to original position, quickly execute left front kick.

(b) Repeat (a), adding right front kick. Return foot to original position.

(c) Advancing, execute a right front kick, upper level, followed instantly by a left front kick, upper level. Repeat alternately.

(d) Advancing, execute a right front kick, upper level, followed instantly by a left front kick, lower level. Repeat alternately.

NOTE: In the following two exercises be sure to withdraw kicking leg swiftly to opposite knee before lowering to floor. Practice them diligently, for they help develop good balance.

13. Execute left front kick; lower left foot as far as possible to the front without breaking balance, then quickly slide-shift right foot forward, recovering forward stance. Continuing across training hall, reverse direction on instructor's command and repeat this pattern executing right front kick.

14. Begin as in 9. When end of training hall has been reached and, for example, student is in the forward stance, he will execute a left front kick, bringing left foot down to the rear as far as possible without breaking balance, and quickly slide-shift right foot backward into left forward stance.

NOTE: As in any attack, be sure to shift body weight toward target. Keep supporting leg bent and body erect, with buttocks firmly forward beyond heel of supporting foot. With increased skill and positive equilibrium the student should project his body weight still farther forward. This provides additional forward thrust from pressure against floor applied by supporting foot.

1 : 12(c) ⟶

12(d)

↓

1 : 13 ⟶

1 : 15 ⟶

15. Alternately execute two consecutive front kicks before lowering attacking leg to the floor.

16. (a) Execute right front kick and, as right foot is withdrawn to opposite knee, simultaneously pivot one half-turn counterclockwise on left foot and lower kicking leg backward to the floor, momentarily reassuming forward stance; immediately execute right front kick.

(b) Right front kick; returning kicking foot to original position, quickly execute left front kick; as foot is withdrawn to opposite knee, simultaneously pivot one half-turn counterclockwise on ball of right foot, lowering kicking leg forward; execute right front kick; withdraw kicking foot to opposite knee and pivot counterclockwise on ball of left foot, reversing direction, and execute right front kick, lowering kicking foot forward.

(c) Right front kick; returning kicking foot to original position, quickly execute left front kick; as foot is withdrawn to opposite knee, simultaneously pivot one half-turn clockwise on ball of right foot, lowering kicking leg forward; execute right front kick; pivot counterclockwise on ball of left foot, reversing direction, and lower foot to rear; then execute right front kick.

(d) Right front kick; returning kicking foot to original position, quickly execute left front kick; as foot is withdrawn to opposite knee, simultaneously pivot one half-turn clockwise on ball of right foot, lowering kicking leg to the rear; execute right front kick; pivot counterclockwise on ball of left foot, reversing direction, and execute right front kick, lowering kicking foot to the rear.

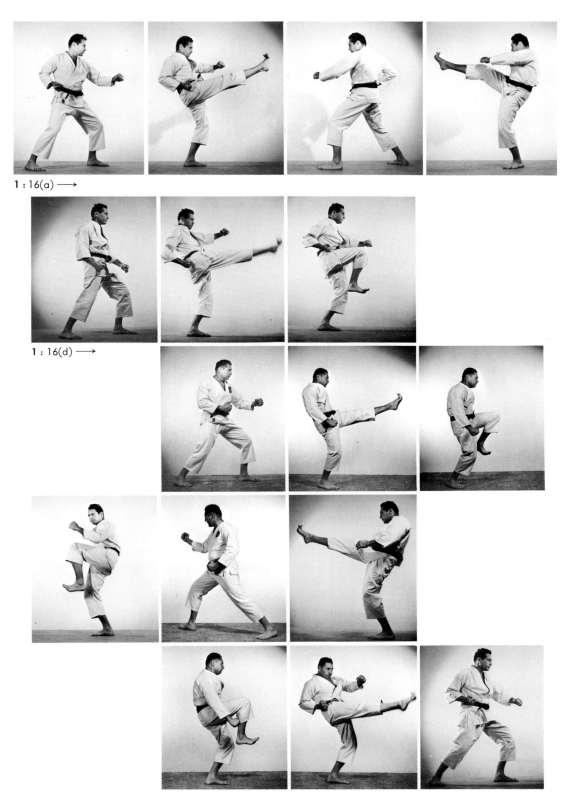

1 : 16(a) ⟶

1 : 16(d) ⟶

1 : 17(a) ⟶

17. (a) Execute right front kick and, withdrawing kicking foot, place it to the left of left foot; then slide-shift left foot to the rear into left forward stance.
    (b) Execute right front kick and, withdrawing kicking foot to opposite knee, simultaneously execute a low backward hop to assume left forward stance.
18. Execute left front kick and, withdrawing left foot to opposite knee, quickly execute right front kick, attempting to do so before left foot touches floor.
    NOTE: This prepares the student for the flying front kick in which the right front kick is performed with the left foot still in the air. This technique should be practiced until the student is able to execute the kick simultaneously with the withdrawal of the opposite foot.

(Forward Stance)

19. (a) Alternately execute front kick with each foot. Supporting foot must remain flat, with entire leg and supporting buttock firm. At completion of kick hips are strongly tucked forward, with buttocks and lower abdomen firmly tensed. Each kick must be fully committed, stretching out for distance without leaning backward or moving arms loosely about. Attempt to keep body weight from shifting to supporting leg. Lower kicking foot forward to floor; then regain original stance.

1 : 17(b)

1 : 18

1 : 19(a)

1 : 19(c) ⟶

1 : 19(b)

(Straddle-Leg Stance)

    (b) (*1*) Repeat 12 (a), kicking front and center. With each repetition, lower kicking foot sideways to floor to regain original stance.

        (*2*) On a single count execute the right, then left front kick.

        (*3*) Execute the right, then left front kick with ten repetitions each.

(Open-Leg Stance)

    (c) (*1*) Left slide-step forward and to the left oblique, simultaneously pivoting forty-five degrees clockwise on ball of left foot. Immediately execute right front kick: then, lowering kicking foot to floor, resume original stance.

        (*2*) Right slide-step forward and to the right oblique, repeating the pattern given in (*1*).

NOTE: The legs are our most powerful weapons of attack. Their effectiveness is obvious in that they are longer and stronger than our arms. Understood in this light, intense concentration must then be placed on their development. Powerful legs are all-important for the maintenance of balance in any technique and to sustain a high level of endurance during prolonged periods of physical activity. When employing the foot attack, the proper place for the hands is hip level or above with elbows in close to the body. This provides superior control for both balance and blocking or hand attacks.

2. **Front-Thrust Kick** (Forward Stance)

    1. Raise right foot beside left knee. Thrust right foot straight forward, locking knee. Bring right foot back beside left knee before lowering it to the ground.

    Striking area—sole or heel of the foot.

    NOTE: The front-thrust kick is extremely powerful.

3. **Side-Thrust Kick** (Open-Leg Stance)

    1. Locking the knee, move left foot straight sideways approximately twelve inches. Twist left hip clockwise and, extending the heel, point toes of left foot forty-five degrees to the right. Center body weight over supporting leg and raise left foot straight up to hip level and parallel to the floor.

    NOTE: This exercise will strengthen the hip and stretch the thigh muscles, enabling the student to properly perform the side-thrust kick.

2. The class forms a single line, facing forward in close-leg stance with arms raised to the sides at shoulder level and holding each others' wrists for balance.

  (a) Raise left foot to opposite knee.

  (b) Execute left side-thrust kick to the left side, simultaneously turning head in direction of kick. (Make certain left knee is locked when leg is fully extended.)

  (c) Return left foot to opposite knee.

  (d) Lower left foot to floor.

  (e) When proficiency has been achieved, perform this exercise in two counts by combining (a) with (b) and (c) with (d).

Striking area—knife-edge of the foot.

(Forward Stance)

3. (a) Raise right foot to opposite knee and execute right side-thrust kick to the right side, simultaneously turning the head in the direction of the kick.

  (b) Raise left foot to opposite knee, then execute left side-thrust kick. Return left leg to opposite knee before placing it forward on the floor.

NOTE: Attempt to keep foot of supporting leg from turning outward when kicking.

3 : 3(a)   3 : 3(b)

3:4(a) ⟶

4. (a) Two students face each other. One student turns to left oblique; with right hand grasps partner's outstretched left hand at wrist. In two counts, deliver side-thrust kick to partner's midsection. When proficient, perform this exercise without holding wrist

   (b) Face partner, assuming open-leg stance; left slide-step forward to the left oblique, executing right side-thrust kick to partner's midsection.

   (c) Repeat (b) and, pivoting clockwise slightly on ball of left foot, add left reverse punch, lower level.

(Open-Leg Stance)

5. Smoothly left slide-step forward, simultaneously lifting both arms forward to shoulder level.

   NOTE: This exercise enables the student to advance smoothly and quickly when performing the side-thrust kick.

6. Right slide-step forward, raising left knee. Keeping upper body erect over bent knee, execute left side-thrust kick straight sideways, leaning body in direction of attack. Return kicking foot to opposite knee before lowering it to original stance. Left then right slide-step back to original position, then repeat to the opposite side. Alternately perform this exercise fifty times, with each of the last ten movements accompanied by a kiai.

   NOTE: On initial forward slide-step the body is considerably lowered, remaining so until completion of kick. This exercise can be executed in a limited area since only one slide-step is performed per pupil.

3 : 4(b) ⟶

3 : 4(c)

6 ↓

3 : 5 ⟶

3 : 7 ⟶

3 : 8 ⟶

3 : 9 ⟶

4 : 1 →

(Straddle-Leg Stance)

7. Left slide-step to the right, placing that foot just past right leg. Quickly raise right foot to left knee and execute right side-thrust kick straight to the side. Bring kicking foot back to left knee before lowering into original stance.

8. With a low hop to the right, place left foot in space vacated by the right, simultaneously raising right foot alongside left knee; execute right side-thrust kick straight to the side; quickly repeat to the left, executing left side-thrust kick to the side.

9. Standing in place, execute left side-thrust kick straight to the side; with a low hop to the right, place left foot in space vacated by the right, simultaneously raising right foot alongside left knee; execute right side-thrust kick to the side.

4. Side-Thrust Kick Development (Close-Leg Stance)

1. Arms extended down and out from sides, fists turned inward; raise the right foot to left knee. Snapping head to the right, quickly execute right side-thrust kick, returning right foot to left knee before lowering to the side.

   NOTE: Perform twenty repetitions before repeating with opposite foot.

4 : 2

4 : 4

4 : 5

5:1

→

(Straddle-Leg Stance)

2. Arms extended down and out from sides, fists turned inward, head facing direction of kick. Repeat 1, maintaining low, strong stance. Allow only minimal weight-shift onto supporting leg.

NOTE: This exercise should be performed by the entire class at the end of every training session. One student will loudly count from one through ten with each kick. Then each student will in turn take up the count. A minimum of fifty side-thrust kicks with each foot should be performed in this manner.

3. Students form opposing lines one arm's length apart. Alternately execute the side-thrust kick, knee level. Opposing student shifts to the side as soon as kick commences.

(Forward Stance)

4. (a) Slide right foot up to a position perpendicular to and immediately behind left foot and execute left side-thrust kick.

(b) Repeat (a), substituting low hop for sliding movement and immediately executing the kick.

NOTE: This technique effects a rapid shift to a new line of attack.

5. Alternately execute the right, then left side-thrust kick across the training hall.

NOTE: As the right foot is raised to the opposite knee, the student simultaneously pivots one quarter-turn counterclockwise on the ball of left foot; after executing kick, foot is withdrawn and then placed forward and down while the student simultaneously pivots one quarter-turn clockwise on the ball of his left foot, assuming the left forward stance. He then executes the left side-thrust kick etc., reversing direction of turns.

5. Side-Snap Kick (Open-Leg Stance)

1. Raise left foot to right knee, pointing left knee to left oblique. Snap foot upward rather than thrusting straight to the side.

2. Substituting side-snap kick, repeat all exercises pertaining to side-thrust kick.

Striking area—knife-edge of foot.

NOTE: The side-thrust kick cannot be used effectively when in close proximity to an opponent. In such situations, the side-snap kick should be substituted.

FOOT TECHNIQUES **167**

6. Round Kick (Open-Leg Stance)

1. Hold both hands palms down, somewhat to the rear. Alternately kick each palm with side of corresponding foot, being careful that the leg is kept parallel to the floor when palm is struck and that the upper body remains erect.

(Forward Stance with partner in left forward stance)

2. (a) With left hand holding partner's outstretched right hand at the wrist for balance, lift right foot up to the rear with knee bent and straight to the side, and leg parallel to the floor. Utilizing power enhanced by a hip-swiveling motion, snap leg forward, so that knee acts as a fulcrum. Kick toward left side of opponent's body. Return kicking leg to previous raised position before lowering into original position.
   Striking area—ball of foot.
   (b) An alternate method of executing the round kick would be with the ankle arched and toes curled downward strongly.
   Striking area—instep.
   NOTE: Kicking to the far side of an opponent's body weakens the attacker's balance and also exposes much of his body to counterattack. As the knee swings forward in an elevated arc, the round kick employs the same principle as does the front kick.

3. Perform (a) without holding partner's wrist.

4. Perform 3 across training hall, lowering kicking foot forward to the floor as partner alternately slide-steps to the rear.

5. Perform exercise 4, executing two consecutive round kicks before lowering attacking foot to the floor.

6. (a) Execute left round kick, and, placing left foot down in original position, immediately execute right round kick, lowering kicking foot forward.
   (b) Execute left side-thrust kick, and, placing left foot down in original position, immediately execute right round kick, lowering foot forward.

7. Execute left round kick. Lowering kicking foot to the rear, simultaneously deliver right reverse punch.

(Forward Stance)

8. Students form opposing lines.
   LINE A: Lightly execute left, then right round kick to opponent's midsection.
   LINE B: After first round kick has landed, quickly left slide-step to rear.
   At termination of second round kick, repeat above sequence reversing roles.
   NOTE: There is to be no pause until instructor's command to stop. Light contact is permissible during this exercise.

6 : 1 ⟶

6 : 2(b)

6 : 6(b)
↓

6 : 2(a)

→

9. Resuming forward stance after each technique, simultaneously left jab and half right slide-step forward, adding the left:
   (a) round kick
   (b) front kick
   (c) side-snap kick forward
   (d) side-thrust kick forward
   (e) slide-step backward
   NOTE: This versatile exercise and its components should be practiced singly with several repetitions of each.
10. Execute right round kick; left side-thrust kick; right reverse punch.

7. **Rear Kick** (Close-Leg Stance)

1. Raise right foot beside left knee. Turning head to the right, and, directing gaze backward, thrust kick to the rear. Quickly snap right leg back to left knee before lowering to original stance. Striking area—heel or sole.
   NOTE: Leaning too far forward while kicking weakens the stance.

(Forward Stance)

2. Execute right rear kick and recover original stance.
3. Execute two consecutive right rear kicks and recover original stance.
4. Repeat 2, using left foot and remembering to turn head to the left before executing kick.
5. Execute right rear kick and, instead of recovering original stance, lower attacking foot forward to the floor. Repeating with left foot, alternately perform exercise across training hall.
6. Modify 2 and 3 by pivoting clockwise on supporting leg after completion of right rear kick and, facing to the rear, lower kicking foot forward to the floor.
   NOTE: The latter exercise provides excellent body-shifting practice.
7. Slide right foot up to a position perpendicular to and immediately behind left foot.
   (a) Execute left rear kick.
   (b) Repeat (a), substituting low hop for sliding movement and immediately executing the kick.

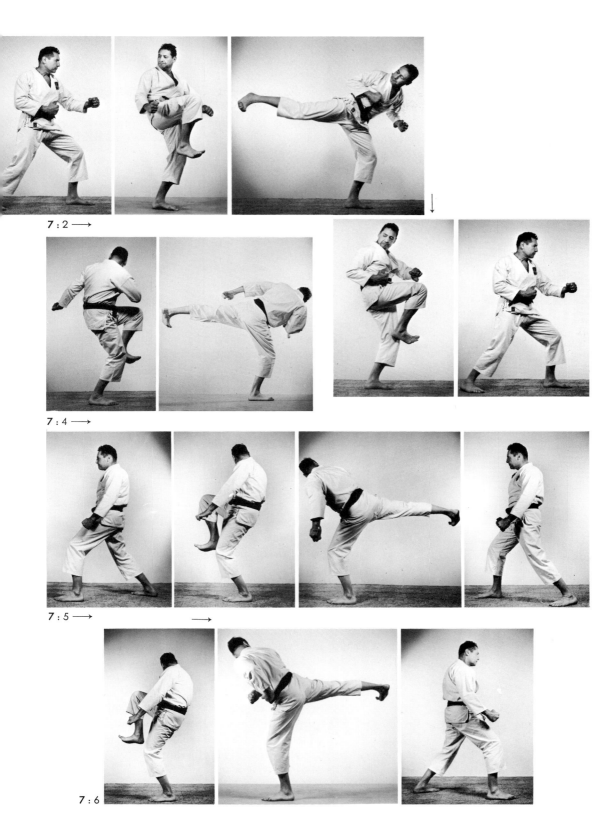

7:2 ⟶

7:4 ⟶

7:5 ⟶   ⟶

7:6

8. Kicking Development (Close-Leg Stance)

1. Whirl counterclockwise one half-turn, raising right foot to opposite knee.
2. Whirl counterclockwise one half-turn, raising left foot to opposite knee.
3. Whirl clockwise one half-turn, raising left foot to opposite knee.
4. Whirl clockwise one half-turn, raising right foot to opposite knee.
5. Repeat 1–4, starting from the left forward stance.
6. Repeat 1–5, adding the appropriate rear kick.
7. Raise right foot beside left knee, left foot firmly in place. Right rear kick ten consecutive times before lowering foot to original stance.
8. Repeat first movement in 7, adding in turn:
   (a) front kick
   (b) front-thrust kick
   (c) round kick
   (d) side-thrust kick
   (e) side-snap kick
9. Right side-snap kick to the side; left round kick; right front kick; left side-thrust kick to the side; right rear kick.
10. Right, then left front kick; right, then left round kick; right, then left side-thrust kick; right, then left rear kick.
11. (a) *Attacker:* Executes right front kick.
    Defender: Moves forward, grasping kicking foot, exerting moderate pressure forward. (Any student whose body easily yields should assume from this indication that his attack did not terminate with maximum body tension. Each of the various foot attacks should be similarly tested.)
    (b) Students form opposing lines. Each student in one line will raise his right leg and place his foot against opponent's abdomen. On command students push forward from supporting leg, attempting to generate maximum thrust. Partners will then advise as to relative power.
       (*1*) Repeat, substituting the side-thrust kick.
       (*2*) Repeat, substituting the rear kick.
    (c) Place the sole of the foot against your opponent's midsection, directly to the front, with leg parallel to the floor and the knee locked. Flex the toes strongly upward, stretching the upper body forward toward opponent.
    NOTE: This aids in developing a strong front-thrust kick.
    (d) Place outer edge of foot[2] against your opponent's midsection, to the side, holding leg parallel to floor. Flex toes strongly upward, stretching upper body sideways toward opponent.
    NOTE: (c) and (d) prove an excellent aid in developing strong front- and side-thrust kicks. Keep supporting leg, abdomen, latissimus dorsi, and buttocks firmly tensed with knee bent.
    (e) Repeat (c), thrusting ball of foot forward.
    NOTE: This aids in developing a strong front kick.

[2] The "knife-edge," a label which conveys the slicing, driving action it performs.

8 : 1 ⟶

8 : 3 ⟶

8 : 11(a)   (b)

(c)   (d)

(Forward Stance)

12. Two students face each other and hold a uniform belt fully extended between them at knee level. Without touching the belt a third student executes:
    (a) front kick
    (b) side-thrust kick
    (c) side-snap kick
    (d) round kick
    (e) rear kick
    NOTE: Repeat each several times before continuing.

13. (a) Right front kick, withdrawing kicking foot beside left knee; with low hop onto right foot, immediately execute left side-thrust kick to the left side.
    (b) Execute left side-thrust kick, then right front kick.

PART 2 : TRAINING **174**

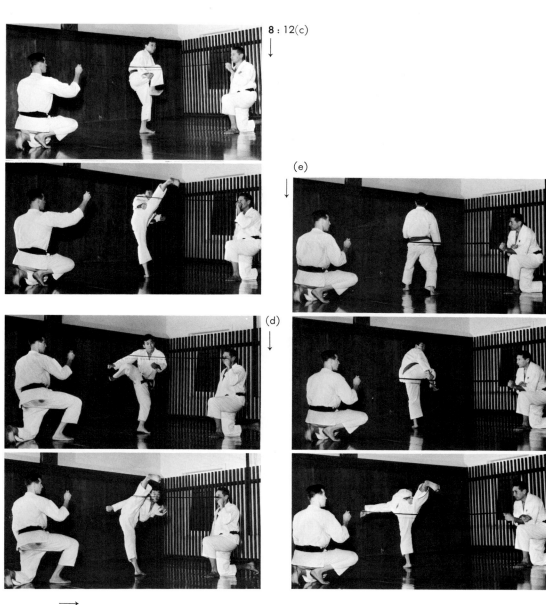

8 : 12(c)

(e)

(d)

8 : 13(a)

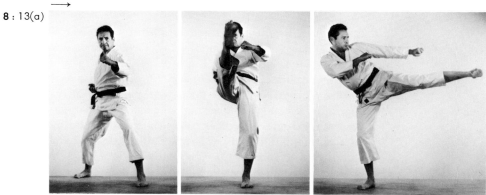

14. Right side-thrust kick to the side; lower kicking leg to the floor, placing it down at right angles to the left instep; immediately execute left side-thrust kick.

    NOTE: Repeat this exercise, completing a circle clockwise and then counterclockwise.

15. (a) Execute right front kick, followed in one continuous movement by right side-thrust kick to the side. Placing right foot down parallel to the left, move the left foot to the rear, assuming a left forward stance. Repeat the foregoing with the left foot.

    NOTE: With a large group this exercise can be performed in a limited area, since the activity does not involve a slide-step in either direction.

    (b) Right front kick, lower level; withdrawing kicking foot to opposite knee, quickly execute right side-thrust kick, upper level.

    (c) Right front kick, lower level; withdrawing kicking foot to opposite knee, quickly pivot one half-turn counterclockwise on ball of left foot; execute right rear kick; pivot one half-turn counterclockwise on ball of left foot, lowering kicking foot to the rear and simultaneously executing right reverse punch.

16. Execute in one continuous exercise:
    (a) right front kick
    (b) right side-thrust kick to the side
    (c) right round kick

17. Execute in one continuous exercise:
    (a) right front kick
    (b) right side-thrust kick to the side
    (c) right rear kick

18. Right front kick; right side-thrust kick to the side; right rear kick; right round kick.

19. Execute right front kick; right side-thrust kick to the side; withdrawing kicking foot to opposite knee, lower to floor, quickly executing left rear kick.

20. Combine exercises 16, 17, 18, and 19, concluding each exercise by placing right foot to the floor in original position.

21. Right front kick; withdrawing kicking foot to opposite knee, execute right side-thrust kick to the right side; withdrawing kicking foot to opposite knee, pivot one half-turn counterclockwise on ball of left foot and execute right rear kick; lower right foot beside left and execute left rear kick; pivot one half-turn counterclockwise on ball of right foot and lower left foot forward to floor.

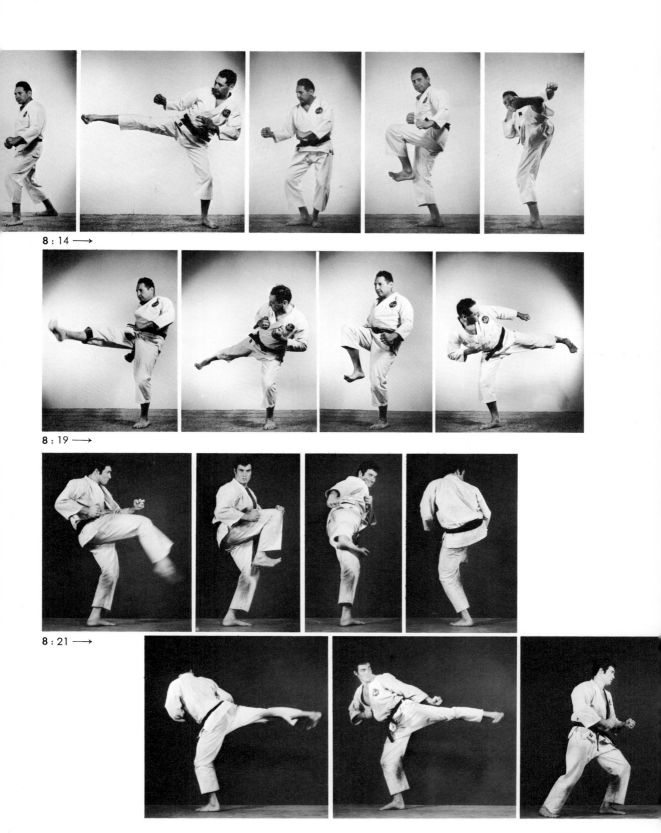

8 : 14 ⟶

8 : 19 ⟶

8 : 21 ⟶

9:1 ⟶

10

9. Stamping Kick (Forward Stance)

1. Raise right foot alongside left knee and, in one continuous exercise, execute front-, side-, and rear-stamping kicks, returning kicking foot to left knee between each consecutive kick.
2. Execute two consecutive stamping kicks in each of above directions before lowering attacking foot to the floor.
   NOTE: The stamping kick, delivered in a manner similar to the thrust kick, strikes an opponent's leg at knee level or below.
3. (a) Execute right front-stamping kick; then, without lowering foot to floor, follow with a right front kick.
   (b) Repeat (a) to the side.
   (c) Repeat (a) to the rear.
   (d) Combine (a)–(c) in one continuous exercise.

10. Knee Kick (Forward Stance)

Attacker: Delivers right lunge punch to the upper level.
Defender: Using both hands, grasps attacking wrist (to hold opponent in close and to give added impact to the counterattack), and then quickly executes the right knee kick.

NOTE: This technique is executed by thrusting the knee either straight up to the front or sideways to the front in an arc. The knee kick should be used only when in close proximity to an opponent.

11 ⟶

12 : 2 ⟶

12 : 1

11. Sweeping Kick (Forward Stance)

With right foot execute sweeping motion along the floor, then up, striking opponent's left ankle or knee. (The knife-edge of the foot should be turned down for this kick.)

NOTE: In contradistinction to other kicks this requires that the ankle be arched and the toes curled downward strongly. It is used primarily as a diversionary or unbalancing kick.

12. Flying Kick (Forward Stance)

1. The flying side-thrust and flying front kicks are executed by leaping high, with both legs pulled up as close to the body as possible and elbows held close before delivering the kick with the foot closest to the opponent. The kicking student is most vulnerable when dropping to the floor. He should land in a strong stance ready to block or attack.

2. It will then prove advantageous to pivot quickly to a final position, facing the rear or side of the opponent.

NOTE: Flying kicks are generally best suited for execution by the lighter, more agile student. Due to the added time requirement, this technique is best utilized as an occasional surprise attack.

When proficiency in foot attacks has been achieved, the student need not feel restricted to the kicking techniques with which he has become familiar. Under certain conditions he may require a greater latitude of expression. The following kicks (which can and should be varied to confuse the opponent) will supply this necessary factor:

Round Kick. This kick can also be executed at an angle which places it midway between the front and round kick, providing an attack that is swift, powerful, and more difficult to block.

Side-Thrust Kick. This movement can begin as a front kick. When the kicking foot nears the opponent, quickly pivot to the side on the ball of the supporting foot, executing the side-thrust kick instead.

Under emergency conditions imposed in free-style sparring, the student will frequently find that speed often takes priority over perfect form. In this case, rather than lifting the attacking foot to the opposite knee prior to the delivery of the side-thrust kick, execute it directly from the floor and on a diagonal and rising line at the opponent.

At this point the student will start to put into practice with a partner the different blocks and attacks. It is recommended that students proceed at a slow pace emphasizing the precise application of technique. After the student's reaction to any single or combination attack becomes reflexive, then and only then should he strive for speed. Let the defending partner remember that his role is never a passive one. Although he may not always be called upon to execute a specific technique, he must ready himself to withstand any onslaught. He commences this by rigorously tensing the abdominal area as each attack is initiated by his opponent. In working from the text it would be most helpful if a third party were to read instructions aloud to the sparring partners. If the student is enrolled in an accredited karate school, he should follow his instructor's directions, utilizing this material for home study.

That animus which inspires the karateist's attack should not suddenly cease with the termination of that technique. Even though the actual physical movement is abruptly checked, the compelling feeling should continue to be one of an intensive drive forward. An opponent confronted by this spectacle is put at a psychological disadvantage while the attacker himself is better equipped to withstand any retaliatory action. Nor should this spirit commence with his initial movement. It is contained within the student constantly; somewhat prior to the overt movement the feeling projects itself to audience and opponents alike in an overwhelming intensity of face and physique. The explosive force of the action which follows, be it block or attack, finds its character in the preliminary state of mind. The most potent concentration of physical power possible (*kime*) will be produced at the precise moment of contact.

■ Combination Foot and Hand Attacks

1 : 1 ⟶

- 1 -

(Forward Stance)

1. Right front kick; returning kicking foot to original position, simultaneously execute right reverse punch.[1]
2. Right lunge punch; then quickly execute left front kick, followed by left reverse punch.
3. Slide-stepping forward, alternately execute front kicks. When end of training hall has been reached and, for example, student is in forward stance, he will perform the following: left slide-step backward; left front kick; lowering kicking foot to the rear, simultaneously execute left reverse punch; right slide-step backward; right front kick; lowering kicking foot to the rear, simultaneously execute right reverse punch.
4. Right front kick and simultaneous left spear-hand attack. Returning kicking foot to original position, simultaneously execute right reverse punch.
5. Repeat 4, lowering kicking foot forward to the floor and simultaneously executing right reverse punch.
6. Right front kick, and lowering kicking foot forward to the floor, quickly execute left lunge punch, then right reverse punch.
7. Right front kick, and lowering kicking foot forward to the floor, simultaneously execute right reverse punch; left front kick, and lowering kicking foot forward to the floor, simultaneously execute left reverse punch.

[1] If at first there is difficulty in performing this exercise, it will be advisable to practice it omitting the front kick, by simply raising the foot to knee level.

182

1 : 8 ⟶

8. Left front kick; return kicking foot beside right knee; pivot one quarter-turn clockwise on right foot and execute left side-thrust kick, followed by right reverse punch.

NOTE: If the left front kick is evaded by an opponent who slide-shifts backward and then quickly forward, he will move into the left side-thrust kick and right reverse punch.

- 2 -

1. Left front kick, and, lowering kicking foot forward, quickly execute right front kick. Returning kicking foot to original position, simultaneously execute right reverse punch.
2. Left front-thrust kick; right front kick; right reverse punch, simultaneously lowering kicking foot to the rear.
3. Right round kick and left reverse punch.
4. (a) Right front kick, left round kick, and left reverse punch.
   (b) Right front-stamping kick to opponent's left leg at knee level or below; left round kick, upper level, and then right reverse punch, lower level.
   (c) Right side-stamping kick to opponent's leg at knee level or below; left round kick, right side-thrust kick, then left reverse punch.
   (d) Right front-stamping kick, to opponent's left leg at knee level or below; return kicking foot to opposite knee and quickly execute right front kick, left round kick, right side-thrust kick, then left reverse punch.
5. Left front kick, right round kick, left round kick, and right reverse punch.

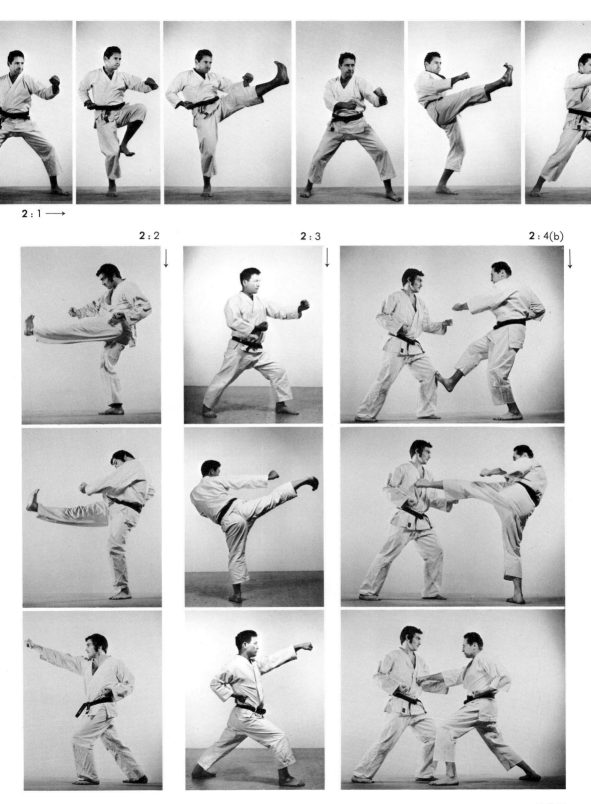

2 : 1 ⟶

2 : 2

2 : 3

2 : 4(b)

2 : 6(a)

2 : 7

3 : 1 ⟶

3 : 3

⟶

6. (a) Right front-lunge kick, and, lowering kicking foot rear, simultaneously execute right reverse punch; right, then left round kick; right rear kick, then right reverse punch.

(b) Right front kick, and, lowering kicking foot forward, execute right reverse punch; left, then right round kick; pivoting one half-turn counterclockwise on ball of right foot, execute left rear kick; withdraw kicking foot to opposite knee; pivoting one half-turn counterclockwise on ball of right foot, lower left foot forward, simultaneously executing a right reverse punch.

7. Right front kick, and, lowering kicking foot forward, pivot counterclockwise on balls of both feet, reversing direction; right front kick, left side-thrust kick, right reverse punch, left jab, right front kick, then right reverse punch.

- 3 -

1. Right reverse punch, right front kick, then right reverse punch.
2. Right reverse punch, upper level; right side-thrust kick; left reverse punch, lower level.
3. Right front kick, left side-thrust kick, and right reverse punch.
4. Execute the right, then left side-thrust kick, and then right reverse punch.

3 : 5(a)

5. (a) Right front kick; withdrawing kicking foot to opposite knee, execute right side-thrust kick, then left reverse punch.

   (b) Right front or front-stamping kick; withdrawing kicking foot to opposite knee, pivot one half-turn counterclockwise on ball of left foot; execute right rear kick; withdraw kicking foot to opposite knee; pivoting one half-turn clockwise on ball of left foot, lower right foot forward and simultaneously execute left reverse punch.

6. (a) Execute right reverse punch, left front kick, right front kick, then left and right reverse punches to the upper and lower levels respectively.

   (b) Execute right reverse punch, upper level; right front kick; left reverse punch, lower level; then left downward block, simultaneously right slide-stepping backward.

7. Execute right reverse punch; left front kick; with a low forward hop, place the right foot in the space vacated by the left; execute a left side-thrust or rear kick, then a right reverse punch.

8. Execute right reverse punch; left front kick; withdrawing kicking foot to opposite knee, immediately execute right flying front kick, then left and right reverse punches to the upper and lower levels respectively.

9. (a) Right round kick, left side-thrust kick, then right reverse or lunge punch.

   (b) Right front kick, right reverse punch, left round kick, right reverse punch.

   (c) Right front kick, left round kick, right side-thrust kick, left reverse punch.

   (d) Right side-snap kick, left side-thrust kick, right reverse punch.

10. (a) Slowly and without power at first execute the right front, left round, right side-thrust kicks, and pivoting one half-turn counterclockwise on ball of right foot, left rear kick.

    (b) Repeat exercise (a), combining each kick with a suitable hand attack.

    (c) Right round kick; pivoting one half-turn counterclockwise on ball of right foot, execute left rear kick; pivoting one half-turn counterclockwise on ball of left foot, execute the right front kick, then right reverse punch.

    (d) Substituting the right side-thrust kick for the right round kick, repeat (c) ending with either the right reverse or lunge punch instead of the right front kick and right reverse punch.

    (e) Right front kick, right reverse punch; pivoting one half-turn counterclockwise on ball of right foot, execute left rear kick; quickly snap kicking foot back beside opposite knee; pivot one half-turn counterclockwise on ball of supporting foot, and lower left foot forward; then execute right lunge punch.

    (f) Substituting right lunge punch for right front kick and right reverse punch, repeat (e).

    (g) Left round kick; right side-thrust kick; pivoting one quarter-turn counterclockwise on ball of left foot, lower right foot; execute left rear kick; pivoting one half-turn counterclockwise on ball of right foot, lower left foot forward; then right reverse or lunge punch.

3 : 8 ⟶

3 : 12 ⟶

(h) Right round kick; left side-thrust kick; pivoting one quarter-turn clockwise on ball of right foot, lower left foot; execute right rear kick; pivoting one half-turn clockwise on ball of left foot, lower right foot forward; then left reverse punch.

(i) Right front-stamping kick; lower kicking foot forward, pivot one half-turn counterclockwise on ball of right foot and execute left rear kick; lower kicking foot to the rear; pivot one half-turn counterclockwise on ball of left foot and quickly deliver right front kick; then right reverse punch.

11. Right lunge punch; right front kick; left reverse punch; right round kick; pivoting one half-turn clockwise on ball of right foot, execute left rear kick, then right reverse punch.

12. Left jab and simultaneous right round kick; right reverse punch and simultaneous left round kick; left and right reverse punches to the upper and lower levels respectively.

FOOT AND HAND ATTACKS **189**

4 : 1 ⟶

5 : 1 ⟶

- 4 -

1. Right front kick; returning kicking foot to original position, simultaneously execute a right reverse punch. Pivoting counterclockwise one quarter-turn on left foot and at the same time, raising right foot to left knee, execute a right side-thrust kick, followed by left reverse punch.

- 5 -

1. Left front kick with simultaneous left jab; right lunge punch, upper level, and left reverse punch, lower level.

- 6 -

1. Right front kick; lowering kicking foot forward, execute right lunge punch; standing in place, execute the left upper-, then right lower-level reverse punches.

- 7 -

1. Right lunge punch; left front kick; left and right reverse punches to the upper and lower levels respectively.
2. Right lunge punch; left front kick; right reverse punch; right side-thrust kick; then left reverse punch.

6:1 ⟶

7:2 ⟶

8:2

- 8 -

1. Left front kick; right round kick; left reverse punch; pivoting one half-turn counterclockwise on ball of left foot, execute right rear kick; withdrawing kicking foot to opposite knee and, pivoting one half-turn clockwise on ball of left foot, execute left reverse punch.
2. Left front kick; right round kick; left reverse punch; right rear kick; withdrawing kicking foot to opposite knee and, pivoting one half-turn clockwise on ball of left foot, execute left reverse punch.

- 9 -

1. Half right slide-step forward and simultaneous left jab; left front kick; right front kick; left side-thrust kick, and right reverse punch.

- 10 -

1. Left lunge jab, right front kick, then right reverse punch, simultaneously lowering kicking foot to the rear.
2. Left lunge jab, right reverse punch, then right front kick.
3. Left lunge jab, right front kick; lowering kicking foot forward to the floor, simultaneously execute right reverse punch, upper level. Standing in place, execute the left reverse punch, lower level; left side-thrust kick and then right reverse punch.

NOTE: The initial forward movement in 9 and 10 quickly closes the distance between opponents.

9:1 ⟶

10:1

10:3 ⟶

11 : 1 ⟶

12 : 1 ⟶

- 11 -

1. Right front-thrust kick; left side-thrust kick; right round kick; left rear kick; pivoting one half-turn counterclockwise on ball of right foot, execute right reverse punch.
2. Left side-thrust kick and simultaneous left back-fist strike; lower left foot to rear (assuming left forward stance), simultaneously executing right reverse punch; deliver left front kick, then left reverse punch.

- 12 -

1. Right front kick, then return kicking foot alongside left knee. Immediately (without returning foot to floor) leap forward delivering a right reverse punch.
2. Right front kick, then return kicking foot alongside left knee. Perform leap as in 1, following immediately with left side-thrust kick, then right reverse punch.
NOTE: Leap is to be performed with knees flexed while maintaining low center of gravity.

13:2 ⟶

14:1 ⟶

- 13 -

1. Right side-thrust kick to the right oblique; left side-thrust kick to the left oblique; right round kick, then left reverse punch forward.
2. Right lunge punch; left side-thrust kick, then right reverse punch (both the latter to the left oblique).
3. Right front kick, lowering kicking foot forward; with a low hop place left foot in space vacated by the right as right foot is snapped up beside left knee; then right side-thrust kick to the right oblique.

   NOTE: When attacked, an alert opponent may frequently slide-shift to either side. This exercise will enable the student to change the direction of his attack swiftly to compensate for his opponent's defensive movement.

- 14 -

1. Right front kick; standing in place, quickly execute a right forward, then left upward elbow attack.

15 : 1 ⟶

- 15 -

1. Left side-thrust kick; right reverse punch; standing in place, quickly execute a left forward and right upward elbow attack, right front kick, and left side-thrust kick.

- 16 -

1. Left slide-shift to the rear, assuming the cat stance; left front kick, then right reverse punch.

- 17 -

1. Right front kick and simultaneous left jab; lower kicking foot forward to floor and simultaneously execute right reverse punch; with low hop forward, place left foot in space vacated by the right and deliver right side-thrust or rear kick, then left reverse punch.
2. Right front kick; left reverse punch, upper level, then right reverse punch, lower level; left front kick; right reverse punch, upper level, then left reverse punch, lower level.
3. Right front kick; right reverse punch, upper level, left and right reverse punches, lower level; left front kick; left reverse punch, upper level, right and left reverse punches, lower level.

- 18 -

1. Left lunge jab, upper level; taking a shorter than normal right slide-step, deliver a right lunge punch, upper level; keeping the right fist extended at the opponent's face, deliver a left front kick, quickly followed by a left upper, then right reverse punch, lower level.
2. Left jab, simultaneously right slide-stepping forward and continuing smoothly into a right lunge punch; left front kick; left, then right reverse punch to the upper and lower levels respectively.
3. Left lunge jab, upper level; right reverse punch, lower level; right front kick, right lunge jab, then left reverse punch to the upper and lower levels respectively.

16 : 1

17 : 1 ⟶

18 : 1 ⟶

20 : 1 ⟶

- 19 -

1. Right front kick; left side-snap kick; right side-thrust kick; left round kick; right reverse punch.

- 20 -

1. Right front kick and then right back-fist strike, terminating in the side straddle-leg stance.
2. Left front kick; withdrawing kicking foot to opposite knee, pivot one quarter-turn counterclockwise on ball of right foot; deliver the left back-fist strike to the rear, terminating in the side straddle-leg stance.
3. Right front kick; right lunge punch, lower level; pivot one quarter-turn counterclockwise on ball of left foot; deliver right back-fist strike, upper level, terminating in the side straddle-leg stance.
4. Right side-thrust kick and simultaneous right back-fist strike, followed by a left reverse punch—all delivered to the right oblique.
5. Left side-stamping kick; left back-fist strike, upper level, and right reverse punch, lower level.
6. Left side-stamping kick, simultaneously withdrawing left fist to a position above its counterpart at right hip; quickly place left foot forward and down, simultaneously delivering a left back-fist strike, upper level, and a right reverse punch, lower level.
7. Left side-stamping kick; place left foot forward and down, simultaneously delivering left and right hook punches to the upper and lower levels respectively.

20 : 2 ⟶

20 : 3 ⟶

20 : 6 ⟶

⟶

20 : 7

20 : 8(a) ⟶

8. (a) *Attacker:* With a low forward hop, place right foot in space vacated by the left; left side-stamping kick to opponent's left leg at
knee level or below with simultaneous left jab, upper level; then
right reverse punch, lower level.

   (b) Repeat (a), delivering the left side-thrust kick to opponent's right
leg at knee level or below.

   (c) With a low forward hop, place right foot in space vacated by the
left; left side-stamping kick to opponent's left leg at knee level or
below; right front kick, and then right reverse punch.

   (d) Right front kick, and, lowering kicking foot to rear, simultaneously execute right, then left reverse punch; with a short low hop,
place right foot in space vacated by left; left side-thrust or rear
kick, and, lowering left foot forward to floor and pivoting clockwise, execute right rear kick, then left reverse punch.

   (e) With a low forward hop, place the right foot in the space vacated
by the left; execute left side-stamping kick to opponent's left leg
at knee level or below with simultaneous left jab, upper level;
right side-thrust kick; right back-fist strike, upper level, then left
reverse punch, lower level.

   (f) With a low forward hop, place the right foot in the space vacated
by the left; execute left side-stamping kick to opponent's left leg
at knee level or below with simultaneous left jab, upper level;
right round kick; pivoting counterclockwise one half-turn, lower
right foot next to left; observing opponent over left shoulder,
quickly execute left rear kick; retracting foot to opposite knee,
pivot counterclockwise on right foot, executing left back-fist
strike, then right reverse punch to the upper and lower levels
respectively.

   (g) With a low forward hop, land on both feet; repeat to the rear,
then quickly forward again landing on left foot, executing left jab
and simultaneous right sweeping kick to opponent's left leg at knee
level or below; left round kick, then right reverse punch.

   (h) With a low forward hop, place the right foot in the space vacated
by the left; execute left round kick, upper level, then right reverse
punch, lower level.

20 : 8(c) ⟶

20 : 8(d) ⟶

21 : 1 ⟶

- 21 -

1. Right front kick, and lower right foot forward to floor; raising left foot to opposite knee, right flying front kick, right reverse punch, left upward elbow attack, right forward elbow attack, and left reverse punch.
2. Right front kick, lower kicking foot forward to floor, and raise left foot to opposite knee; right flying front kick, left reverse punch, right reverse punch, and left upward and right forward elbow attacks.
3. Right front kick; quickly bring right foot back beside left knee, simultaneously executing the left flying front kick, then right reverse punch.

- 22 -

1. Quickly slide right, then left foot straight back (maintaining original interval); right front kick, then right reverse punch, simultaneously lowering kicking foot to the rear.
2. Quickly slide right, then left foot straight back (maintaining original interval); right lunge punch.

- 23 -

(Left Forward Stance)
1. Right flying-front kick; right reverse punch, lower level; left reverse punch, upper level, and right upward elbow attack.
2. Left side-thrust kick, right round kick, and left reverse punch.
3. Right slide-step to the rear, simultaneously executing the left inward block; left side-thrust kick, then right reverse punch.

21 : 2 ⟶

⟶

23 : 2

FOOT AND HAND ATTACKS **203**

(Forward Stance)

1. *Attacker:* Delivers right lunge punch to the upper level.
   Defender: Executes right front kick, right reverse punch, and, standing in place, the left forward and right upward elbow attacks.

1. *Attacker:* Delivers right lunge punch to upper level.
   Defender: Executes left side-stamping kick, striking attacker's right leg at knee level or below. (This halts attacker's forward slide-step.)
2. *Attacker:* Delivers right lunge punch to the upper level.
   Defender: Executes left side-stamping kick to attacker's right leg at knee level or below; right front kick, then right reverse punch.
3. *Attacker:* Delivers right lunge punch to the upper level.
   Defender: Executes left jab and simultaneous left side-stamping kick to attacker's right leg at knee level or below; right front-thrust kick, left round kick, then right reverse punch.
4. *Attacker:* Delivers right lunge punch to the upper level.
   Defender: Executes right front kick; lowers kicking foot to rear, immediately dropping to right knee (with left foot in place) and executes right reverse punch; with a short low hop, places right foot in space vacated by the left; left side-thrust kick; pivoting clockwise on left foot, observes attacker over right shoulder and executes right rear kick, then left reverse punch.

26

1. (a) With a rapid slide-step, snap right foot forward to a position slightly ahead of the left; follow instantly with a left jab and simultaneous left front kick, then right reverse punch.
   (b) Class forms opposing lines which alternately perform (a).
   (c) In free-style sparring the above technique may be preceded by a right reverse punch and simultaneous kiai.
   (d) Feint right reverse punch, simultaneously executing a kiai; then repeat (a).

24 : 1 ⟶

25 : 1

26 : 1(c) ⟶

(e) Feint right reverse punch; execute left jab with simultaneous half right slide-step forward; left front kick, then right reverse punch, upper level.

(f) Feint right reverse punch, simultaneously executing a kiai; deliver left jab, simultaneously executing half right slide-step forward; left front kick and simultaneous right reverse punch.

(g) Feint right lunge punch, simultaneously executing a kiai and half right slide-step forward; left jab and simultaneous left front kick, then right reverse punch.

(h) Feint right reverse punch; left jab and simultaneous half right slide-step forward; left side-thrust kick, then right reverse punch.

(i) Feint right lunge punch, simultaneously executing a half right slide-step forward; left side-thrust kick, then right reverse punch.

2. Right front kick, lower level; left round kick, upper level, then right reverse punch, lower level.

(a) (*1*) Left jab and simultaneous right sweeping kick to opponent's left leg at knee level or below; lowering kicking foot forward, deliver a simultaneous right reverse punch and left front kick, then left reverse punch.

(*2*) Feint right reverse punch; left jab and simultaneous left side-stamping kick to opponent's left leg at knee level or below; pivoting one quarter-turn counterclockwise on ball of left foot, execute right side-snap kick, then left reverse punch.

(*3*) Feint right reverse punch; left jab and simultaneous left side-stamping kick to opponent's left leg at knee level or below; right round kick; left reverse punch.

(b) (*1*) Right front-stamping kick to opponent's left leg at knee level or below; quickly bring right foot back beside opposite knee; right front kick to opponent's midsection; then right reverse punch, upper level.

(*2*) With a low forward hop, place right foot in space vacated by the left; left side-stamping kick to knee level or below; without lowering foot, quickly draw kicking leg up to the rear with knee bent and leg parallel to the floor and execute left round kick, then right reverse punch.

(*3*) Repeat (*2*), and, after executing left side-stamping kick, quickly return kicking foot beside opposite knee; left side-thrust kick, right front kick, then right reverse punch.

(*4*) Repeat (*3*), and, after returning kicking foot beside opposite knee, quickly pivot one half-turn clockwise on ball of right foot and execute left rear kick.

(c) (*1*) Right sweeping kick to opponent's left leg at knee level or below; without lowering foot, quickly draw kicking leg up to the rear with knee bent and leg parallel to the floor; right round kick, left front kick, then left reverse punch.

(*2*) Right sweeping kick to opponent's left leg at knee level or below; without lowering leg, quickly return kicking foot beside opposite knee; right side-thrust kick, left front kick, then left reverse punch.

26 : 1(e)
↓

26 : 2(a) *1* ⟶

26 : 2(b) *1*
↓

26 : 2(g) ⟶

(d) (*1*) Feint right reverse punch; left jab and simultaneous left front kick; right lunge punch.

(*2*) Feint right reverse punch; left jab and simultaneous right front- or side-stamping kick to opponent's left leg at knee level or below; left round kick, lower level; right round kick, upper level, then left reverse punch, upper level.

(e) Feint right reverse punch; deliver left jab with simultaneous right slide-step forward; left front kick, then right reverse punch, lower level.

(f) Left front kick and simultaneous left jab; right front kick and simultaneous right reverse punch; left lunge punch, then right reverse punch.

(g) Left front kick and simultaneous right reverse punch; right front kick and simultaneous left reverse punch; right reverse punch, then left lunge punch.

3. Right front kick and simultaneous right reverse punch; then right back-fist strike, upper level, and simultaneous left reverse punch, lower level.

4. Right lunge punch, then right back-fist strike, upper level; left reverse punch, lower level; left front kick and simultaneous right reverse punch; then left reverse punch.

5. Right front kick; lower kicking foot to rear; right front kick and right reverse punch; left and right reverse punches; left side-thrust kick; right round kick, then left reverse punch.

6. Right lunge punch; right flying side-thrust kick; right forward elbow attack; then left lunge punch.

7. Left jab; right lunge punch; left slide-stepping forward into the right side straddle-leg stance, execute a left back-fist strike; right slide-step forward, executing a right outward knife-hand strike; left reverse punch.

8. Right front kick, simultaneously raising open right hand, palm inward, to right ear; execute right knife-hand strike downward to left side of opponent's neck; left reverse punch, upper level, simultaneously withdrawing opposite hand to the right side; quickly execute right ridge-hand attack, upper level.

26 : 3 ⟶

26 : 4 ⟶

26 : 6 ⟶

9. Right front kick, simultaneously raising open right hand, palm inward, to right ear; execute right knife-hand strike downward to left side of opponent's neck; left reverse punch, simultaneously moving right hand across body to left ear; quickly execute right knife-hand strike forward, upper level.

10. Left lunge jab, upper level; right slide-step forward to the right oblique; slide left foot to the right, assuming the left forward stance; raising left fist, palm inward, to right ear, simultaneously execute right close punch, lower level; left bottom- or back-fist strike, upper level, simultaneously withdraw fist above right hip; right reverse punch, lower level; right sweeping kick to opponent's left foot; left reverse punch, upper level.

11. Left lunge jab, upper level; right, then left slide-step forward to the right oblique; raising left fist, palm inward, to right ear, simultaneously execute right close punch, lower level; left bottom- or back-fist strike, upper level, simultaneously withdrawing right fist above right hip; right reverse punch, lower level; right sweeping kick to opponent's left leg at knee level or below; left reverse punch, upper level.

12. Feint a right reverse punch; left jab and simultaneous right front kick; left side-thrust kick; right round kick; whirling counterclockwise, lower right foot and quickly execute left rear kick; pivoting counterclockwise on ball of left foot, execute right reverse punch.

13. *Attacker:* Delivers right lunge punch to the upper level.
    Defender: Executes a blocking left lunge jab, upper level; raises left fist, palm inward, to right ear, simultaneously executing right close punch, lower level; left bottom- or back-fist strike, upper level, simultaneously withdrawing right fist above right hip; right reverse punch, lower level; right sweeping kick to attacker's right leg at knee level or below; left reverse punch, upper level.

- 27 -

1. Right slide-step to the rear, and, pivoting clockwise one quarter-turn on ball of left foot, assume side straddle-leg stance, simultaneously executing the left downward block; slide right foot sideways, placing it beside the other foot; execute left side-thrust kick; assume forward stance, pivoting counterclockwise one quarter-turn on ball of right foot; right front kick, then quickly right reverse punch, simultaneously lowering kicking foot to the rear.

2. (a) Repeat 1 through forward stance; then execute right lunge punch, upper level, then left reverse punch, lower level.
   (b) Repeat 1 through forward stance; then execute right reverse punch, lower level, then left reverse punch, upper level.
   (c) Repeat 1 through forward stance; then execute right lunge punch; right slide-step backward, simultaneously executing the left inward block; left jab, then right reverse punch, lower level.
   (d) Repeat 1 through forward stance; then execute right front kick; right reverse punch, upper level; left round kick, then right reverse punch, lower level.

27 : 1 ⟶

(e) Repeat 1 through forward stance; then execute right round kick, followed by left reverse punch.

(f) Repeat 1 through forward stance; then execute right side-thrust kick, followed by left reverse punch.

(g) Repeat 1 through forward stance; then execute right side-snap kick, followed by left reverse punch.

(h) Repeat 1 through left downward block; left slide-stepping to the rear, assume the left forward stance, simultaneously executing the right inward or outward block, then left lunge punch.

(i) Repeat (h) through the inward/outward block; left front kick, then left and right reverse punches to the upper and lower levels respectively.

(j) Repeat (h) through the inward/outward block; left side-thrust kick; left back-fist strike, then right and left reverse punches to the upper and lower levels respectively.

NOTE: 1–2(j) should also be practiced by left slide-stepping forward or right slide-stepping to the rear into a forward stance and omitting the side straddle-leg stance.

■ Combination Blocking, Foot, and Hand Attacks

1 ⟶

(Open-Leg Stance)

1. Right slide-step to the rear, simultaneously executing left downward block, followed immediately by right front kick. Lower kicking foot forward to the floor, then resume original position. Repeat, alternating between left and right. Repeat, substituting the following for indicated block:
   - (a) rising block
   - (b) inward block
   - (c) outward block
   - (d) knife-hand block
2. Repeat 1, substituting the following for indicated block:
   - (a) side-thrust kick
   - (b) side-snap kick
   - (c) round kick
3. Add a reverse punch to 1 and 2, repeating each several times before continuing.
4. Repeat 1–3, kicking with forward foot.
5. Repeat 1 and 2, adding a back-fist strike.
6. Repeat 1–4, adding a back-fist strike with either hand.
   NOTE: These exercises can be performed in a limited area since the activity does not involve more than one slide-step in either direction.
7. Right slide-step to the rear, executing a left knife-hand block, quickly followed by a right knife-hand block downward to the right; deliver right side-thrust kick, then left reverse punch, both to right side.
8. Right slide-step to the rear, simultaneously executing a right outward block, followed immediately by a right side-thrust kick to right side.

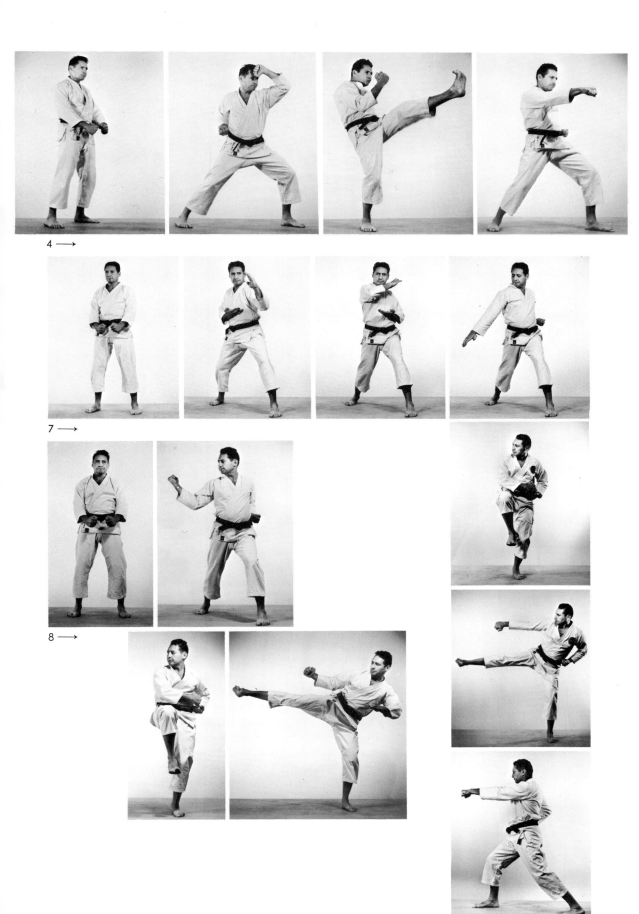

4 ⟶

7 ⟶

8 ⟶

1 ⟶

3 ⟶

The following exercises are to be executed in one smooth and continuous pattern. Keep the arms from moving loosely about during each exercise. (Forward Stance)

1. Right slide-step forward, executing the right inward block; left side-thrust kick, then right reverse punch.
2. Right slide-step forward, executing the right rising block, left front kick, and left reverse punch.
3. Right slide-step forward, executing the right outward block, left front kick, then left reverse punch.
4. Right slide-step forward, executing the right inward block, left front kick, then left reverse punch.
5. Right slide-step forward, executing the right downward block, left front kick, then left reverse punch.
6. Left front kick, then right reverse punch; standing in place, execute left outward block, right front kick, then right reverse punch.
7. (a) Right slide-step forward and simultaneously execute right outward block; standing in place, execute the left outward block, left front kick, then right reverse punch.
   (b) Right reverse punch, left outward block, right front kick, then right reverse punch.
   (c) Right slide-step forward, executing the right rising block; left round kick, and, lowering kicking foot forward, assume right side straddle-leg stance; left back-fist strike; right lunge punch.

7(a) ⟶

7(b) ⟶

7(c) ⟶

8 ⟶

8. Right slide-step forward, simultaneously executing right knife-hand block; right front kick; lowering kicking foot to floor, simultaneously execute left spear-hand attack. When the end of the training hall is reached and, for example, the student is in the forward stance, he will perform the following:

(a) right knife-hand block, simultaneously sliding left foot backward; right front kick, and lowering kicking foot to rear, simultaneously execute left spear-hand attack;

(b) right knife-hand block, simultaneously sliding left foot backward; left front kick; lowering kicking foot to the rear, simultaneously execute left spear-hand attack;

(c) combine exercises (a) and (b).

9. (a) *Attacker:* Delivers right lunge punch to the upper level.
   Defender: Executes left knife-hand block and simultaneous right front kick, then right reverse punch.

(b) *Attacker:* Delivers right lunge punch to the upper level.
   Defender: Executes left outward block and simultaneous left front kick, then right reverse punch.

(c) *Attacker:* Delivers right lunge punch to the upper level.
   Defender: Executes left outward block and simultaneous right front kick, then right reverse punch.

(d) *Attacker:* Delivers right lunge punch to the upper level.
   Defender: Holding both hands high to the sides of his face, blocks attack, simultaneously executing right front kick, right downward elbow attack, left reverse punch, then right upward elbow attack.
   NOTE: Use caution, as the sternum area is extremely vulnerable.

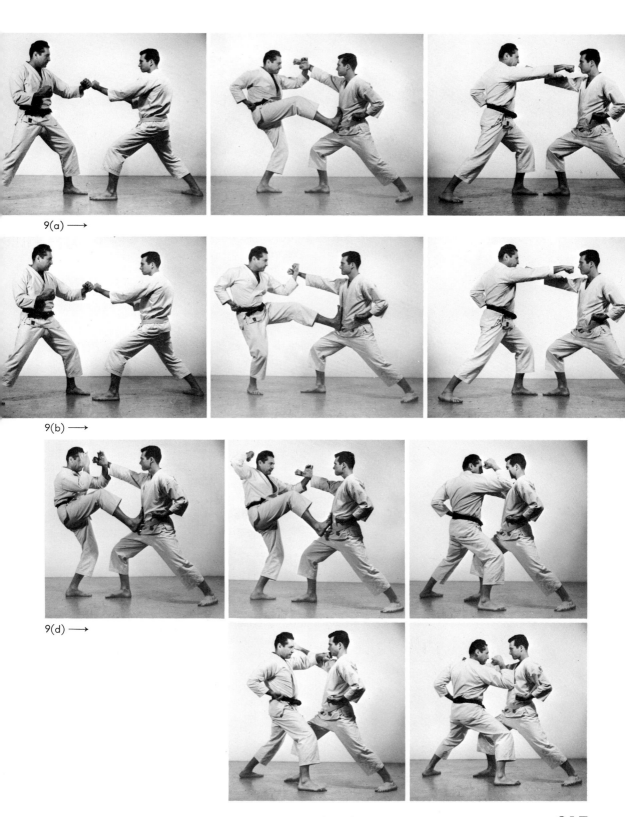

9(a) ⟶

9(b) ⟶

9(d) ⟶

9(e) ⟶

(e) *Attacker:* Delivers right lunge punch to the upper level.
  Defender: Pivoting one quarter-turn counterclockwise on ball of left foot, simultaneously executes right downward or rising block, then right side-thrust kick to attacker's armpit.

(f) *Attacker:* Delivers right lunge punch to the upper level.
  Defender: Executes left outward block and simultaneous left side-thrust kick; then quickly delivers right upward, then left forward elbow attack.

(g) *Attacker:* Delivers right lunge punch to the upper level.
  Defender: Executes left outward block; then, grasping attacking arm, counterattacks with right, then left round kick.

(h) *Attacker:* Delivers right lunge punch to the upper level.
  Defender: Executes left outward block, simultaneously slide-shifting left, then right foot forward; then quickly delivers right forward elbow attack.

(i) *Attacker:* Delivers right lunge punch to the upper level.
  Defender: Executes left outward block, simultaneously sliding right foot close behind and at right angles to left foot; left front (or round) kick; right front kick; right reverse punch.

(j) *Attacker:* Delivers right lunge punch to the upper level.
  (Open-Leg Stance)
  Defender: Right slide-steps backward, executing left knife-hand block, and, quickly shifting into the side straddle-leg stance, counterattacks with the left:
  - (*1*) knife-hand strike
  - (*2*) spear-hand attack
  - (*3*) back-fist strike
  - (*4*) bottom-fist strike
  - (*5*) rear-elbow attack
  - (*6*) side-thrust kick

NOTE: (*1*)–(*6*) are to be practiced singly with several repetitions of each. These are just a few of the many combinations possible. Students at advanced levels of proficiency should experiment to develop logical combinations, but never to the detriment of correct form and adequate power.

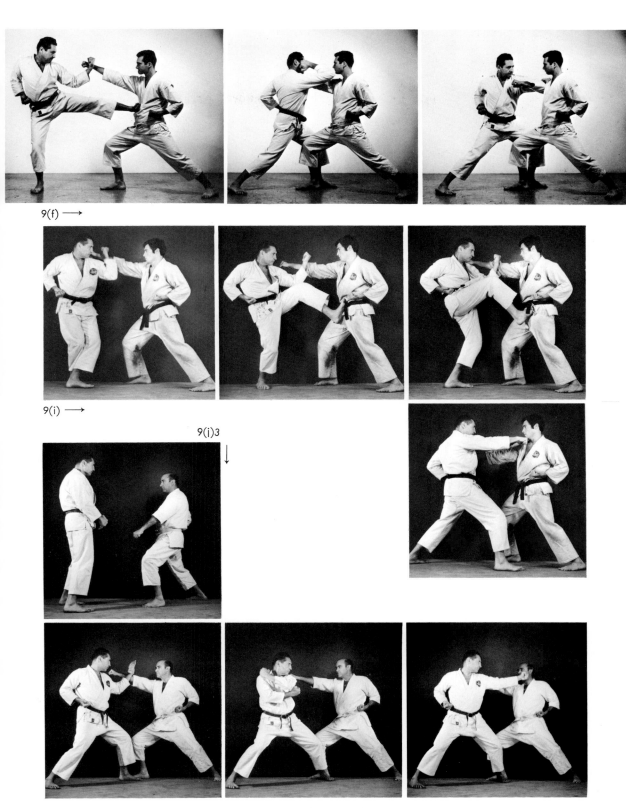

9(f) ⟶

9(i) ⟶

9(i)3 ↓

■ Defense Against Foot Attacks

1 ⟶

(Forward Stance)

1. *Attacker:* Executes right front kick.
   Defender: Blocks with left side-stamping kick, then quickly counterattacks with right reverse punch.
2. (a) *Attacker:* Executes right or left front kick, then right reverse punch.
   Defender: Dropping to right knee, delivers downward cross-arm block, punching attacker's shinbone or knee with right fist; quickly executes left rising block, then right reverse punch, lower level.
   (b) *Attacker:* Executes right front kick.
   Defender: Delivers downward cross-arm block, punching attacker's shinbone or knee with right fist, then delivers simultaneous left close punch and right reverse punch to the lower and upper levels respectively.
3. *Attacker:* Executes right side-thrust kick.
   Defender: Slide-shifts left, then right foot slightly to the left; thrusting left hand downward rigidly, sweeps attacking leg forward and to the right; then delivers right reverse punch.

2(a) ⟶

2(b) ⟶

3 ⟶

4. *Attacker:*   Executes either right front- or side-thrust kick.
   (a) *Defender:* Raises left knee across body, protecting abdomen; then counterattacks with right reverse punch.
   (b) *Defender:* Repeats block as in (a), executing left side-thrust kick, then right reverse punch.
   (c) *Defender:* Raises left knee across body, and, holding left forearm vertical, snaps elbow down to knee; then counterattacks with right reverse punch.
   (d) Repeat block as in (c); then counterattack with left side-thrust kick.
   (e) Repeat block as in (c); then counterattack with left side-thrust kick, followed by right reverse punch.
   (f) (*1*) Raise left foot to right knee, simultaneously executing a left jab, then right reverse or lunge punch.
   (*2*) Raise left foot to right knee, simultaneously executing a left jab; lowering left foot forward, execute right front kick, then right reverse or lunge punch.
   (*3*) Raise left foot to right knee, simultaneously executing a left jab; quickly drawing raised foot back and up to the rear with knee bent and leg parallel to the floor, execute a left round kick, then right reverse punch.
   NOTE: By maintaining a strong stance on the supporting leg the above technique can also be used when the student attempts a front kick that is blocked.
   (g) *Attacker:* Executes right front- or left side-thrust kick.
   (Side Straddle-Leg Stance)
   Defender: Raises knee of leading leg upward to the side, meeting elbow of corresponding arm with forearm held vertical. Stays low on supporting leg keeping weight solidly centered between legs as body shifts sideways toward attacker. Follows immediately with a back-fist strike.
   NOTE: In this instance unusual force should be employed by both students in an attempt to break each other's balance. This exercise constitutes one of the more helpful progressions from basic training into free-style sparring.
NOTE: (a)–(g) are simple and highly effective methods of blocking the front- and side-thrust kicks. Be sure that the supporting leg is solidly planted and that counterattack swiftly follows each block.

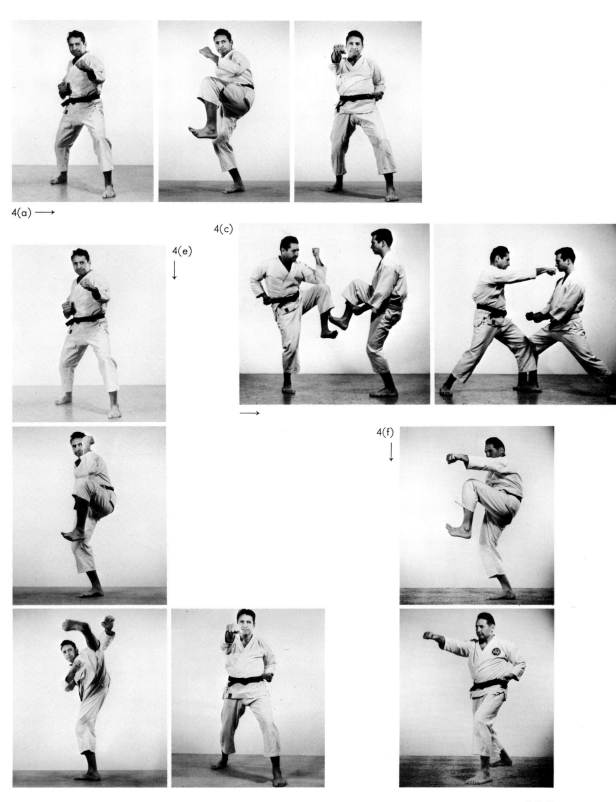

4(a) ⟶

4(c)

4(e)

⟶

4(f)

5. (a) *Attacker:* Delivers right front kick.

   Defender: Slide-shifts right, then left foot backward out of range; quickly slide-shifts left, then right foot forward; then executes right front kick.

   (b) *Defender:* Slide-shifts right, then left foot to the right, executing left downward block; counterattacks with right reverse punch.

   (Left Forward Stance)

   (c) (*1*) *Defender:* Slide-shifts left, then right foot to the left, executing right downward block; counterattacks with left reverse punch.

   NOTE: Students should develop a facility for moving backward deftly to either side to avoid any rapid multiple kicking attack. Blocking from the side, as in (b) and (c), involves relatively less danger from a possible follow-through punch. Advanced students can perform this variation of the downward block from the forward stance by a half-right forward slide-step to the left oblique, immediately shifting left foot to the rear and simultaneously executing the right downward block.

   (Forward Stance)

   (*2*) *Defender:* Left slide-steps to the rear, simultaneously executing right downward block, then counterattacks with left reverse punch.

   NOTE: The downward block should be executed with sufficient power to turn the opponent's body sideways.

   (*3*) *Defender:* Left slide-steps to the rear, simultaneously executing right downward block; left slide-steps forward, immediately executing right reverse punch.

   (Left Forward Stance)

   (d) *Defender:* Slide-shifts left, then right foot to the left, simultaneously executing a right downward block; then quickly slide-shifting both feet forward, counterattacks with a right back-fist strike, upper level, then left reverse punch, lower level.

   (Forward Stance)

   (e) (*1*) *Attacker:* Executes right front kick.

   Defender: Keeping left foot in place, slide-shifts right foot quickly to the left, placing himself at a forty-five degree angle to attacker; delivers right reverse punch, lower level.

   (*2*) *Attacker:* Delivers right front kick; right reverse punch.

   Defender: Executes left downward block; left blocking lunge jab, upper level; right reverse punch, lower level.

   NOTE: If, instead, defender's left foot is withdrawn, the resulting interval between opponents will be too great for an effective counterattack.

5(a) →

5(b) ↓

5(c)1 ↓

5(c)3 →

■ Helpful Hints

4(a) ⟶

For Students:

1. Do not lean away from the direction of the kick.
2. Do not attempt a kick employing the rear leg while in the cat or back stance.
3. (a) Normally, when practicing the front, round, side-thrust, snap, and rear kicks, the kicking leg should attack high enough so that it will be parallel·to the floor or even higher. This will tend to develop speed; in actual sparring the kicking height should be modified to avoid being trapped in opponent's grasp.

   (b) In kicking (unless otherwise indicated) the kicking foot should always be withdrawn to the opposite knee before lowering to floor.

4. (a) In executing the front kick, strongly thrust the knee of the kicking leg toward the opponent's abdomen before snapping the foot forward. The technique of swiftly and vigorously closing the distance between opponents should be applied when initiating any attack. Too often, the student fails to approach an opponent closely enough during an attack, thereby forfeiting the effectiveness of maximum contact.

   (b) Likewise, with the lunge punch, when the gap to be closed is unusually wide, the student must eliminate this handicap before channeling his utmost effort into the attacking fist.

5(a)

5(b)

5(c)

5(d) ⟶

5. (a) A weak stance when executing the reverse punch. Notice the loss of shocking power by recoil action through the bent elbow and supporting knee.

   (b) A strong stance when executing the reverse punch. Here the attacking elbow is firmly locked and the supporting knee tensed but not locked.

   (c) A weak stance with accompanying poor balance is created when an attacking student leans forward while executing either the reverse or lunge punch. This will enable his opponent to pull him forward easily, by grasping the attacking hand.

   (d) When executing either the reverse or lunge punch the body weight should be distributed over both legs with slight emphasis on the forward leg, the shoulders squared, with punching arm thrust slightly forward, upper body held erect, and lower abdomen and buttocks firmly tensed. In the event that the attacking arm is pulled forward, it can then be bent at the elbow to deliver a forearm attack, lower level, followed (with opposite hand) by a reverse punch, upper level.

6(a)

6(b) ⟶

6. (a) Many students make the mistake of turning the supporting foot out immediately preceding a forward movement. This error will invariably inform an alert opponent of the intended move. Be sure to keep the supporting foot firmly in place until the advance has been nearly completed.

(b) Another common error associated with the forward movement is to turn or bend the knee of the supporting leg inward. The knee must remain in vertical alignment over the toes.

7. When a student is closer to his opponent than double arms' length, he should consider himself as being within the danger zone. An attack should immediately be launched or the student should quickly withdraw to double arms' length apart from his opponent. This spacing (*ma*), however, varies according to each student's intuitive estimate of his opponent's capability. Judging the proper spacing between oneself and one's opponent must be made part of each student's acquired ability before he can become proficient in sparring.

NOTE: It is not enough that the student develop a feeling of intense energy and power in and of himself alone. He must make the danger zone an extension of himself by imbuing it with that same intensity, in a sense creating his own personal "force field."

8. Never leave the hand outstretched longer than necessary. An alert opponent grasping the wrist can quickly slide-step forward and execute an inward block against the elbow, causing severe damage.

9. When sparring it is preferable to grasp an opponent's training uniform rather than a limb; this will allow better control and make it more difficult for him to extricate himself.

10. In each of the basic exercises the student must perform as though facing an opponent with deadly intent. Half-hearted application of blocks and attacks is little more than worthless. The feeling within must be one of impending disaster whenever the student carelessly executes a weak block or attack.

7

8 ⟶

11. Although the inclination may be to hold one's breath while performing a series of blocks and/or attacks, an effort should be made to breathe continuously, exhaling in a controlled manner (which frequently ends in a kiai). Beyond this method of breathing during blocks and/or attacks, the acceptable breathing pattern is one of brevity in which expansion and contraction are confined to the lower abdomen rather than the rib cage.

12. At the conclusion of the last exercise in any series, students should make a concerted effort to be in an extremely low, strong stance. It would be well to execute a form occasionally exaggerating one's normal low stance. This will correct the tendency to rise.

13. At the instructor's command of *kamaete* (assume stance), students are to assume immediately the indicated stance. From this instant until the start of the next command, students should stand immobile as if in anticipation of an attack.[1]

---

[1] Too often there are seen during this interval certain nervous movements, such as clenching and unclenching of fists. These are to be eliminated.

For Instructors:

1. At the instructor's command of *kaete* (reverse direction), students should turn, then immediately repeat the exercise sequence. In the event that the exercise does not commence with a block, then the downward block should be employed:
(Forward Stance)
Front kick, reverse punch; reverse direction and immediately execute the downward block, front kick, reverse punch and simultaneous kiai.
NOTE: The above should be executed when practicing blocking, hand or foot attacks, or any combination thereof.

2. During class no concentration on specific attack techniques should be permitted until all are thoroughly assimilated.

3. Students may be able to perform a single block or attack well even if their level is low. Therefore, students should progress by ironing out difficulties which will almost certainly appear during a combination block-and-attack exercise.

4. The training program may be stepped up to prepare students for events (i.e., promotionals, summer training, tournaments, etc.) by alternating each exercise with the more arduous calisthenics to build endurance. Thus the command to execute the front kick across the training hall and back might be followed by an order to perform ten push-ups; from there to the lunge punch, then a series of ten squats and so forth. Rest periods should be kept at a minimum for the most beneficial results.

5. Each basic training exercise is performed on the instructor's command: that is, counting steadily from one through ten, then repeating. A more advanced expression of this would be the performance of three movements in succession, followed by a kiai in response to each command. When the class has attained some degree of proficiency, the instructor will change the count from an even tempo to an unpredictable one. By constantly changing the rhythm, he will help develop in the student a highly flexible response.

6. Never teach any technique about which there is the least doubt. One error taught to a group might easily be compounded, as instructors emerge from that group and themselves add to the original error mistakes of their own. With the passage of time karate will thus be corrupted.

7. Ideally the instructor must not be dependent upon teaching as his main income. If he is, the instructor-student relationship will inevitably suffer. It is obvious that more often than not the student will be catered to and indulged, in an effort to hold his interest. The instructor must be particularly careful not to mold the quality of his guidance to the student's whims, but rather should stimulate the student to enlarge his capacity for progress. An honest attempt should be made under all conditions to maintain the highest, and consequently the most Spartan, level of instruction. Teachers should feel deeply a commitment to karate which compels them to follow an unwavering line of duty.

■ Development of Powerful Punch

"For every action there is an opposite and equal reaction."[1] This is a basic principle of physics, and is of course applicable to our punching techniques. The movement of the punching arm contains the action while the motion of the opposite hand, as it is brought swiftly back to the hip, produces the reaction. With the proper muscular contraction and expansion we are able, through speed of motion, to convert static force into shocking power; concentrated body weight plus speed of motion are combined to produce a given striking power. Diligent practice of basic training and forms will develop the necessary muscular coordination. The principle described is applicable to kicking and blocking techniques as well.

The following indicates the principle of the power punching technique. Students of physics will recognize the formula used: for example, force (shocking power) equals mass (body weight) times velocity squared (punching speed).

MASS or pounds of body weight	$\times$ (multiplied by)	VELOCITY^2 or punching speed^2	$=$ (equals)	FORCE or shocking power
150	$\times$	2 miles per minute^2	$=$	600 foot-1bs.
175	$\times$	2 miles per minute^2	$=$	700 foot-1bs.
150	$\times$	3 miles per minute^2	$=$	1350 foot-1bs.

The figures used above are arbitrary and do not allude to karate exclusively. They merely indicate the relationship of shocking power to punching speed.

When delivering the punching attack, a typical student weighing 150 pounds (mass), and possessing a speed of motion (velocity) designated by the unit of two miles per minute squared, will create a shocking power of x degrees of energy. A gain of 25 pounds of muscle tissue, with no increase in attacking speed, will add only one-sixth additional shocking power to his potential. However, with weight unchanged, the mere addition of one unit of speed more than doubles the shocking power of the student's punch.

Practically speaking, the student who not only builds muscular weight but concentrates on the development of punching speed can vastly increase the shocking power of his punch. Basically, this is what takes place at the moment of attack. We should think of the lower abdominal area as a kind of reservoir of physical power. Upon a signal from the brain our kiai activated, forcing a contraction of the lower abdomen, which starts the flow of power surging outward. Here again in the kiai we observe the phenomenon of action and reaction. Accelerated by a swift hip-twisting motion in combination with a strong forward movement of the leading knee and hip, this power is then transmitted through the attacking fist.

When the fist strikes the opponent his body immediately contracts as the shock waves enter. In making contact with an opponent, a portion of the shock waves' direction is then reversed through the body and down the leg, striking the ground. At this point the shocking power that is not yet dissipated again reverses direction, returning along its previous path. The opponent's body will have expanded by this time to again come in contact with the attacking fist, which has not yet been withdrawn, creating a secondary reaction. This double entry of shocking power delivered with such lightning rapidity is largely responsible for the internal injury associated with the karate punch.

In delivering a punch, one should not limit its effectiveness by concentrating on the area being attacked. Instead the effort should be projected to a point beyond. The object, then, is not merely to strike the surface of the opponent's body, but, preceding the attack, to move in close enough so that the student need not overextend himself to follow through. The student should imagine that his fist is going to penetrate several inches beyond the target surface. It should be noted that shocking power is dissipated when any portion of the body is moving in opposition to the direction of attack. In order to produce the greatest possible degree of shocking power, both body weight and actual attack must be channeled in the same direction. When kicking, if the body is inclined away from the direction of the kick, or if when punching, the attacking arm is bent at the elbow, or the supporting leg is bent at the knee, there will be a resultant loss of shocking power.

In boxing, contestants are sometimes observed to be jabbing or punching with little effect. This may be a strategy to amass points toward a favorable decision, or perhaps even to harass an opponent. By contrast, in karate each attack must be powerfully and decisively delivered so that the issue can be then and there decided. This thought is to be projected throughout one's entire training experience. Therefore it must be kept in mind that mere shallow repetition is not sufficient; the ideal prevails that each movement shall be initiated with precision, power, and speed.

The student must then work toward the development of a consistently high level of power. As the author has stated earlier, the karateist should consider the lower abdominal area to be a reservoir of strength. His ensuing movements will benefit from this procedure, since each action will draw directly upon a constant central source. This approach will result in a more cohesive, smoothly coordinated performance.

The novice, while executing the lunge punch, must consciously strive for a steady, smooth forward slide-step. Without this firm supporting action his punching power will suffer. Also, the student must not rely upon whatever momentum may accompany the forward slide-step because in so doing he will inevitably reduce his maximum punching potential. In executing the lunge punch it is imperative to drive the central abdominal region straight at an opponent's midsection. This strengthens one's technique and closes the gap rapidly between opponents.

The beginning student tends to overemphasize the importance of speed while punching or kicking in the performance of an attack. Superficially, it may seem that speed of punch or kick is the most essential factor, and many a student may attempt to concentrate his efforts in this area to the detriment of others. In reality, success results from a fusion of a wide range of highly developed skills, several of which in combination can outweigh punching or kicking speed alone: creating an opening; closing the distance; application of power; surprise; coordination; punching through; and stance. These terms will be dealt with in future chapters.

PUNCHING EXERCISES

(Open-Leg Stance) Left hand outstretched with the right fist held above the right hip.

1. Alternately deliver a reverse punch to the upper level on each count.
   NOTE: Commence slowly, punching lightly, and concentrate on building speed. Do not tense the shoulders or arms. However, the pectoral and latissimus dorsi muscles, lower abdomen, and buttocks should be firmly tensed at completion of each punch. When the instructor is satisfied that a correct pattern has been established, then this exercise should be performed with maximum power.
2. Repeat 1, executing a right, then left reverse punch to the upper level on each count.
3. Repeat 1, executing three alternate reverse punches to the upper level on each count.
4. Repeat 1, executing four alternate reverse punches to the upper level on each count.

1 $\longrightarrow$

3 $\longrightarrow$

5. Repeat 1, executing five alternate reverse punches to the upper level on each count.

NOTE: In multiple punching exercises be sure to use a consistent level of speed and power. The objective in breathing technique is an even, unbroken expulsion of air throughout each multiple punching exercise.

(Open-Leg Stance) Right hand outstretched with the left fist held above the left hip.

1. Deliver left reverse punch to the upper level, followed by right and left reverse punches in quick succession to the lower level.
2. Deliver left reverse punch to the lower level, followed by right and left reverse punches in quick succession to the upper level.
3. Deliver left reverse punch to the lower level, followed by right and left reverse punches in quick succession to the lower level.

4

1 ⟶

4. Deliver left reverse punch to the upper level, followed by right and left reverse punches in quick succession to the upper level.

5. Combine 1–4 in one continuous exercise.

6. Repeat 1–4 in quarter-turns clockwise, completing a circle.

7. Repeat 1–4 in quarter-turns counterclockwise, completing a circle.
   NOTE: The initial punch in exercises 1–4 should be one of concentrated force, followed by the two powerful alternate punches with the accent on speed.

8. Repeat 1–7, starting with the left hand outstretched and the right fist held above the right hip.

(Open-Leg Stance)

1. Right reverse punch to left oblique, then move right fist to the left shoulder.

2. Right sideward bottom-fist strike, then move opened right hand, palm upward, straight to the front.

3. Right backward elbow attack.

4. Repeat 3 with left hand.

5. Alternate right and left forward reverse punches.

6. Right reverse punch high to left oblique.

7. Left reverse punch high to right oblique.

8. Combine 1–7 in one continuous exercise.
   NOTE: When proficiency in basic punching exercises has been achieved, repeat in straddle-leg stance.

2 ⟶

3

4 ⟶

5

6

7

(Open-Leg Stance)

1. With right arm on top, bend hands across chest at shoulder level.
2. Execute double sideward bottom-fist strike.
3. Right slide-step forward, executing double inward bottom-fist strike.
4. Right slide-step backward into the open-leg stance.
5. Right slide-step forward, executing double reverse punch.
6. Right slide-step backward, simultaneously pivoting to the left on ball of left foot.
7. Right front kick; execute the vertical double punch.
8. Right slide-step backward, simultaneously pivoting to the right on ball of left foot.
9. Left front kick; execute the vertical double punch.
10. Left slide-step backward into open-leg stance.

11. Execute upward double reverse punch.
12. Move left fist to position above left hip, bending right arm across chest at shoulder level.
13. Execute right reverse punch downward to the left rear.
14. Move right fist to position above right hip, bending left arm across chest at shoulder level.
15. Execute left reverse punch downward to the right rear.
16. Resume open-leg stance.
17. Deep knee bend and simultaneous double reverse punch, downward to the outside of each leg.
18. Rising, immediately execute right, then left reverse punch.
19. Resume open-leg stance.
20. Execute double reverse punch overhead to the rear.

21

22 ⟶

23

21. Bend forward, executing double reverse punch downward between legs.
22. Execute backward elbow and simultaneous spear-hand attacks on left, then right side.
23. Resume open-leg stance.
24. Combine 1–23 into one continuous exercise.

NOTE: All attacks in the punching exercises must be powerfully executed. Wherever practical, the student's eyes should be focused in the direction of each attack. These exercises are designed to develop continuity and power in addition to practical attack training. Each one of the punching exercises should be performed at every training session. The punching exercises are an excellent example of dynamic tension since, instead of actually striking an object, it becomes necessary to use our own muscle power to stop each attack in midair.

PUNCHING BOARD

1

1. **Construction**

The punching board is easily constructed, using two-inch-thick hardwood cut to the dimensions of four inches by seven feet. The board is beveled down so that the last foot, which becomes the striking surface, is one-half inch thick. This is necessary so that the punching board will spring back upon contact. The punching board should be imbedded approximately three feet in the ground and packed at its base with rock and dirt. The top should be on a level with the student's solar plexus. The striking surface is best padded with a two-inch thickness of sponge, covered with canvas or burlap, which should then be bound at the top and bottom with rope.

2. **Application**

(Forward Stance)

Stand close enough to the board so that the fist will extend two inches beyond. Lower the body with right arm raised to shoulder level. The outstretched hand should touch the center of the padded area. Keeping the body low, execute the reverse punch, then quickly withdraw the attacking hand. The attacking surface should consist of the knuckles of the index and middle fingers. This will produce a greater concentration of power at the point of contact, increasing the potential

2 ⟶

for internal damage. New students should begin with two sets of twenty-five repetitions daily, gradually increasing the number of repetitions to fifty and finally to two sets of seventy-five repetitions with each hand. All the various hand attacks should also be practiced with the punching board. Be sure to twist the hips with a swift, dynamic motion, driving the leading knee and hip forward, ending with the shoulders squared and the punching arm thrust slightly forward at the moment of contact. Kiai with each punch and inhale when withdrawing the attacking hand.

NOTE: It is imperative that the student's body be tensed when striking the punching board so that the internal organs will not be excessively jarred. Avoid using any punching board that is immobile. The resulting recoil of shocking power can produce an unhealthy reaction. It should be kept in mind that overdeveloped knuckles alone do not signify a karate expert. For the individual who wants primarily to stay in good physical condition, the use of the punching board can well be eliminated. Certainly no growing boy should be allowed to risk deforming his hands. The age of eighteen should be considered the minimum for commencement of this aspect of training.

■ Special Exercises

1 ⟶

REACTION SPEED

(Forward Stance)

1. Instructor, facing the class and without warning, suddenly executes right reverse punch. Students attempt to surpass the instructor's punching speed with:
   - (a) reverse punch
   - (b) front kick
   - (c) side-thrust kick
   - (d) rising block
   - (e) inward block
   - (f) outward block
   - (g) reverse punch added to techniques (b)–(f)
   NOTE: Repeat each several times before continuing.

2. Instructor, facing the class and without warning, suddenly executes any kick. The students attempt to surpass the instructor's kicking speed with:
   - (a) reverse punch
   - (b) any kick
   - (c) any appropriate block
   - (d) reverse punch added to (b) and (c)

4(g)2 $\longrightarrow$

3. Instructor, facing the class, calls out specific kicks to be executed. At the completion of each kick, the students resume their original stance. Repeat, adding a reverse punch to each kick.

(Open-Leg Stance)

4. Instructor, facing the class, consecutively calls out any block and its direction of execution, that is:
   (a) forward (slide-step forward and block)
   (b) backward (slide-step backward and block)
   (c) left side (left slide-step to the left, pivoting on the ball of the right foot and block)
   (d) right side (right slide-step to the right, pivoting on the ball of the left foot and block)
   (e) rear (pivot to the rear on the ball of the opposite foot to the blocking arm used and block)
   (f) add a reverse punch to each block

(Forward Stance)

   (g) All students will immediately follow the instructor's command to proceed.
       (1) *Attacker:* Delivers a right reverse punch to the upper level.
           Defender: Attempting to beat attacker's punching speed, executes in turn:
           (*a*) right front kick
           (*b*) left front kick
           (*c*) left side-thrust kick
           (*d*) right round kick
       (2) *Attacker:* Standing to rear of defender, delivers a right reverse punch to the upper level.
           Defender: Executes right rear kick; pivoting clockwise on ball of left foot, delivers left reverse punch to the lower level.

4(g)3 ⟶

(3) *Attacker:* Standing to the rear of defender, delivers right reverse punch to the upper level.

Defender: Executes right rear kick, then left rear kick, and, pivoting counterclockwise on ball of right foot, delivers a right reverse punch, lower level.

(4) *Attacker:* Standing to right of defender, delivers right reverse punch to the upper level.

(Open-Leg Stance)

Defender: Turning head to the right, simultaneously left slide-steps forward, executing the right outward block, then counterattacks with right side-thrust kick to the side.

(Forward Stance)

(5) *Attacker 1:* Standing to right side of defender.

Attacker 2: Standing to left side of defender.

Attacker 3: Standing directly in front of defender. Each attacker simultaneously delivers right lunge punch to the upper level.

(Open-Leg Stance)

Defender: Left slide-steps forward, simultaneously executing a left outward block and right front kick, quickly followed by a right side-thrust kick to the side. With a low hop to the left, places right foot in the space vacated by the left, instantly executing left side-thrust kick to the side.

(6) Repeat (1) through (5) without the instructor's command of execution. The attacking student's kiai signifies the beginning of his forward movement, thus alerting defender.

NOTE: (4), (5), and (6) stress the peripheral vision so important to the student engaged in sparring. Even while directing his gaze forward, a student should be aware of any attack originating from either side.

4(g)4 ⟶

4(g)5 ⟶

1(a) ⟶   1(b) ⟶

PUNCHING SPEED

(Straddle-Leg Stance)

1. Arms bent to the front, with elbows lightly resting on abdomen, fists clenched.

   (a) On the instructor's command to proceed, alternately thrust each fist forward to the upper level, quickly withdrawing that arm to its original position.

   (b) Bend arms across chest, fists down, with right arm on top. Deliver right bottom-fist strike to the right side, simultaneously bringing left fist back to left hip.

   (c) Deliver back-fist strike in the same manner as in previous exercise.

(Forward Stance)

   (d) Students form parallel lines six feet apart, facing each other. On instructor's command to proceed, each student delivers the reverse punch, attempting to be first in execution.

   (e) Students form parallel lines six feet apart, facing each other. Without the instructor's command, first one side and then the other will individually execute the reverse punch. This is done at each attacking student's discretion, independent of the class. The opposing student, fixing his gaze at eye level, will attempt to anticipate the attack and beat his partner to the punch.

(Open-Leg Stance)

   (f) Students form parallel lines slightly more than one arm's length apart, facing each other. On instructor's command to proceed, one line right slide-steps forward, executing a right lunge punch to the lower level, while the opposing line right slide-steps backward, executing a right reverse punch to the upper level. Both lines attempt to be first in execution.

   (g) Repeat, reversing levels of attack.

   NOTE: In exercises (f) and (g) be sure to avoid contact.

1(f) ⟶

1

ENDURANCE

(Open-Leg Stance)
1. Perform deep knee bend;[1] upon rising, execute right front kick. Repeat deep knee bend and, upon rising, execute left front kick.
2. Perform deep knee bend; upon rising, execute a right, then left front kick. Repeat deep knee bend and, upon rising, execute a left, then right front kick.

---

[1] Deep knee bends, squats, and "duck walks" are to be practiced in moderation. Medical studies on the effects of these exercises have revealed the possibility of damage to the supporting tissue of the knee joint.

3

(Open-Leg Stance)

   3. Execute right front kick and simultaneous left reverse punch; lowering kicking foot to the floor, quickly execute a right, then left reverse punch. Continue with left front kick and simultaneous right reverse punch; lowering kicking foot to the floor, quickly execute a left, then right reverse punch.

(Forward Stance)

   4. One student, starting from the right, will count loudly from one through ten, simultaneously executing a front kick in unison with the class (on each ten count, add the right reverse punch and simultaneous kiai). Each student will in turn repeat the count.

     NOTE: As each kick is completed, the foot is brought back to its original position in the forward stance. The class should practice each kick, block, and attack in this manner with at least one hundred repetitions. The instructor should check each student, paying particular attention to balance, low stance, tenseness of abdominal and underarm muscles.

   5. Being careful to maintain the correct forward stance, hop forward, then backward several inches, repeating in an unbroken rhythm. When forward, the front foot will lead by a fraction of a second; to the rear, the back foot will lead. This is a very low hop. Shifts in direction will heighten the benefits of this exercise.

     NOTE: In preparation for competition, perform for three minutes then rest one. Repeat.

1

2

3(a) $\longrightarrow$

3(b)

STANCE

(Straddle-Leg Stance)
1. Remaining tense, hold the straddle-leg stance for a length of time at the instructor's discretion.

    NOTE: There are schools which require a beginning student to be able to remain in this stance for fifteen minutes before he can receive additional training.

(Back Stance)
2. Lift one leg, balancing low on the other for a length of time at the instructor's discretion.

(Open-Leg Stance)
3. (a) toe raises
   (b) flat-footed squats
   (c) Combine (a) and (b) in one exercise.
   (d) Combine (a), (b), and 2 under Endurance (p. 247) in one exercise.

(Forward Stance)
4. For the following exercise students of similar weight should be paired off: Slide-step across training hall, supporting partner astride the shoulders.

1(a)

1(b)

1(c)

1(d)

2(c)

PUNCHING POWER

1. Basic Push-Ups
   - (a) knuckles (index and middle fingers only)
   - (b) crossed palms
   - (c) knife-hand
   - (d) fingertips

     As strength increases, the number of fingers used to support the body may be gradually reduced to four, then three, and later, if possible, two.

     NOTE: Perform (a) and (b) a minimum of twenty repetitions daily; (c) and (d) at the instructor's discretion.
2. Advanced Push-Ups
   - (a) Combine the above in units of ten to produce an unbroken exercise (i.e., forty push-ups).
   - (b) Assume position as in 1 (a); then "walking" on the fists, drag body across training hall.
   - (c) Students line up in pairs: one student lies face down on floor and, as partner grasps his ankles, he elevates his body, supporting it with his arms; then he "walks" with palms or fists down across training hall.

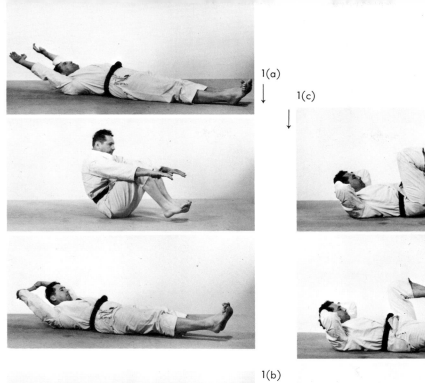

1(a)

1(c)

1(b)

ABDOMEN

1. Sit-Ups (Prone Position)
    (a) Raise upper body, simultaneously lifting knees to chest, and thrust arms toward the toes. Return to original position but do not allow feet to touch the floor.
    (b) Perform with partner as illustrated.
    NOTE: Perform a minimum of thirty-five repetitions daily.
    (c) With hands clasped behind head, draw knees up to chest. Alternately execute front-thrust, then side-thrust kicks in unbroken succession. Perform a minimum of twenty-five repetitions daily.
    NOTE: Exercises requiring special equipment have been pointedly avoided. However, the efficacy of the following exercise is such that it seemed wise to include it.
2. Acquire a dumbbell bar, two ten-pound barbell plates, and two collars with which to hold the plates at the center of the bar.
(Kneeling Position)
    Grasping the bar with hands as far apart as possible, extend body slowly to arms' length; draw up slowly to original position.
    NOTE: Perform a minimum of ten repetitions daily.

1(a)

1(b) ⟶

LEGS

1. "Duck Walks"
    (a) forward and backward
    (b) hopping low, forward, and backward
    (c) hopping low alternately to right, then left side

    (d) Lying on stomach with legs bent at the knee, partner applies resistance as legs are lowered and raised.

(Forward Stance)

2. (a) Using right leg for leverage, shift body weight onto front foot with a rapid forward thrusting motion. Do not lift the right heel off the floor.

    NOTE: This exercise develops the leg muscles responsible for strong, swift forward-shifting movements.

(Open-Leg Stance)

    (b) *Basic.* Hands on hips with one foot extended forward, resting on heel, toes strongly flexed:
    (*1*) downward
    (*2*) upward

    (c) *Advanced.* Balancing on one foot, raise opposite leg from the floor and repeat above.

    NOTE: Perform a minimum of fifty repetitions daily.

(Open-Leg Stance)

    (d) (*1*) With an erect posture, spring nimbly off the floor, landing lightly on the balls of feet. Repeat ten times; lowering body into squatting position and holding this posture, repeat hopping movements.

    (*2*) Repeat first half of (*1*); then lowering body into squatting position, hop first forward, then back, repeating ten times.

    (*3*) Repeat first half of (*1*); then lowering body into squatting position, hop first to one side, then to the other, repeating ten times.

    (*4*) Combine (*1*), (*2*), and (*3*) into one continuous exercise.

    (*5*) At conclusion of (*4*), leap once in place as high as possible.

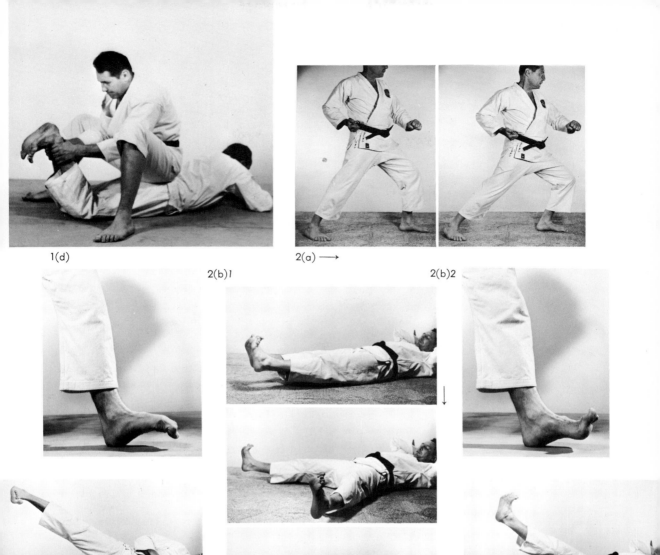

1(d) 2(a) ⟶ 2(b)1 2(b)2

2(e)1 2(e)2 2(e)3

(e) (*1*) Lie flat on left side, raising right leg vertically with heel extended and toes flexed upward.

(*2*) Lying on back, raise feet slightly off floor and, with heels extended and toes flexed, stretch legs out to both sides, maintaining same distance from floor, then bring together.

(*3*) Lying on back, head slightly raised, with arms on floor at sides, raise and lower legs alternately, keeping knees locked. Vary speed from slow to fast.

NOTE: Repeat up to thirty-five repetitions daily. These are excellent groundwork for the kick since they strengthen hip muscles.

3. Roadwork (Barefooted)
    (a) Run forward one and three-quarters miles.
    (b) Run backward one-quarter mile.
    (c) Alternate (a) and (b).
        NOTE: Course used should be unpaved and its surface, if uneven, will tend to produce better results. The author has noticed during summer-training roadwork that those who adopted a flat-footed gait were capable of sustained activity. The feet were not raised high off the ground while running and very short steps were taken.
(Open-Leg Stance)
4. Twist trunk clockwise, simultaneously touching left knee to floor, then repeat to the left.
(Straddle-Leg Stance)
5. Pointing toes of both feet outward, perform repeated deep knee bends down to knee level only.

NECK

1. Wrestler's bridge:
    (a) forward
    (b) backward
        NOTE: Perform a minimum of fifty repetitions daily.
2. With partner:
    (a) downward
    (b) backward
    (c) sideways
    (d) upward
        NOTE: Perform a minimum of ten repetitions in each direction. Each student resists as his partner exerts slow and steady pressure during the complete range of the neck extension. No student engaged in any combative sport should possess a weak neck or flabby midriff. The effectiveness of a jabbing or punching attack to the head or abdomen is pronounced if either is weak.

1(a)

1(b)

2(a)

2(b)

2(c)

1(a) →

1(b) →

2(a)

2(b)

2(c)

2(d)

WRIST AND FOREARM

(Open-Leg Stance)
1. Holding hands straight out at shoulder level, strongly open and close fists with:
   (a) palms down
   (b) palms up
   (c) Alternate (a) and (b).
   NOTE: Perform a minimum of thirty-five repetitions daily.
2. Wrist push-ups:
   (a) fingers forward
   (b) fingers backward
   (c) fingers inward
   (d) fingers outward

1 ⟶

2 ⟶

LEG STRETCHING

(Close-Leg Stance)
1. Turn head to the left. With knee locked, raise left leg straight up and to the side. Keep body erect and foot parallel to the floor.
2. With short hops to the sides, spread feet widely apart. Keeping body erect, tense inner thighs and hop-slide feet toward each other.

1(a) $\longrightarrow$

BLOCKING SPEED

(Open-Leg Stance)

1. (a) *Attacker:* Delivers right reverse punch to the upper level.

      Defender: Executes left outward, right outward, and left downward blocks in rapid succession; then counterattacks with right reverse punch to the upper level. Attacker withdraws right hand to position above right hip and repeats this pattern.

   (b) Students form opposing lines. First student attacks with right reverse punch, leaving arm extended. Partner executes any appropriate block with right arm and counterattacks with left reverse punch, leaving arm extended. First student executes any appropriate block with right arm and counterattacks with left reverse punch, leaving arm extended. Repeat, increasing speed.

2. Students form opposing lines. Opponents alternately attack and block, executing reverse punches to the upper, middle, and lower levels, defending with rising, inward, outward, and downward blocks.

3. Opponents place both hands on each other's upper arms. Using short light movements, they block and attack with no predetermined plan. Repeat, assuming starting position.

1(b) ⟶

3 ↓

4. Students form opposing lines.

    Attacker: On instructor's command to begin and at his own pace, will alternately deliver a designated right or left lunge punch, lower level, returning to open-leg stance between attacks.

    Defender: Arms bent to the front, with elbows lightly resting on abdomen, hands unclenched. As soon as attack begins, right or left slide-steps backward, simultaneously executing a downward block (keeping hands unclenched) and upward palm-heel attack.

              NOTE: Do not let elbows bend outward. As in boxing, judo, or wrestling, opposing students should attempt to control that strategic area within their opponent's shoulder width, rather than allow their arms to be maneuvered to the outside. This exercise illustrates the contrast between early development, with its weak irresolute mental condition coupled with an overcompensation in a rigid physical demeanor, and the advanced level—a strong mind in a relaxed, flexible but ready body.

        Begin and end above exercises on instructor's command. Start slowly and increase speed as proficiency is acquired. In a short time forearms will be noticeably strengthened and relatively impervious to pain caused by encounters with opponent.

1(a) 1(b)

1(c) ⟶

2 ⟶

DISTANCE CONTROL

1. *Attacker:* Stopping short of contact, delivers reverse punches to:
   (a) upper level
   (b) lower level
   (c) alternate upper and lower levels

   Defender: Remains motionless, keeping his eyes fixed unflinchingly on attacker's eyes, thereby gaining important visual control.
   (Forward Stance)

2. With partner holding an upright pencil as target, execute right reverse punch, stopping just short of contact.

   NOTE: The student holding the pencil should vary distance and height.

1(a) 1(b) 1(c)

1(d) 1(e)

MUSCLE TONE

1. The following exercises are excellent for developing the student's strength and endurance. For maximum benefit, he should concentrate mentally and physically upon the muscles involved. A towel or uniform belt should be used.

   (a) Grasping belt vertically in front of diaphragm with hands slightly apart, raise upper hand while resisting with lower; then reverse.

   (b) With partner grasping ends of belt and resisting, hold belt at middle and curl upward; then have partner pull downward against resistance.

   (c) With partner grasping ends of belt and resisting, hold belt at middle and pull upward with a rowing motion; then have partner pull downward against resistance.

   (d) Stand next to partner, facing same direction, with both in straddle-leg stance. Each grasps belt in front at chest level, one palm up and one down. They then alternate, pulling and resisting, horizontally.

   (e) Students face each other two feet apart in a half-squat. Holding belt between them, they alternately pull and resist with a rowing motion.

1(f)

1(g)

1(h) ⟶

(f) Partners sit, legs apart, one partner's feet placed firmly above the other's ankles. Holding belt between them, they alternately pull and resist with a rowing motion.

(g) One partner lies face downward. The other sits astride him, facing the same direction. The supine partner reaches backward as far as possible overhead, keeping arms parallel. While partner resists, he pulls belt forward. Direction and resistance are then reversed.

(h) Using belt and maintaining straddle-leg stance, repeat movements in exercises 2 (a)–(c) in the section devoted to neck development (page 254).

NOTE: The student can on his own initiative develop helpful exercises with the uniform belt.

(i) The student will derive great benefit from practicing blocks, punches, and kicks in a pool, lake, or any other body of water, since the additional resistance thus provided heightens the effectiveness of each exercise.

2

(Forward Stance)

2. Students form parallel lines an arm's length apart facing each other.

(a) Partners place both hands directly under each other's arms with thumbs facing up against chests. Maintaining low center of gravity, one line pushes steadily forward against maximum resistance. Be sure to remain erect with elbows locked and latissimus dorsi tensed. It would be helpful, in maintaining the proper posture, to feel as if the student were leading with the abdomen.

(b) Reverse roles and repeat.

(c) Both lines push forward simultaneously on the instructor's command of execution.

NOTE: This is an outstanding overall conditioner.

2 ⟶

3(a)

3(b)

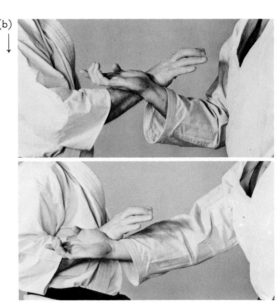

BLOCKING POWER

(Forward Stance)
1. Each student holds his arm in knife-hand position against partner's blocking arm as long as possible, applying maximum pressure.
2. Repeat 1, substituting outward, inward, downward, and rising blocks in consecutive exercises.

(Open-Leg Stance)
3. Students form parallel lines an arm's length apart facing each other.
    (a) Students extend the open right hand forward with palm up. Arms make contact at thumb side of wrist with applied tension.
    (b) One side inverts hand, hooking opposing wrist, pressing down and back. Withdrawing elbow should brush side.
    (c) Repeat, reversing roles.
    (d) Both lines repeat simultaneously.

NOTE: This is the proper method of performing the knife-hand block, calculated to break opponent's balance.

To increase the efficacy of various special exercises, such as push-ups, sit-ups, muscle tone, and leg raises, the performance speed should be varied from deliberately slow to very rapid. In performing such an exercise slowly the student will be putting the principle of "dynamic tension" to work. He will build his functional strength and long-term endurance as a result of faithful application. When his pace is accelerated the benefits of increased blood circulation, greater lung capacity, and reduced reaction time will be realized. A combination of these two markedly different approaches produces the most favorable program for good general conditioning.

PART 3
SPARRING

■ Sparring (kumite)

BASIC SPARRING

What are the origins of basic sparring? Basic sparring was not always part of karate. The training that Master Funakoshi received consisted almost exclusively of the practice of kata. After he himself became a teacher he had his students practice single blocks and attacks from each kata as independent units. He felt that this approach (i.e., the polishing of each technique) would inevitably result in more perfectly executed kata. This, together with later combinations of techniques, is what we have come to call basic training. The next significant major development under Master Funakoshi's direction was the practice of these exercises against an opponent. Of course we are now referring to basic sparring (kihon kumite).

In gohon and sambon kumite (see chart, p. 268) the student must learn to execute the first block while thinking of the next one, and so on, until he envisions his counterattack while he is executing the last block. If inordinate emphasis is placed on blocking the opponent's initial attack, then any subsequent attack will be more difficult to cope with. The inherent benefit of these two exercises (gohon and sambon) is the development of a strong feeling of attack against an opponent, and for the defender an equally strong attitude while retreating.

New students practicing gohon, sambon, kihon ippon, and jiyu ippon kumite should attack and counterattack with the lunge and reverse punches respectively. After proficiency has been acquired, kicking techniques can then be substituted for, as well as alternated with, various hand attacks. In gohon and sambon kumite, the attackers step forward, striking alternately with hand or foot, or in combination thereof. Since each attack is precise, it must be delivered as a distinct unit before the next attack begins. During the last attack, defender blocks and then delivers a counterattack which must stop short of actual physical contact.

267

Type	Number of Attacks	ATTACKER	KUMITE (SPARRING)				DEFENDER	
		Movement Preceding Attack	Weapon Used	Area Attacked	By Whom	Contact	Block Required	Counter-attack (no contact)
Gohon kumite	Five	None	Desig.[1]	Desig.	Desig.	Perm.[2]	Yes	Yes, free choice weapon and area
Sambon kumite (basic)	Three	None	Desig.	Desig.	Desig.	Perm.	Yes	Yes, free choice weapon and area
Sambon kumite (advanced)	Three	No res.[3]	Desig. in first attack only	Desig. in first attack only	Desig.	Perm. in first attack only	Yes	Yes, free choice weapon and area
Kihon ippon kumite (basic)	One	None	Desig.	Desig.	Desig.	Perm.	Yes	Yes, free choice weapon and area
Jiyu ippon kumite (semifree style)	One	No res.	Desig.	Desig.	Desig.	Perm.	Yes	Yes, free choice weapon and area
Jiyu ippon kumite (free style)	One	No res.	No res.	No res.	Desig.	Not perm.	Yes	Yes, free choice weapon and area
Jiyu kumite (free style)	No limit	No res.	No res.	No res.	Not desig.	Not perm.	No	Remain active until point is called

[1]Desig. = designated   [2]Perm. = permitted   [3]Res. = restrictions

SEMIFREE AND FREE-STYLE SPARRING

Basic sparring ushered in evolving forms which we refer to as semifree and free-style sparring. These were a natural, more fluid outgrowth of the predetermined patterns found in basic sparring. Semifree sparring provides the most realistic testing ground for attacker as well as defender. Constant danger is an inherent factor since the attacker is free to move about before launching his attack and (in contrast with free-style sparring) contact is permitted. This element of freedom of movement heightens the intensity of this phase of sparring.

Free-style sparring, though relatively new,[1] is the most advanced phase of training. It dominates any tournament because of the excitement, individual skill, spirit of competition, and spontaneous action involved. As indicated by its name, neither attacker, weapon used, nor area attacked is predetermined. Unlike basic sparring, wherein attacker makes an earnest attempt to strike a designated area, nothing in this case is predetermined. Although the attack should be strong and well executed, it must stop short of contact. (Of course, students are not permitted to participate in free-style sparring until they have demonstrated sufficient ability to block and to exercise control over their own attack.)

Good form and maximum effort are of paramount importance. The victor, not employing these, should not assume competence. Ideally the objective in free-style sparring should be not merely to win, but rather to demonstrate good form and to try one's very best. Any loss incurred under this regimen has within itself the seeds of future victory, whereas any compromise of good form intended to produce momentary advantage will in all likelihood serve to retard the student's progress. A student should not slacken his effort because an opponent appears to lack the same degree of skill as his own. Instead, everyone should be approached as if he had great potential.

Karate ni sente nashi (There is no first attack in karate). This phrase attests to two underlying concepts which should be adhered to. In the first place it is understood that when outside the training hall the karateist never provokes an attack;[2] second, rather than employing the attack as an end in itself, the karate master has schooled himself to hold his stance with patience, imperceptibly inching forward until his opponent, no longer able to stand the suspense, either attacks first or weakens his position by retreating. Our opponent's actions, thus precipitated, create the desired opening.

The counterattack in any type of sparring must be delivered with optimum speed, force, and skill as if it were a matter of survival. The defender should feel that if his counterattack proves lacking in any respect, then his opponent's next attack will be a fatal one. Every iota of physical, mental, and spirtual energy must flow through the attacking limb.

The final attack in any series should be so effectively executed that the defender will be unable to deliver a worthy counterattack. Any subsequent attack will overwhelm him.

---

[1] Only as recently as 1937 did Master Shigeru Egami initiate free-style sparring among the black-belt holders at Waseda University.

[2] Master Funakoshi taught that all *kata* (forms) start with a block, demonstrating the precept that one does not initiate the attack but rather anticipates it when it comes.

APPLICATION

(Forward Stance)

Attacker stands six feet apart from and facing defending student.

1. Instructor designates a specific attack and block to be delivered on command of execution.
2. Delivers attack and appropriate block of own choice on instructor's command of execution.
3. Repeat 1 and 2 without instructor's command of execution. Attacker launches technique, choosing a time at his discretion, while defender responds swiftly with appropriate block, attempting to exceed opponent's attacking speed.
4. Repeat 1–3, with opposing sides changing roles.
   NOTE: Contact is to be avoided at this level of development; therefore students shall not face each other less than six feet apart.

Attacker stands slightly more than an arm's length apart from and facing defender. Any closer interval gives an advantage to attacker; wider spacing on the other hand, benefits defender.

1. *Attacker:* Executes right front kick, then left lunge punch.
   (Left Forward Stance)
   Defender: Right slide-steps to rear, simultaneously executing left downward block; left slide-steps to rear, simultaneously executing right rising block.
2. *Attacker:* Executes right front kick and right reverse punch, then left lunge punch.
   (Left Forward Stance)
   Defender: Right slide-steps to rear, simultaneously executing left downward block; sliding left foot back to other foot, rapidly withdraws right foot, assuming forward stance and simultaneously executing left outward block, then left slide-steps to rear, recovering original stance and simultaneously executing right rising block.
3. *Attacker:* Delivers three lunge punches alternately to the upper level.
   (Open-Leg Stance)
   Defender: Slide-stepping backward, alternately executes the left, right, then left rising blocks; concluding with a right reverse punch, upper level.
   Repeat with defender executing any combination of blocks, concluding with a right reverse punch, lower level.
4. *Attacker:* Delivers in rapid succession the right, left, and right lunge punches to the upper level.

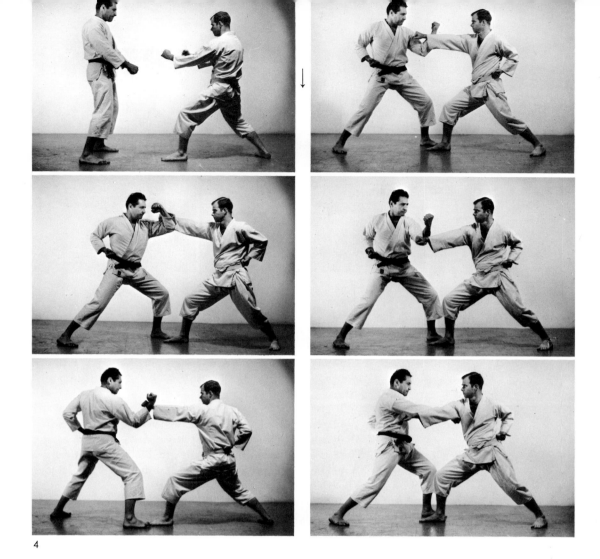

4

(Open-Leg Stance)

Defender: Slide-stepping backward, executes in succession the left rising, right inward, and left inward blocks, then quickly counterattacks with a right reverse punch.

NOTE: Remember to stress the strength and precision of that first backward movement. Failing this, the student will discover that his subsequent backward steps are progressively weaker.

5. *Attacker:*   Delivers three alternate lunge punches to the upper level.

(Open-Leg Stance)

Defender: Left slide-steps backward, executing the right outward block; sliding right foot back to other foot, rapidly withdraws left foot, assuming left forward stance, and at the same time executing right outward block; right slide-steps backward, executing left rising block; concludes with a right front kick.

8 ⟶

6. *Attacker:*   Delivers three alternate lunge punches to the upper level.

(Open-Leg Stance)

   Defender: Right slide-steps backward, executing the left outward block; sliding left foot back to other foot, rapidly withdraws right foot, assuming forward stance, and at the same time executing left inward block; left slide-steps backward, executing the right rising block; concludes with a left front kick.

7. Repeat 5 and 6, with defender moving backward obliquely to either side rather than straight to rear; conclude with any foot or hand attack or combination thereof.

NOTE: Moving back as in 7 serves a twofold purpose: It eliminates the second slide-step, gaining precious time; moving backward on the oblique disrupts attacker's forward momentum since he must necessarily change his line of attack. As the student learns to improvise he may want to rely more heavily upon this very rapid backward movement, substituting it for all backward slide-steps.

8. *Attacker:*   Delivers right lunge punch to the lower level.

(Open-Leg Stance)

   Defender: Right slide-steps backward, executing left inward block, then counterattacks with right reverse punch.

9. *Attacker:*   Delivers right lunge punch to the lower level.

(Open-Leg Stance)

   Defender: Left slide-steps forward to the left oblique, immediately right slide-stepping straight to the left. Executes a left inward block and counterattacks with right reverse punch.

NOTE: All blocking techniques, wherever applicable, should be executed by right or left slide-stepping backward, flexibility being the keynote.

10 ⟶

11 ⟶

10. *Attacker:*   Delivers right lunge punch to the upper level.
(Open Leg Stance)
    Defender: Right slide-steps backward, executing left outward block, then counterattacks with right reverse punch.

11. *Attacker:*   Delivers right lunge punch to the upper level.
(Open-Leg Stance)
    Defender: Right slide-steps backward, executing left rising block, then grasping attacker's right arm, pulls forward and down, breaking his balance and simultaneously counterattacking with right reverse punch.

12 →

12. *Attacker:*   Delivers right lunge punch to the upper level.
    (Open-Leg Stance)
    Defender: Left slide-steps forward to the left oblique, immediately right slide-stepping straight to the left. Keeping both feet in place and twisting torso counterclockwise, executes right outward block, then counterattacks with a left reverse punch.

13. *Attacker:*   Delivers right lunge punch to the lower level.
    Defender: Sliding right, then left foot backward to the right oblique, executes left downward block, then counterattacks with right reverse punch.

14. *Attacker:*   Delivers right lunge punch to the upper level.
    (Open-Leg Stance)
    Defender: Left slide-steps backward and, pivoting counterclockwise on ball of right foot, brings left foot around parallel to right, assuming side straddle-leg stance. Executes in one continuous movement the right inward block and, sliding both feet forward, the right backward elbow attack.

15. (a) *Attacker:* Delivers right lunge punch to the upper level.
    (Open-Leg Stance)
    Defender: Right slide-steps backward, executing in one continuous movement the left knife-hand block and the left, then right spear-hand counterattacks to the upper and lower levels respectively.
    NOTE: Substitute palm-heel attack for left spear-hand attack, upper level, to eliminate risk to eyes.

13 →

14 →

↓

15(a)

15(b) ⟶

(b) *Attacker:* Delivers right lunge punch to the upper level.

    Defender: Slides right foot to the left approximately eighteen inches. Immediately moves left foot to the rear, to assume left forward stance, and simultaneously executes right knife-hand block. Grasping sleeve of attacking arm with right hand, pulls forward and down; then, in same motion, delivers right palm-heel attack, upper level.

(c) Repeat (b), but, after grasping sleeve of attacking arm with right hand and pulling forward and down, immediately grasp same sleeve with left hand before delivering right palm-heel attack, upper level.

    NOTE: Alternatives are offered wherever practical as versatility and adaptability should be the keynote.

16. *Attacker:* Delivers left lunge jab to the upper level.

    Defender: Left slide-steps forward, executing right outward block; right slide-steps forward, delivering right bottom- and right back-fist counterattacks to lower and upper levels respectively.

17. *Attacker:* Delivers right lunge punch to the upper level.

    Defender: Executes right, then left round kick, followed by right reverse punch.

18. *Attacker:* Delivers right lunge punch to the upper level.

    Defender: Left, then right slide-steps forward and slightly to the left oblique, executing left sweeping block and simultaneous right reverse punch.

19. (a) *Attacker:* Delivers right lunge punch to the lower level.

    Defender: Left slide-steps forward, simultaneously executing left pressing block, then left back-fist strike and right reverse punch.

(b) *Attacker:* Delivers right lunge punch to the lower level.

    Defender: Left slide-steps forward, executing left pressing block; left back-fist strike; left knife-hand strike, and simultaneous right reverse punch or right index-finger jab.

    NOTE: Use extreme caution.

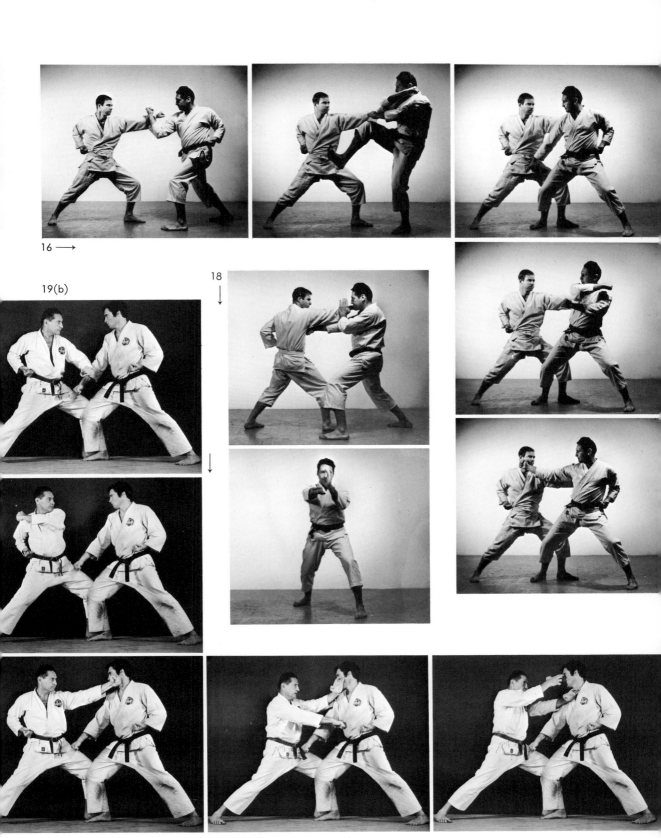

16 →

19(b)

18
↓

↓

20 ⟶

20. *Attacker:* Delivers right lunge punch to the upper level.

　　Defender: Leaps high in the air and, tilting upper body forward, executes left pressing block against right forearm; then counterattacks with right reverse punch while still in the air. Drops to the side, grasping attacking arm from this advantageous position.

　　NOTE: The lower the stance the higher the leap. Main portion of body weight will be forward, increasing the crushing power of this block. Exercises 19 and 20 require split-second timing as they must be executed before attacker's lunge punch has gained momentum.

21. *Attacker:* Delivers right lunge punch to the upper level.

　　Defender: Left slide-steps forward, executing blocking left jab.

22. *Attacker:* Delivers right lunge punch to the upper level.

　　Defender: Left slide-steps forward into side straddle-leg stance and simultaneously counterattacks with a left jab.

23. *Attacker:* Delivers left lunge jab to the upper level.

　　Defender: Left slide-steps forward, executing left rising block and, grasping sleeve of attacking hand, pulls forward and down, simultaneously counterattacking with a right reverse punch.

24. *Attacker:* Delivers right lunge punch to the upper level.

　　Defender: Left slide-steps forward, executing left rising block; then right slide-stepping forward, counterattacks with right upward elbow attack.

25. *Attacker:* Alternately delivers right front-, left side-thrust, and right round kicks.

　　(Open-Leg Stance)

　　Defender: Alternately slide-stepping backward, delivers in succession left downward, right sweeping (fist held downward), and left outward blocks.

21

22

23 ⟶

24 ⟶

26. *Attacker:*   At a slightly accelerated pace, delivers in succession any combination of five attacks.

(Open-Leg Stance)

Defender: Slide-steps backward, refraining from blocking until attacker's last attack, which is blocked and counterattacked with any appropriate technique.

NOTE: This exercise gives one student an opportunity to practice his delivery of multiple attacks while the other, maintaining a low center of gravity, learns to slide-step backward adroitly.

27. Students form parallel lines an arm's length apart facing each other. Practice restrained attacking and blocking techniques of their own choice while remaining within close proximity.

NOTE: This exercise provides excellent training in reflexive responses.

28. *Attacker:*   Alternately delivers three lunge punches, upper level.

Defender: Slide-shifts backward and assumes the cat stance with each attack.

29. *Attacker:*   Alternately delivers two lunge punches to the upper level.

Defender: Slide-shifts backward to the right oblique with the first attack, then slide-shifts backward to the left oblique with the next attack; counterattacks with any combination of hand and/or foot techniques.

(Forward Stance)

(a) *Attacker:* Alternately delivers front kick.

(Open-Leg Stance)

    Defender: Continues to slide-step backward without blocking.

(b) Repeat (a), with attacker substituting side-thrust kick and round kick.

(c) Repeat (a) and (b), with defender executing any appropriate block and counterattack.

(d) *Attacker:* Confining himself to foot attacks, selects any three and, slide-stepping forward, delivers them in succession.

    Defender: Slide-steps backward, executing any appropriate block for each attack.

(e) *Attacker:* Substituting hand attacks, repeats (d).

    Defender: Slide-steps backward, executing any appropriate block for each attack.

NOTE: When practicing karate forms, the student should inject a sense of realism by imagining several concurrent attacks from multiple opponents. Conversely, while sparring, the student should imagine that he is practicing karate forms and perform each block or attack with precision. Each technique should be deliberate, for, after skill is attained, speed may then be developed.

29 ⟶

30(a) ⟶

(Forward Stance)

30. (a) *Attacker:* Delivers right lunge punch to the upper level. Standing in place, executes a left reverse punch to the lower level, then right reverse punch to the upper level.

     Defender: Standing in place, executes left rising, inward, and outward blocks, then right reverse punch, upper level.

  (b) *Attacker:* Delivers right lunge punch to the upper level. Standing in place, executes a left reverse punch to the upper level, then right reverse punch to the lower level.

     Defender: Standing in place, executes left rising, inward, then downward blocks.

  (c) *Attacker:* Delivers right lunge punch to the upper level. Standing in place, executes a left reverse punch to the upper level, then left front kick.

     Defender: Standing in place, executes left rising, inward, then right downward blocks, simultaneously left slide-stepping to the rear.

  (d) To the last block in (a), (b), and (c), defender will add the appropriate reverse punch.

31. Repeat 30, with attacker delivering a lunge punch with each attack. Defender blocks all three attacks with his left hand, while edging backward to his original stance.

32(a) ⟶

32. (a) *Attacker:* Delivers right lunge punch to the lower level and, standing in place, left and right reverse punches to the upper and lower levels respectively.

    Defender: Standing in place, executes in rapid succession, left inward, right outward, and left downward blocks; counterattacks with a right reverse punch, upper level.

(b) *Attacker:* Delivers right lunge punch to the upper level and, standing in place, left and right reverse punches to the upper and lower levels respectively.

    Defender: Standing in place, in rapid succession executes left outward, right outward, and left downward blocks; counterattacks with a right reverse punch, upper level.

(c) Repeat 32 (a) and (b), with attacker delivering a lunge punch with each attack. Defender alternately slide-steps backward with the second and third blocks.

33. *Attacker:* Delivers left lunge jab to the upper level and, standing in place, a right reverse punch to the lower level.

    Defender: Executes left rising, then left downward block; counterattacks with right reverse punch.

34. *Attacker:* Delivers right lunge punch to the lower level and, standing in place, a left reverse punch to the upper level.

    Defender: Executes left downward, then left rising block; counterattacks with right reverse punch.

35. *Attacker:* Delivers right lunge punch to the lower level and, standing in place, a left reverse punch to upper level.

    Defender: Executes left downward, then right rising block; counterattacks with left reverse punch.

36. *Attacker:* Delivers right lunge punch to the upper level and, standing in place, a left reverse punch to the lower level.

    Defender: Executes left rising, then right downward block; counterattacks with a left reverse punch.

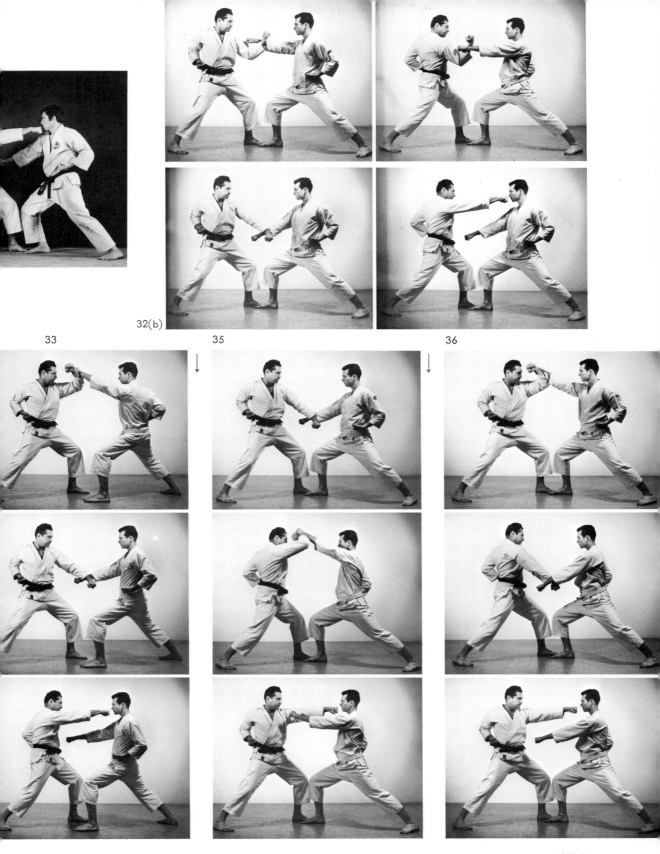

32(b)   35   36

33

 37 ⟶

38 ⟶

37. *Attacker:* Delivers right lunge punch to the upper level.

Defender: Executes left rising block; then counterattacks with right reverse punch, upper level.

Attacker: Standing in place, defends himself against the counterattack with a left rising block and delivers right reverse punch, upper level.

(a) Repeat 37, with attacker substituting a right lunge punch, lower level, and defender using the left downward, inward, or outward block.

(b) Repeat, alternating between the various blocks and attacks during each individual exercise.

(c) *Attacker:* Delivers right lunge punch to the lower level.

Defender: Executes left downward block; then counterattacks with right reverse punch, lower level.

Attacker: Executes left downward block; then right reverse punch, lower level.

38. *Attacker:* Delivers right lunge punch to the upper level.

Defender: Executes left rising block and counterattacks with right reverse punch, upper level.

Attacker: Standing in place, defends himself against the counterattack with a left outward block and delivers right close punch, upper level.

39(b) ⟶

39(c)
↓

39. (a) *Attacker:* Delivers right reverse punch to the upper level, then left reverse punch to the lower level.

    Defender: Executes left rising and left downward blocks; then counterattacks with a right reverse punch, upper level.

(b) *Attacker:* Delivers right lunge punch to the lower level and, standing in place, a left reverse punch to the upper level.

    Defender: Executes left downward and left rising blocks; then counterattacks with a left reverse punch, upper level.

(c) *Attacker:* Delivers right reverse punch to the upper level, then left reverse punch to the upper level.

    Defender: Executes left rising block; right inward block, then counterattacks with a left reverse punch, upper level.

    Attacker: Standing in place, defends himself against the counterattack with a right rising block, then delivers a left reverse punch, lower level.

40(a) ⟶

40. *Attacker:*　Delivers right lunge punch to the upper level.

　　Defender:　Without blocking, immediately executes the following, always attempting to exceed opponent's attacking speed: left front kick, right front kick, left side-thrust kick, right side-thrust kick, right round kick, left rear kick, right rear kick, and left side-stamping kick.

　　NOTE: Each of the above kicks is preceded by attacker's lunge punch.

　　Repeat the above eight kicks, following each kick with a reverse punch.

It will be beneficial for defender to combine various kicks (at his own or instructor's discretion) in one continuous exercise as illustrated below:

　(a) *Attacker:*　Delivers right lunge punch to the upper level.

　　Defender:　Executes left front-thrust kick, quickly followed by right front kick; lowering kicking foot to the rear, counterattacks with a right reverse punch, upper level.

　(b) *Attacker:*　Delivers right lunge punch to the upper level.

　　Defender:　Executes right, then left round kick.

　　NOTE: Since the foregoing exercises preclude any block by defender, he must have landed his kick before attacker is midway through the lunge punch.

　(c) *Attacker:*　Delivers right reverse punch to the upper level, then left reverse punch to the lower level.

　　Defender:　Executes left rising and right downward blocks; then counterattacks with a left reverse punch, upper level.

　　Attacker:　Standing in place, defends himself against counterattack with a right rising block, then delivers left reverse punch, lower level.

41. *Attacker:*　Delivers right lunge punch to the upper level.

　　Defender:　Left slide-steps slightly to the left and executes right round kick. Pivoting counterclockwise on ball of left foot, places right foot down to rear of attacker, executing either the left side-snap or side-thrust kick, then right reverse punch.

　　NOTE: The distance between opponents determines which kick is to be used.

40(b) →

40(c)

↓ 41 →

42. (a) *Attacker:* Delivers right lunge punch to the upper level, then left palm-heel attack to the chest.

   Defender: Slides right, then left foot slightly to the right, executing left outward block, then quickly counterattacks with a right reverse punch, lower level.

   NOTE: The objective of this exercise is to exceed the speed of attacker's palm-heel attack. Prior to the attack, intending a lateral movement, defender must not reveal it by the slightest motion.

(b) *Attacker:* Delivers right lunge punch to the upper level.

   Defender: Simultaneously executes left rising block and right front kick. Returns kicking foot to position beside left knee before placing it down parallel to left foot. Draws left foot up beside right knee and delivers left side-thrust kick, followed by right reverse punch.

(c) *Attacker:* Delivers right front kick.

   Defender: Executes left downward block, then sliding both feet forward into the side straddle-leg stance, delivers left back-fist strike, upper level.

(d) *Attacker:* Delivers left lunge jab to the upper level. (Left Forward Stance)

   Defender: Left slide-stepping backward into the side straddle-leg stance, simultaneously executes right rising block; then delivers right back-fist strike, upper level.

42(b) ⟶

42(c) ⟶

42(d) ⟶

42(f) ⟶

42(e)

(e) *Attacker:* Delivers right lunge punch to the upper level.

Defender: Executes left rising block.

Attacker: Sliding both feet forward into the side straddle-leg stance, delivers right back-fist strike to the upper level.

(f) *Attacker:* Delivers right lunge punch to the upper level.

Defender: Left slide-stepping back into side straddle-leg stance, executes right inward block, withdraws right fist, palm inward, to left ear, then delivers right back-fist counterattack.

Attacker: Executes left palm-heel block to opponent's attacking arm, then delivers right reverse punch, lower level.

43. *Attacker:* Delivers right lunge punch to the upper level.

Defender: Executes left inward block.

Attacker: Delivers right back-fist strike to the lower level.

44. *Attacker:* Delivers right lunge punch to the upper level.

Defender: Executes left outward block.

Attacker: Delivers left back-fist strike to the upper level.

45. *Attacker:* Delivers right lunge punch to the upper level.

Defender: Sliding right foot to the left, pivots clockwise on ball of left foot, executing left inward block and simultaneous right reverse punch.

PART 3 : SPARRING **290**

43 44

45 ⟶

Attacker: Delivers right back-fist strike to the upper level.

Defender: Without withdrawing left hand, delivers extended left jab, upper level (twisting torso clockwise), before attacker's second attack has been completed.

      NOTE: Each movement, though swiftly executed, must be performed with precision while keeping the body erect, being especially careful not to lean forward. These exercises are part of advanced training and prepare the brown-belt holder for participation in free-style sparring.

46. (a) *Attacker:* Rapidly delivers a series of alternate lunge punches to the upper level.

     Defender: Slide-steps backward in a straight line, executing any appropriate arm block for each attack.

   (b) Repeat with defender shifting first left, then right foot slightly to the right (approximately six inches) before executing block. Partners will eventually complete a circle in this manner.

   (c) Repeat (a) and (b), with attacker substituting a lunge punch, lower level.

47. (a) Rapidly slide-step forward, alternately delivering five lunge punches to the upper level; then rapidly slide-step backward, alternately executing five rising blocks.

   (b) *Attacker:* Slide-stepping forward, alternately delivers five lunge punches to the upper level.

     Defender: Slide-steps backward, alternately defending with the rising block, concluding with a reverse punch counterattack, lower level.

   (c) Repeat (a) and (b), with attacker substituting the lunge punch, lower level, and defender a downward block.

   (d) Repeat (a)–(c) as defender blocks with the hand corresponding to the one used by attacker.

48(a)2 ⟶

48. (a) (*1*) *Attacker:* Right slide-steps forward.
     Defender: Slides left, then right foot quickly forward to the left oblique, maintaining the forward stance.
    (*2*) *Attacker:* Delivers right lunge punch to the upper level, using maximum speed within the limitations of good form. The line of attack must not deviate to the point to which defender is expected to move.
     Defender: Does not execute a block but instead right slide-steps forward to the right oblique, describing a quarter-arc which places him at right angles to attacker and once again in a forward stance. (This movement involves such split-second timing that defender's left foot merely pivots counter-clockwise as his right simultaneously slide-steps forward to the right oblique and similarly pivots.)

(b) (*1*) Repeat (a) *2*, with defender right slide-stepping to the left rear, describing a quarter-arc which places him at right angles to attacker, once again in a forward stance.
    (*2*) Repeat, as defender simultaneously executes the left jab, lower level.

(c) Repeat (a) *2*, with defender counterattacking with a right: close punch, reverse punch, forward elbow attack, and upward elbow attack.
    NOTE: Each technique in the above exercise should be practiced singly with several repetitions.

(d) Repeat (c) without the instructor's command of execution. The attacking student's kiai signals the beginning of his forward movement, thus alerting defender.

49(a) ⟶

(Open-Leg Stance)

Students form parallel lines at arm's length facing one another and commence on the instructor's command of execution.

49. (a) *Attacker:* Delivers right front kick.

   Defender: Right slide-stepping to the left rear, pivots clockwise on ball of left foot, bringing right foot around parallel to the left, assuming side straddle-leg stance. Simultaneously, using left arm with fist turned down and to the rear, rigidly sweeps attacking leg forward and to the right.

(b) *Attacker:* Delivers left front kick.

   Defender: Left slide-stepping to the rear, pivots counterclockwise on ball of right foot, sliding left foot around and parallel to the right to assume side straddle-leg stance. Simultaneously, using right arm with fist turned down and to the rear, rigidly sweeps attacking leg forward and to the left.

(c) *Attacker:* Without the instructor's command of execution, delivers either left or right front kick.

   Defender: Right or left slide-steps back into side straddle-leg stance, executing right- or left-handed block regardless of the front kick chosen by attacker.

   NOTE: Repeat (a)–(c) until the instructor's command to cease. Attacker must disregard defender's presence, concentrating on delivering his attack straight forward with maximum speed and no facial expression to betray the attack. Defender meanwhile studies attacker's eyes, waiting for signs indicating the attack. When it comes, he quickly and smoothly slide-steps backward to either side, and out of attacker's path; with a properly timed and vigorous block, he will precipitate attacker's loss of balance, exposing him to effective counterattack.

   The defending block should, for the most favorable result, be executed with the left or right hand as indicated in (a) and (b).

(d) Repeat (a)–(c), with attacker substituting the side-thrust kick for the front kick.

(e) (*1*) *Attacker:* Delivers right lunge punch, upper level.

Defender: Right or left slide-steps to the rear, executing any appropriate arm block.

(*2*) Repeat (*1*), with attacker substituting right lunge punch, lower level.

(*3*) Repeat (*1*) and (*2*). Attacker keeps eyes lightly closed until attack has commenced.

NOTE: This exercise provides a new dimension to sparring since it deprives defender of the foreknowledge of time of attack through any inadvertent eye movements. It also demands of attacker a shifting of dependence upon his eyes to a greater emphasis on muscular coordination.

(Forward Stance)

(*4*) *Attacker:* Delivers right lunge punch to the upper level.

Defender: Executes any appropriate arm block; then improvises any hand or foot counterattack, either singly or in combination.

NOTE: For the purpose of developing spontaneity it should be stressed that attacker's move be made without any preliminary retraction of the striking arm. To prevent an anticipated and thus easily avoided attack, students must make certain that in consecutive attacks they do not lapse into a rhythmic pattern. It is better to delay an attack until the right psychological moment.

(Forward Stance)

(f) (*1*) *Attacker:* Repeats (e) *1–4* attacking with right foot.

Defender: Begins by left slide-stepping forward and slightly to the left; then repeats the entire sequence in exercise (e).

(Left Forward Stance)

(*2*) *Attacker:* Repeats (e) *1–4*, attacking with left foot.

Defender: Begins by right slide-stepping forward and slightly to the right; then repeats sequence in (b).

NOTE: Defender's initial forward movement must be powerfully and unhesitatingly executed. The mental image should be one of the entire body strength flowing through the defending arm. Keep the center of gravity low with shoulders relaxed, but the latissimus dorsi and abdominal muscles tensed.

(*3*) *Attacker:* Delivers front kick (either left or right).

Defender: Executes any block and counterattack.

NOTE: Attacker can precede his kick by any chosen feint, then deliver the front kick. This is continued until the command to stop is given. Repeat, substituting various foot and hand attacks in place of the front kick.

50 $\longrightarrow$

(Forward Stance)

50. *Attacker:*   Delivers right front kick.

     Defender: Shifts right then left foot swiftly to the right, simultaneously executing the left downward block, followed by a right reverse punch, lower level.

     Attacker: Executes left rising or left outward block.

51. *Attacker:*   Alternately delivers a right lunge punch to the upper level, preceding each attack by a body feint or by moving counterclockwise in a semicircle around defender.

     Defender: Whirls in place to face in opposite direction, executing a rear kick with either foot whenever attacker approaches within danger zone.

52. (a) *Attacker:* Moves forward executing continuous front kicks.[3]

       Defender: Moves backward and/or to either side executing the appropriate downward block for each attack.

(Open-Leg Stance)

   (b) Students form opposing lines one arm's length apart.

      (*1*) On instructor's command to begin, the indicated partner will initiate the following: right slide-step forward, simultaneously executing right straight punch, lower level.

      NOTE: The attacks are to be delivered lightly and swiftly with contact tolerated. Defender is to block, then counterattack vigorously, stopping short of contact.

      (*2*) Repeat (*1*), left slide-stepping forward, simultaneously executing left straight punch, lower level.

      (*3*) Repeat, choosing from exercises (*1*) or (*2*) at random.

      (*4*) Repeat (*1*)–(*3*), substituting straight punch, upper level.

(Forward Stance)

   (c) Students are to engage in free-style sparring, executing a wide variety of foot and hand attacks with emphasis on form and speed rather than on power.

[3] Participants may wish to protect parts in contact (shins, forearms) with improvised padding.

(d) Students engage in an alternate exchange of light, swift, and varied kicking techniques, stopping just short of contact. Defender does not block but moves about evasively.

NOTE: It is important that there should be a steady even tempo in this exercise. As soon as a student has obviously completed his attack, defender assumes the alternate role. This close interaction without any preset pattern will cultivate an ability to react speedily.

(e) Students form opposing lines. On instructor's command, each pair will engage in a three-minute period of free-style sparring. In this instance feather-light techniques are to be used, with contact now permissible. This will be followed by a one-minute period of normal free-style sparring (maximum power, no contact). Partners are then rotated to provide the opportunity for maximum exposure.

NOTE: Under the instructor's watchful eye in regular free-style sparring, students may feel hampered and cautious about attempting the wide gamut of alternatives. This exercise will provide a more relaxed atmosphere for exploring less frequently used techniques.

(f) *Defender:* Lies on back, withdrawing one or both legs to a position protecting groin.

Attacker: Proceeds using any technique.

(g) Each student grasps the other's jacket. Maintaining hold and using light or no contact at all, practice sweeping, stamping, and knee kicks; elbow, forearm, and forehead attacks, and initiate throwing techniques without actual completion.

(Proceed on the instructor's command of execution)

53. (a) *Attacker:* Delivers right lunge punch to the upper level.

Defender: Left slide-steps forward, quickly sliding the right foot to the left, placing himself at an angle to his opponent's forward line of attack.

(b) Repeat (a), executing the left jab simultaneously with the completion of the right slide-step, then quickly execute the right reverse punch.

(Forward Stance)

54. *Attacker:* After informing opposing student as to what techniques he will use, launches his attack stopping short of contact.

(Open-Leg Stance)

Defender: Blocks and counterattacks.

When defender is no longer able to block the attack effectively, roles are exchanged. During this exercise a selection of preferred techniques should be employed.

55(b) ⟶

55. (a) *Attacker:* Executes right lunge punch to the upper level, followed by an unexpected attack of his own choice.

Defender: Blocks these two and delivers appropriate counter-attack.

(b) *Attacker:* Delivers right reverse punch to the upper level.

Defender: Executes double palm-heel thrust to attacker's chest; withdrawing right hand, delivers right reverse punch, upper or lower level.

(c) (*1*) When opponent moves within range, execute left side-stamping kick to his leading leg, at knee level or below, and simultaneous left jab, upper level; then execute right reverse punch, lower level.

(*2*) With a low forward hop, place the right foot in the space vacated by the left and repeat (*1*).

(*3*) With a low forward hop, place the right foot in the space vacated by the left and execute the left side-stamping kick to opponent's leading leg at knee level or below; left back-fist strike, then right reverse punch, lower level.

(d) (*1*) *Attacker:* Delivers right reverse punch to the upper level.

Defender: Slides right foot to the left, pivoting clockwise on ball of left foot, simultaneously executing left palm-heel block and right reverse punch, lower level; then left reverse punch, lower level, simultaneously assuming straddle-leg stance.

(*2*) Repeat (*1*) and as soon as defender delivers reverse punch, attacker executes left downward block, then right reverse punch. Both students continue this exchange avoiding contact. This is done with one controlled exhalation of air.

(*3*) *Attacker:* Delivers right reverse punch to the upper level.

Defender: Slides right foot forward to the right oblique; pivoting counterclockwise on ball of left foot, simultaneously executes left outward block, then right reverse punch, lower level.

Attacker: Delivers left downward block, then right reverse punch, lower level.

NOTE: Avoid contact and repeat breath control as in (*2*).

55(d)1

55(d)3

(e) (*1*) During the execution of a front kick, an alert opponent may grasp the kicking leg. Quickly hop in on the supporting foot, forcing the body weight onto the trapped leg and thus at the opponent, and deliver a right reverse punch.

(*2*) Similarly during the execution of a side-thrust kick, an alert opponent may grasp the kicking leg. Spin around to the rear in the direction of the supporting leg, simultaneously crouching low and place palms on floor. From this position, execute a rear kick with the free leg.

(*3*) When sparring, any student landing on his back may recover immediately, thrust himself up and forward on one arm while pushing against floor with both feet, and follow through with a reverse punch with the opposite arm.

(*4*) When sparring, any student landing on his back may quickly withdraw one or both legs to a position protecting the groin. This action would also be necessary before the execution of the front- or side-thrust kick while supine.

NOTE: In the event of falling or being thrown backward it is important to tuck the chin down tightly, keeping head forward so that the skull will not sustain any damaging impact. The student will find that, when thrown, the best position in which he can land will be on the side with the arm extended downward at an angle to absorb the shock. This position presents the least possibility of injury and provides more leverage and maneuverability for counterattack.

Do not remain either completely tense or relaxed when engaged in free-style sparring. A tense condition will soon prove tiring, while the relaxed state could be disastrous if confronted with a sudden attack. Flexibility of thought and action to accommodate the constant adjustment of body tension should be cultivated.

56. Repeat following exercise until instructor's command to stop, then exchange roles:
   (a) *Attacker:* Delivers right lunge punch to the upper level.
   Defender: Executes any suitable hand block, then quickly recovers original stance.
   (b) Repeat, with neither attacker nor defender having to recover original stance.
   (c) Repeat, with defender adding any suitable counterattack.
   (Continuous Attack)
   Beginners should not participate in the following exercise. To increase proficiency and build the endurance of advanced students the instructor will occasionally require them to face several opponents in succession in this manner: An advanced student selected by the instructor will act as defender against single opponents repeating (a)–(c) until instructor's command to stop. Students will take turns against him. Defender will then release his role to another student chosen by the instructor while he joins the ranks of the attackers.

55(e)1

55(e)2

55(e)3 →

→

55(e)4

(d) Repeat, having defender react only with a foot attack.

NOTE: Each student should understand that in this instance his partner intends to modify the force of his actions so that neither will be discouraged from continuing. Otherwise the severity of defender's kick will discourage the quality of future attacks, and similarly attacker must stop his forward movement immediately upon contact with defender's kick, or risk throwing him backward and thereby undermining his confidence during repetitions of the exercise.

(e) Repeat, having defender add any suitable counterattack.

NOTE: To prevent the dangerous pattern of employing a single counterattack and then pausing (thereby providing an opening), students should practice combinations of multiple techniques within each counterattack.

57. Generally speaking, in performing any block the accepted pattern is to retreat a step. This movement provides time to improvise a suitable defense and counterattack. Also, by increasing the distance between opponents, it creates an interval for attacker's power to dissipate itself. A master, having the role of defender, will often perform this startling technique; rather than yielding to or avoiding attacker's forward thrust, he will marshal his total strength and, without equivocation, slide-step forward to execute his block. The hip will swivel forward at the precise instant when the slide-step commences, carrying the body to a position parallel to his opponent. The attack now in progress can very well proceed harmlessly by providing a ready target for counterattack. It goes without saying that split-second timing is imperative for the success of this technique. Because of its devastating potential for both attacker and defender, it should be attempted only by the advanced student. Exercise (b), below, illustrates this point.

(a) (Forward Stance)

Attacker: Delivers right lunge punch to the upper level.

(Open-Leg Stance)

Defender: BASIC—Right slide-steps backward, executing left knife-hand block.

(b) (Forward Stance)

Attacker: Delivers right lunge punch to the upper level.

(Open-Leg Stance)

Defender: ADVANCED—Right slide-steps forward, executing right knife-hand block.

As each attack in basic sparring is directed to a predetermined area, it must be delivered in earnest, inasmuch as defender already knows where the attack is to be directed. Therefore, if defender were actually struck, the fault would be his alone. Students would be doing an injustice to each other if they pulled or otherwise misguided their punches, as maximum efficiency is the desired goal. Most students do not begin to appreciate the absolute necessity of improving their blocking technique until they have actually absorbed an attack.

This will of necessity produce greater effort on their part in blocking any future attack. Repeated practice will, in due time, remove any timidity present in the student's makeup, and thus will enable him to spring forward to the attack whenever the opportunity presents itself. When attacking, the student must learn to disregard his opponent's potential. "If your opponent knocks your teeth out, swallow them and keep fighting" is an old Chinese adage. An opponent may present such a fierce and seemingly invincible spectacle, as to invite timidity if not outright fear. The student thus affected will tend to maintain a greater range (*ma*) than is effective. However, if he has prepared himself for combat by "tightening" his mind, which provides an objective view of his opponent's potential rather than an illogical exaggeration of it, he is psychologically ready.

The importance of maintaining an erect posture cannot be overstressed. Too often there is demonstrated a tendency to lean away from an attack, thus weakening one's stance and suggesting a fear of absorbing a blow. A successful attack under these conditions could be devastating. There is a decided advantage to be gained in holding a resolute and stalwart demeanor. One can then move decisively forward to either side and from there block and effectively counterattack. Of Japanese origin, the maxim "Give the face to your opponent" is pertinent to this strategy.

Free-style sparring is the culmination of the student's entire karate experience, since it constitutes the ultimate proving ground for all the formal theory and training to which he has been exposed. For the first time he is called upon to engage an opponent spontaneously. Here he may use his own initiative to improvise combinations of appropriate techniques, translating his hard-earned knowledge into a flexible, highly effective pattern of attack and defense. The rigid and somewhat inflexible style of the novice evolves in this way into the fluid and far more versatile performance of the black-belt karateist. The thrill of the unexpected and the challenge of combat will now provide a most stimulating atmosphere.

There is a way of confronting one's opponent which should be observed consistently from the outset. It is this: we must sustain the most intense observation of the opponent's eyes. This can best be portrayed by imagining a string drawn taut between the eyes of the contestants. This string must remain tightly drawn—that is to say, the gaze of each partner must not be deflected from its subject or slacken for an instant. That student who excels in this one area will have a twofold advantage. He will be extremely sensitive to his opponent's intentions and, at the same time, present a formidable appearance.

During free-style sparring the student should be quick to observe any inherent weaknesses in his opponent's technique so that he may instantly adjust his own movements to capitalize upon any such weaknesses. In like manner he must strive to avoid deficient areas of his own. This adaptability, although perhaps difficult to cultivate, when once attained will very often provide the margin for success. Given opponents of otherwise equal merit, the victory will go to the more adaptable and perceptive student.

When defending oneself against an attack, the student, generally speaking, should retreat no more than one or two steps in order not to weaken his stance. Blocking effectively and counterattacking strongly is the pattern which all should cultivate while sparring. The student should not wait until the attacking arm or leg is actually near before beginning an appropriate block. Rather, as quickly as possible, the alert student should move into the block so that he will have attained a powerful and positive stance at the moment of impact. Otherwise, a block started too late may be brushed aside with relative ease.

When sparring, it is extremely important that the initial move in an attack brings us close to the opponent so that it and any attacks which may follow will be within striking range. This is especially true in the event that one's opponent decides to retreat.

Stopping a powerful and properly directed attack short of contact during free-style sparring requires far more skill than if one were to strike the opponent. The critical situation most frequently occurs when the distance between the opponents is decidedly closer than the normal sparring interval. This would most often be the case within the framework of a counterattack. The student should now utilize a technique similar to the close or vertical punch, in that he does not have adequate range for the normal follow-through. He will execute his retaliatory attack from this closer range extending the attacking arm only partially, stopping just in time to avoid contact while yet attempting to score a clear point. Remember to withdraw attacking hand quickly.

In delivering the lunge punch there is a striking range within which the attack is most effective. For a few inches beyond, the attack could prove nearly as effective by twisting the shoulders or pushing forward from the rear leg. Students are apt to make the mistake of attacking from too great a distance; when the attack falls short they hold the fist extended in front like a battering ram and continue to charge forward. Even if this appears to the uninitiated to be a valid attack, it should not be considered in this light since the technique is faulty and incorporates much less than maximum power. Begin by closing the distance at once. This will eliminate the weaker alternative of having to stretch forward to insure contact. The actual attack can then be best accomplished by propelling the body forward vigorously (remembering to tense the lower abdomen and buttocks firmly) and driving the knee directly at the opponent's groin. The raised leg will function primarily as a block. Conversely, the student who retreats from a multiple attack must be sure that his initial step is quickly accomplished and that he covers enough distance so that each succeeding attack will not overwhelm him. Bear in mind that each backward step should keep pace with the opponent's advancing one so that the retreating student continually maintains the proper range for counterattack. When slide-stepping backward the student should not rise and terminate the movement suddenly; instead he should remain low in the same dynamic stance ready for any eventuality.

Each individual stance incorporates both good and bad features. The stance that suggests particularly good defensive qualities may be lacking in the offensive and vice versa. The student must be able to analyze instantly and to take immediate advantage of every opportunity presented.

If a student blocks an attack improperly and is consequently struck, he should disregard his momentary failure and counterattack with vigor, uttering an accompanying kiai. His sparring partner should not pause at this moment to offer solicitous words. In the event of a minor injury, students should not be permitted to terminate sparring practice. Younger students expecially will best achieve resolute manhood when required to follow through under painful or unpleasant conditions.

Combination exercises employ the hip-twisting and forward thrust movement necessary to produce accelerated momentum for the performance of each attack. If one link in the chain of attack is weak, then it is all too possible for the entire combination to go awry. When launching a multiple attack consisting of four different techniques, care must be taken that undue emphasis is not placed on any one of them. This ability is best developed through training exercises by emphasizing the initial attack in a combination. Stress should then be shifted to the second, third, and fourth individual attacks in turn. As a result the student will find that he will soon be able to perform each attack precisely and with a consistently high level of power.

Powerfully concentrating each attack during free-style sparring, yet avoiding unnecessary contact, benefits the student by teaching him the proper concepts of distance and timing and develops the ability to control the emotions. The latter strengthens one's resolve to refrain from acts of violence outside the training hall.

If combat outside the training hall proves unavoidable, a student may find himself the victim of a successful attack to a vulnerable area, such as the groin or solar plexus. In this event, it should be kept in mind that several seconds will elapse before physical immobilization. During this brief interval, rather than await the inevitable, the student should quickly launch an all-out counterattack in a final dramatic effort to subdue his opponent.

NOTE: There are distinct advantages innate in both basic and free-style sparring, some of which have been mentioned previously. The latitude for expression apparent in free-style sparring, while it promotes ingenuity and flexibility, does not allow for the refinement of technique. The major emphasis must therefore remain with basic sparring, for it provides the exacting disciplines which must be present if the level of technique is to be raised.

Retreating in a straight line is not good strategy since it permits an opponent to advance strongly, thus increasing the intensity of his attack. Shifting to either side is speedier and forces an assailant to change the direction of attack, slowing his forward momentum and consequently weakening possible resultant contact. A student retreating in a straight line must be sure that each block is executed with maximum power. When shifting to the side, however, a deflecting block will prove ample. It must be kept in mind that a shift too far to the side will require that defender move closer to his opponent before launching a counterattack. No block should be executed as an end in itself but, rather, should be followed by an immediate, strong counterattack. Otherwise, one may just as well turn and run from his opponent. Bear this in mind, however: "To retreat is to invite pursuit."

When faced by the onslaught of an attacking opponent, merely retreating or side-stepping does not constitute the highest level of technique. The advanced student anticipating an attack must react with more courage than that exhibited by the attacker. The Japanese have a saying, "To escape from the rain it is best to plunge into the sea." When an opponent directs a punch or kick at the student the best way to nullify this attack is to move aggressively forward (generally on a slight diagonal approach), turning the body sideways at the proper moment.

(Forward Stance)
    (c) *Attacker:* Executes right lunge punch, lower level.
          Defender: Slides the right foot behind and to the left of the left, and as part of the same movement slides the left foot forward, simultaneously twisting the upper body clockwise.
    (d) *Attacker:* Executes right front kick.
          Defender: Slides the right foot behind and to the left of the left, and as part of the same movement slides the left foot forward simultaneously twisting the upper body clockwise.
    (e) Repeat (c) and (d), with defender commencing in the open-leg stance.
          NOTE: The arms are not used to block in (c), (d), and (e). The body, turned sideways, allows the attacking limb to proceed harmlessly past.

57(d) ⟶

THE ATTACK

One measure of the seasoned karateist is his correct evaluation of an opponent. In the matter of the attack he will assume that it has indeed begun at the instant his opponent closes the distance to within double arms' length, even though no hand or foot attack has yet been launched. Since the opponent's merely moving within the danger zone is tantamount to an attack, the offensive measures taken against him should be considered as a counterattack. In coping with an attack the student should concentrate upon the counterattack rather than upon the block preceding it, otherwise he will find that the block is overemphasized, thereby draining away vital power from his counterattack.

The student must learn to move precisely when his opponent is most off guard. This ability to attack advantageously is best developed by centering the gaze on the opponent's eyes and minutely observing any movement therein, as well as changes in his breathing pattern. With the exception of the skilled karateist, an attacker will indicate his intentions through his eye movements. We may also notice in his eyes a somewhat vacant expression which will indicate a momentary diminution of intensity on his part. Now is the ideal instant for attack. The need for developing this sensitive faculty for interpreting your opponent's intent or frame of mind cannot be overstressed, since the element of timing is of the essence in free-style sparring. This sense of timing also applies in another respect. It is interesting to note that within the normal breathing pattern there are predictable strong as well as weak points. Immediately after exhalation, while the breath is first being drawn in, the body is at its weakest point in the breathing cycle. Knowing this, an alert karateist will gauge his attack accordingly.

When the student has developed peripheral vision, it will not then be necessary to shift his gaze; he need only center it on his opponent's eyes. With the development of this ability, not only will his own attack technique be more successful but when defending himself against an attacker, he will find that he can "beat his opponent to the punch." This principle of extended vision will prove indispensable when students are pitted against multiple opponents.

Students who excel in defensive technique, but who have neglected to develop a good attack, may not do well in free-style sparring. Theoretically, every defensive action should be quickly followed by an attack, for the best defense is actually a good counteroffence.

When concluding an attack, whether or not it succeeds, the student cannot become motionless, even for an instant, expecting his opponent to do the same. He must immediately launch a follow-up attack, or else quickly move into a defensive position until another opportunity presents itself.

A suggested attack for the student beginning free-style sparring consists of five related components. It should flow smoothly in the following sequence: 1) the feint; 2) upsetting opponent's balance; 3) the actual attack; 4) the follow-up attack; and 5) the assuming of a defensive stance or moving into position for the next attack, depending upon how successfully the fourth step has been executed. The following enumerates various possibilities in each category:

SUGGESTED ATTACKS

	I	II	III	IV	V
STRATEGY USED	THE FEINT	UPSETTING OPPONENT'S BALANCE	THE ACTUAL ATTACK	THE FOLLOW-UP ATTACK	RECOVERING POSITION
1.	Eyes	Sweeping kick	Reverse punch	Spear-hand attack	Back stance
2.	Hands	Side-stamping kick	Front kick	Upward palm-heel attack	Forward stance
3.	Feet	Pushing	Forward elbow	Double straight punch	Cat stance
4.	Shoulders	Pulling	Forearm attack	Double hook punch	Straddle-leg stance
5.	Kiai	Changing direction	Knee kick	Knife-hand strike	Slide-step forward/ backward

Actual attacks should be limited to a maximum of four in succession. When more are attempted the student will find that each attack beyond the fourth becomes progressively weaker. Neither should the student begin his attack with his strongest technique and follow it with successively weaker ones, for if this pattern is employed the follow-up will offer little gain for his efforts and little to be feared by his opponent. Ideally, each technique within a multiple attack should incorporate a consistently high level of power.

When the karateist has reached that plateau of excellence where

1 ⟶

his performance is superior, he may well dispense with preliminaries and propel himself abruptly into the actual attack. It must constitute so sudden and potent an onslaught that few opponents could withstand it. Before the attack he will have mentally closed the distance to, then through, his opponent.

CREATING AN OPENING

(Forward Stance)
1. Standing in place, swiftly move upper body in a feint to the left and/or right, then quickly slide-step forward.
2. (a) Attacker shifts left foot abruptly to the left or right, then quickly to the opposite side, before launching a frontal attack.
   NOTE: This device serves to confuse the opponent as to intended direction of the impending attack.
   (b) Attacker shifts left foot abruptly to the right, then quickly to the opposite side; right slide-steps forward, simultaneously executing left palm-heel thrust to defender's fist, sweeping it to the right; right reverse punch or back-fist, strike; right rear-stamping kick to defender's left leg at knee level or below, simultaneously pushing against defender with right hand; then left reverse punch, lower level.
   (c) Attacker shifts left foot abruptly to the right, then quickly a few inches to the opposite side; right slide-steps forward, simultaneously grasping defender's left sleeve, pulling it down and to the rear; right reverse punch or back-fist strike; left rear-stamping kick to defender's left leg at knee level or below, simultaneously pushing against defender with left hand; then left reverse punch, lower level.

3. To slide-step counterclockwise can cause the opponent's left foot to move too far to his left as he attempts to face the new line of attack. As soon as his body thus becomes exposed, right slide-step forward assuming straddle-leg stance, and, slide-shifting both feet forward, simultaneously deliver the right back-fist strike.

4. Deliver right sweeping kick to opponent's left knee and simultaneous left spear-hand attack,[4] upper level; dropping the right foot forward to the floor, sharply press it inward against back of opponent's left knee, breaking his balance; quickly execute right reverse punch, upper level.

5. Keeping right foot in place, execute left slide-step to the rear. This technique often entices an opponent to move in closer, at precisely which time execute one of the following:
   (a) Left or right front kick.
   (b) Pivoting counterclockwise on left foot, deliver right rear kick.
   (c) Left slide-step forward, delivering left forward elbow attack, then right reverse punch to the opponent's chest.
   (d) Right slide-step backward, delivering left reverse punch.

6. Deliver right sweeping kick to opponent's leading ankle, simultaneously grasping his extended hand, then left round kick and right reverse punch.

[4] Substitute left palm-heel thrust.

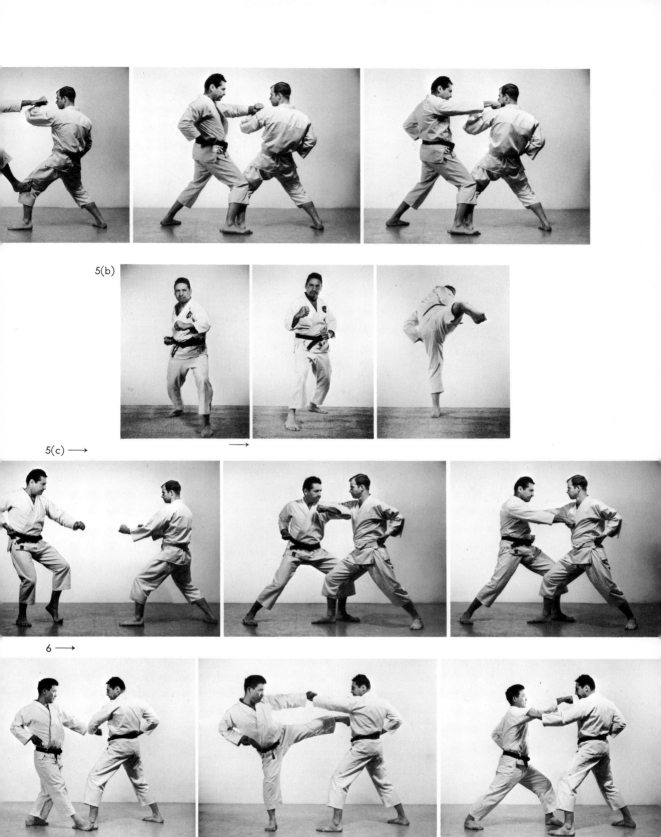

5(b)

5(c) ⟶

6 ⟶

7(a) ↓

7(b) ⟶

7(c)3 ⟶

7. (a) Left jab and simultaneous right sweeping kick to opponent's left knee; left side-thrust kick and right reverse punch.

(b) Left jab and simultaneous right sweeping kick to opponent's left knee; left, then right round kick; left lunge punch.

(c) (1) Left jab, upper level, and simultaneous left front kick, lower level; then right reverse punch, upper level.

(2) Left jab, upper level, simultaneously snapping right foot to position slightly ahead and to the side of left foot; then right reverse punch, upper level.

(3) Left lunge jab, upper level, simultaneously snapping right foot to position slightly ahead and to the side of left; left front kick, then right reverse punch, upper level.

(d) Execute left front kick and simultaneous left jab; with a low hop, make one half-turn clockwise, moving right foot behind and perpendicular to the left; instantly deliver left rear kick, then right reverse punch.

(e) Execute right front kick and simultaneous right reverse punch; with a low hop, make one half-turn counterclockwise, moving left foot behind and perpendicular to the right; instantly deliver right rear kick, then left reverse punch.

7(d) ⟶

7(e) ⟶

8(c) ⟶

11 ⟶

8. (a) Feint a right reverse punch; slide the right foot behind and to the left of the left and, as part of the same movement, slide the left foot forward, simultaneously executing a left lunge jab, upper level; then right reverse punch, lower level.

   (b) Feint a right reverse punch; slide the right foot behind and to the left of the left, simultaneously executing a left jab; left slide-thrust or rear kick, then right reverse punch.

   (c) Execute left lunge jab; with a low hop, make one half-turn clockwise; moving right foot behind and perpendicular to the left, instantly deliver left rear kick.

   (d) Execute right reverse punch; with a low hop, make one half-turn clockwise; moving right foot behind and perpendicular to the left, instantly deliver left rear kick.

9. *Attacker:* Advances to within double arms' length.
   Defender: Launches left side-thrust kick directly from the floor at attacker's left leg at knee level or below.

10. *Attacker:* Executes left palm-heel attack to defender's leading hand, sweeping it aside and simultaneously right slide-stepping forward. Without pausing, moves quickly into side straddle-leg stance, delivering right side-elbow attack.

13(a)1 →

11. *Attacker:* Executes left palm-heel attack to defender's leading hand, sweeping it aside; left slide-stepping forward into side straddle-leg stance, delivers left back-fist strike to the upper level.

12. *Attacker:* Delivers left lunge jab to the upper level; then right slide-steps forward, pressing right foot down on top of defender's leading foot, immobilizing it. (This diversionary technique, shifting the defender's attention to the trapped foot, renders him vulnerable to attack. This principle applies to exercises 1–11 as well.)

13. (a) (*1*) *Attacker:* Half left, then half right slide-steps forward, executing left pressing block against defender's left arm, pinning it to his side; then quickly delivers right reverse punch, upper level. (*2*) *Attacker:* Half left slide-steps forward; right slide-steps forward, executing the left pressing block, then right lunge punch. NOTE: As the lower abdomen and buttocks must be vigorously tensed during this technique, the pressing block is delayed until after the start of the right slide-step. Both foot and arm movements immediately preceding the reverse or lunge punch terminate together.

(b) Feint a right lunge punch, upper level, simultaneously half right slide-step forward; half left slide-step forward, simultaneously executing a left pressing block against opponent's left arm, pinning it to his side; then quickly deliver the right lunge punch, upper level.

(c) Feint a right lunge punch, lower level, simultaneously half right slide-step forward; left lunge jab, upper level; then a series of four vertical lunge punches alternating right with left. (These punches should be coupled with short, rapid slide-steps.)

13(d)   13(e)   13(f)

(d) Slide right foot forward to a position ahead of left, simultaneously raising right fist to left ear, palm inward, as if to deliver the right back-fist strike; instantly execute left front kick, then right reverse punch.

(e) Execute right back-fist strike followed by (d). Repeat several times in reverse order.

(f) Slide right foot forward to a position ahead of left, simultaneously raising right fist to left ear, palm inward, as if to deliver the right back-fist strike; execute left lunge punch, then right front kick.

(g) Execute right back-fist strike, followed by (f). Repeat several times in reverse order.

NOTE: (d), (e), and (f) following one another in any order should set the pattern for many other combinations of techniques that are closely related.

 14(b)

14(d)

↓

The feint is of limited effectiveness unless the student places great emphasis on timing. An explanation of the mechanics involved will serve to illustrate this point: the student feints (with hand, foot, kiai, or any combination thereof), causing a twofold reaction in his opponent. The initial reaction will be an uneasy adjustment to the threat of attack, followed by a secondary reaction involving the regaining of composure and consolidation of stance. The attack, if it is to be successful, must take place before the secondary reaction occurs. (The feint must be followed instantly by the attack.) Simple direct techniques can then be of most value for the attack, for example:

1. Right lunge punch.
2. Left lunge jab and right reverse punch delivered to the upper and lower levels respectively.

NOTE: The techniques in 2 above are to be delivered in such quick succession as to appear nearly simultaneous.

14. (a) *Attacker:* Feints a right, then left reverse punch; quickly executes a right lunge punch, upper level.

    (b) *Attacker:* Feints a right lunge punch; withdrawing the left fist to corresponding hip, simultaneously executes right half slide-step forward; left close or vertical punch, lower level, and simultaneous left slide-step forward; right reverse punch.

    (c) *Attacker:* Feints a right reverse punch, simultaneously withdrawing left fist to corresponding hip; left reverse punch, upper level, and simultaneous right slide-step forward; right reverse punch and simultaneous left slide-step forward; left, then right reverse punch to the upper and lower levels respectively.

    (d) *Attacker:* Feints a right lunge punch, simultaneously executing a half right slide-step forward; left lunge jab; right reverse or lunge punch.

(e) *Attacker:* Feints a right lunge punch, simultaneously executing a half right slide-step forward; left lunge jab; grasping collar of defender's training uniform, pulls down to left rear, simultaneously breaking his balance with left sweeping kick to left foot; right reverse punch, lower level.

(f) *Attacker:* Feints a right lunge punch, simultaneously executing a half right slide-step forward; left back-fist strike, upper level; right reverse or lunge punch.

(g) *Attacker:* Feints a right reverse punch; right front kick and right reverse punch; left lunge punch, then right reverse punch.

Attacker: Feints a right lunge punch and simultaneously half right slide-steps forward; left round kick; right lunge punch.

(h) *Attacker:* Feints a left jab, executes a right reverse punch, upper level, and simultaneously half right slide-steps forward; left front kick and simultaneous left reverse punch; right front kick and simultaneous right reverse punch; left lunge punch, right reverse punch.

Attacker: Feints a left jab, executes a right reverse punch, upper level, and simultaneously half right slide-steps forward; left front kick and simultaneous left reverse punch; right lunge punch; left reverse punch.

(i) Left jab, simultaneously raising right knee to chest level as a feint (this also serves to protect abdomen); right back-fist strike; left lunge punch; right reverse punch.

Attacker: Stamps floor loudly with left foot, simultaneously executing left jab; right lunge punch.

(j) Feint a right reverse punch; left jab, simultaneously raising right knee to chest level; execute right reverse punch, simultaneously lowering leg forward; rapidly slide right, then left foot forward, simultaneously executing right back-fist strike; then left reverse punch to the upper and lower levels respectively, or left back-fist strike; then right reverse punch to the upper and lower levels respectively.

Attacker: Feints a right reverse punch; left jabs, simultaneously raising right knee to chest level; executes right reverse punch, simultaneously lowering leg to rear; right front kick and simultaneous left reverse punch.

Attacker: Feints a right reverse punch; left jabs, simultaneously raising left knee to chest level; executes right reverse punch, simultaneously lowering leg forward.

Attacker: Feints a right reverse punch; left jab, simultaneously raising left knee to chest level; lowers leg forward, immediately executing right lunge punch, upper level.

(k) *Attacker:* Feints a right reverse punch; left jab and simultaneous right front or round kick; right reverse punch, simultaneously lowering kicking foot forward or backward.

14(e) ⟶

14(g) ⟶

14(k) ⟶

Attacker: Feints a right reverse punch; left jab and simultaneous right front-stamping kick to defender's left leg at knee level or below; left round kick, then right front kick and right reverse punch.

(l) *Attacker:* Feints a right reverse punch; left round kick; right lunge punch.

(m) Feint a right reverse punch; left jab and simultaneous right front kick; right reverse punch, simultaneously lowering kicking foot to the rear; with low forward hop, place right foot in the space vacated by the left and execute the left side-thrust kick, then reverse punch.

(n) Feint a right reverse punch; left jab and simultaneous right front kick; right reverse punch, simultaneously lowering kicking foot forward; with low forward hop, place left foot in the space vacated by the right; execute right side-thrust kick, then left reverse punch.

(o) Feint a right reverse punch; left jab and simultaneous half right slide-step forward; right reverse punch and simultaneous left front kick; left reverse punch; with a low forward hop, place right foot in the space vacated by the left; execute left side-thrust kick, then right reverse punch.

(p) Feint a right reverse punch; left jab and simultaneous half right slide-step forward smoothly continuing into a right lunge punch; left front kick, then left reverse punch.

(q) Feint a right reverse punch; left jab, simultaneously raising right knee to chest level; lower right foot forward immediately executing left round kick; right reverse punch.

(r) Feint a right reverse punch; right front kick; execute left jab, simultaneously lowering kicking foot to the rear; right reverse or lunge punch.

(s) Feint a right reverse punch; right front kick; execute left reverse punch, simultaneously lowering kicking foot forward; right reverse punch.

NOTE: When practicing feints, it is wise to work on form as well as speed. A mirror will be helpful.

15. (a) Swiftly reverse foot positions, assuming left forward stance; quickly execute left front kick.

(b) Reverse foot positions twice, swiftly assuming original stance; quickly execute right front kick, then right reverse punch.

BREAKING THE OPPONENT'S BALANCE

(Forward Stance)

1. (a) With leading hand, quickly grasp opponent's left wrist, pulling forward and down, simultaneously delivering the right lunge punch.

(b) With leading hand, quickly thrust opponent's left fist downward; immediately execute right front kick, followed by a right reverse or lunge punch to the upper level.

1(c) ⟶

2(a) ⟶

2(b) ⟶

(c) With a low hop forward, place the right foot in the space vacated by the left, simultaneously thrusting opponent's left fist downward or to the right with left palm; quickly execute the left side-thrust kick.

2. (a) Body feint to the left; if opponent adapts by shifting his stance, rapidly slide-shift both feet to the right. Immediately grasp opponent's left wrist and pull forward and down, simultaneously delivering right reverse or lunge punch from the outside on the diagonal slightly to the opponent's left side.

(b) Body feint to the right; if opponent adapts by shifting his stance, rapidly slide-shift both feet to the left. Immediately execute left palm-heel thrust to opponent's fist sweeping it to the right, simultaneously delivering either the right back-fist strike or reverse or lunge punch from the inside on the diagonal slightly to the opponent's right side.

2(d) ⟶

(c) Keeping the upper body erect and motionless, slide the left foot several inches to the right, then quickly forward several inches to the left oblique, immediately executing a right lunge punch, upper level, on the diagonal (this will be slightly to the opponent's right).

(d) Keeping the upper body erect and motionless, slide the left foot several inches to the left, then quickly forward several inches to the right oblique, simultaneously grasping opponent's left wrist; pull forward, simultaneously executing a right reverse punch.

(e) Keeping the upper body erect and motionless, slide the left foot several inches to the left, then quickly forward several inches to the right oblique, immediately executing a right lunge punch, upper level, on the diagonal (this will be slightly to the opponent's left).

NOTE: The stance must remain low throughout with the supporting leg firmly planted on the floor. Frequently a student will raise his hands to protect the face when attacked at the upper level; therefore, the alert attacker should be able to readily improvise with a lunge punch, lower level. Practice this technique repeatedly with a partner who blocks, bobs, and weaves and/or executes a reverse punch, upper level.

(f) *Attacker:* Slides left foot slightly to the left in a feinting maneuver, then quickly back; slides left, then right foot swiftly forward, executing a left side-stamping kick to defender's left leg at knee level or below while grasping left sleeve; pull forward and down, simultaneously delivering right reverse punch.

NOTE: This technique effectively neutralizes hand and foot attacks.

3. With leading hand, quickly grasp opponent's left wrist, pulling forward and down, simultaneously executing a right sweeping kick to his left leg at knee level or below; then deliver the right lunge punch.

2(f)

3

4 ⟶

4. With leading hand, quickly grasp opponent's left wrist, pulling forward and down, simultaneously delivering the right round kick.
5. Regarding the above exercises in which attacker grasps defender's wrist, if the latter's fist is held unusually high, instead of grasping his wrist attacker should execute a left palm-heel thrust to defender's elbow, forcing his arm up and creating an opening.[5]

   NOTE: When a student's hand or sleeve is grasped by his opponent, he should not try to pull away, thereby giving his opponent an opportunity to attack. Rather than dissipating his energy in an effort to break free, he himself can immediately attack by bending his left arm and executing a left forward or upward elbow attack to his opponent's chest.

(Left Forward Stance)

6. Left slide-step forward, strongly driving left knee against inner thigh of opponent's leading leg, breaking his balance; then deliver right reverse punch.

(Forward Stance)

7. (a) *Attacker:* Delivers right lunge punch to the upper level.
      Defender: Half left slide-steps forward to the left oblique, executing a left sweeping block. Delivers the right side-thrust kick to the back of attacker's right knee, breaking his balance, then counters with a right backward elbow attack.

   (b) *Attacker:* Delivers right lunge punch to the upper level.
      Defender: Half left slide-steps forward to the left oblique, executing a right outward block. Delivers the right side-thrust kick to the back of attacker's right knee, breaking his balance, then counters with a right backward elbow attack augmented by the left hand.

[5] Here we remind the student that the forward stance as taught in Shotokan Karate does not allow for the variation (fist held high) described in 5 above. However, the student who takes part in tournaments should be prepared to cope with many different styles.

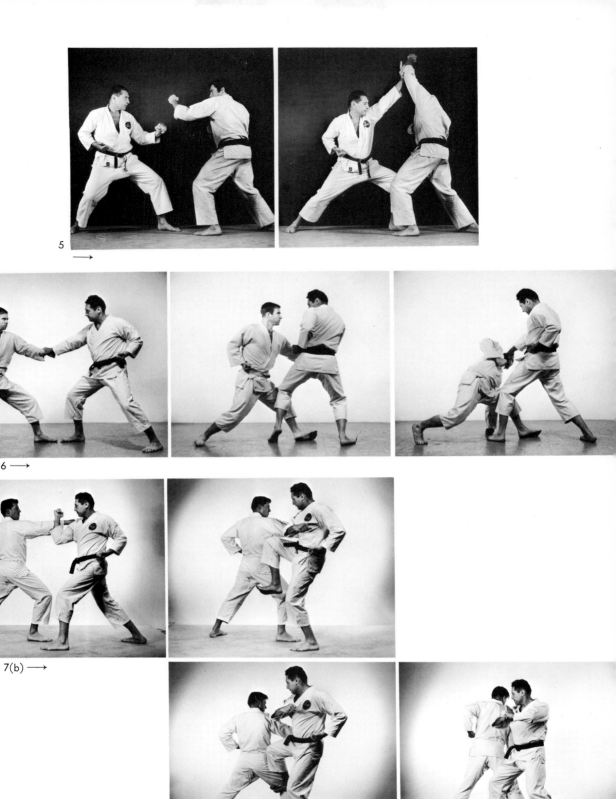

5 →

6 →

7(b) →

7(d) ⟶

(c) *Attacker :* Delivers right lunge punch to the upper level.

Defender : Half left slide-steps forward to the left oblique, executing left sweeping block; delivers right side-thrust kick to the back of attacker's right knee, breaking his balance, then counterattacks with a right bottom-fist strike, upper level.

(d) *Attacker :* Feints left front kick, raising knee sufficiently high to protect abdomen; quickly executes right lunge punch.

Defender : Half left slide-steps forward to the left oblique to evade attacker; omitting block, delivers right backward elbow attack, then right back fist strike.

8. *Attacker :* Delivers right lunge punch to the upper level.

Defender : Half left, then right slide-steps forward and slightly to the left oblique, twisting his body clockwise, then hooks left foot behind attacker's right ankle. Pulls foot forward, breaking his balance, then counterattacks with a right reverse punch.

9. *Attacker :* Delivers right lunge punch to the upper level.

Defender : Executes left rising block.

Attacker : Bends right foot inward against back of defender's left knee, breaking his balance, then delivers left reverse punch.

10. *Attacker :* Delivers right lunge punch to the lower level and left palm-heel attack to the upper level; keeping left hand at defender's face as long as possible, alternately delivers in rapid succession a right then left reverse punch to the lower level.

8

9 →

10

11(a) ⟶

11. (a) *Attacker:* Delivers right sweeping kick to the side of defender's left knee; continues sweeping movement, pivoting counterclockwise on ball of left foot to assume a position beside defender; delivers the left side-snap kick, then right reverse punch.

   (b) *Attacker:* Delivers right sweeping kick to defender's left leg at knee level or below; placing right foot forward, quickly executes left front kick, then right reverse punch.

   (c) *Attacker:* Delivers right sweeping kick to defender's left leg at knee level or below; lowering kicking foot forward, executes left side-stamping kick to defender's right leg at knee level or below and simultaneous left back-fist strike, upper level, then right reverse punch, upper level.

12. *Attacker:* Delivers right lunge punch to the upper level.

   Defender: Left slide-steps backward; executes right sweeping kick to attacker's right ankle, breaking his balance; then counterattacks with a left reverse punch, or, grasping attacker's right sleeve, pulls forward, simultaneously executing a right reverse or vertical punch, upper level.

13. *Attacker:* Delivers right lunge punch to the upper level, keeping right fist rigidly forward (prolong this position) at defender's face; then executes left lunge punch, upper level, in the same manner, followed by a right reverse punch, lower level.

11(b) ⟶

11(c) ⟶

12 ⟶   ⟶

13

14(a)1 ⟶

14(a)3 ⟶

14(c)

14. (a) (*1*) *Attacker:* Delivers right lunge punch to the upper level.

        Defender: Executes left outward block; grasps attacker's right sleeve, simultaneously pulling him off balance; delivers right forward elbow attack to side of attacker's face.

    (*2*) *Attacker:* Delivers right lunge punch to the upper level.

        Defender: Executes left outward block; grasps attacker's right sleeve, simultaneously pulling him off balance; delivers a right upward elbow attack to attacker's abdomen.

    (*3*) *Attacker:* Delivers right reverse punch to the upper level.

        Defender: Executes left outward block; grasps attacker's right sleeve and left slide-steps to rear, simultaneously pulling him off balance; delivers right inner forearm attack to back of attacker's neck.

  (b) Repeat (*3*), with attacker delivering right lunge punch to the upper level.

  (c) Repeat (b), with defender sliding both feet slightly to the left, simultaneously executing the right outward block; grasping attacker's right sleeve, right slide-steps to rear, simultaneously pulling him off balance; deliver left inner forearm attack to back of attacker's neck.

15 ⟶

16 ⟶

17 ⟶

15. *Attacker:* Delivers right lunge punch to the upper level.
    Defender: Keeping left foot in place, slides right foot to the left, then quickly executes left sweeping kick to attacker's right heel, breaking his balance.
    Attacker: Delivers right back-fist strike to the upper level, even though his balance may be upset.
16. *Attacker:* Delivers right lunge punch to the upper level.
    Defender: Half left slide-steps forward, grasping attacker's throat with a choking thrust of the left hand. Maintaining throttling grip, continues left; then right slide-steps forward with short swift movements accompanied by repeated attacks to the upper level with the right fist.
17. *Attacker:* Delivers right lunge punch to the upper level; remaining low, simultaneously executes right palm-heel thrust against defender's chest and sweeps his right foot back against defender's left heel with hooking motion.

18(a) ⟶

18(b)

18. (a) *Attacker:* Delivers right lunge punch to the upper level.

       Defender: Executes left inward block; quickly places left foot in back of and parallel to attacker's right foot, both now facing in the same direction; sharply presses left foot inward against attacker's leg, breaking his balance.

  (b) Repeat, facing opponent at close quarters.

19. (a) *Attacker:* Delivers left side-stamping kick to defender's left leg at knee level or below; quickly executes right front kick, then right reverse punch.

  (b) *Attacker:* With low forward hop, places right foot in space vacated by the left and executes left side-stamping kick to opponent's left leg at knee level or below; right front kick and simultaneous left jab, then right reverse punch.

  (c) *Attacker:* Delivers right lunge punch to the upper level.

      Defender: Executes left rising block, left forward palm-heel thrust to right side of chest with simultaneous half left slide-step forward, then right reverse punch, lower level.

20. (a) *Attacker:* Slides left foot forward, then right foot coupled with right reverse punch feint; executes left lunge jab, upper level, then right reverse punch, lower level.

  (b) *Attacker:* Slides left foot forward, then right foot coupled with left feinting jab; executes right reverse punch, upper level, simultaneously left slide-stepping forward, then left reverse punch, lower level.

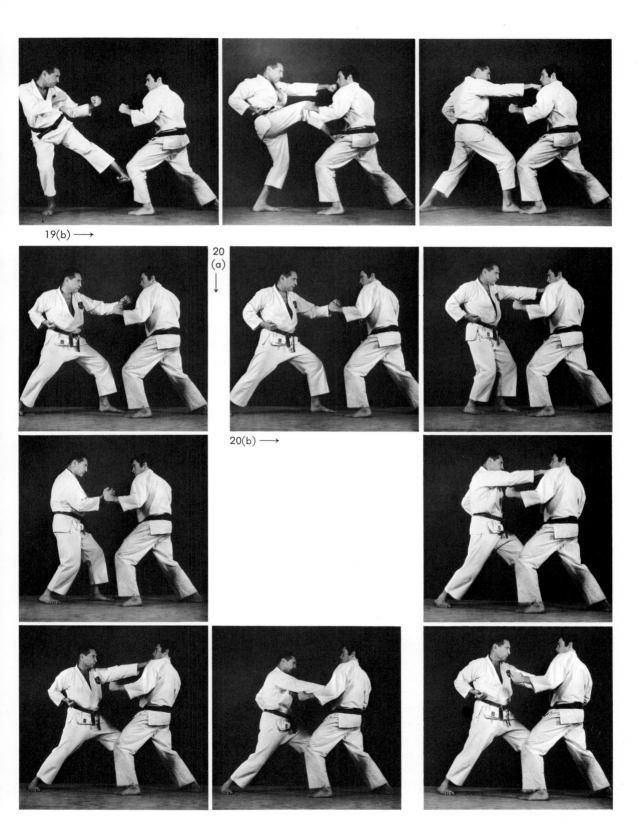

19(b) ⟶

20 (a) ↓

20(b) ⟶

21. *Attacker:* Delivers right sweeping kick to defender's left leg at knee level or below; left side-stamping kick to defender's right leg at knee level or below and simultaneous left jab, then right reverse punch.

22. *Attacker:* With left hand, grasps defender's leading left hand, pulling down and to the left, simultaneously executing a right sweeping kick to his left leg at knee level or below; lowering right foot forward to the floor, executes right reverse punch, upper level, then right back-fist strike and left reverse punch to the upper and lower levels respectively.

CLOSING THE DISTANCE

(Forward Stance)

1. (a) Commence right slide-step forward, stopping when right heel is just in front of left toes and execute:
   (*1*) left front kick
   (*2*) right reverse punch
   (*3*) combine (*1*) and (*2*) in a single exercise
   (b) Straightening right leg, propel the body strongly forward, simultaneously raising right leg beside the left knee. Lower right foot to the rear.
   (c) Repeat (b), adding a right front kick before lowering foot to the rear.
   (d) Execute right lunge punch to the upper level and immediately left slide-step forward into close-leg stance.
   (e) Repeat (d), progressing into left front kick, then left reverse punch.
   (f) (*1*) Repeat (d), progressing into right front kick, then right reverse punch.
   (*2*) Repeat (*1*), progressing into left front kick, then left reverse punch.
   NOTE: (a)–(f) develop the proficiency necessary for rapid forward movement.

2. Students form parallel lines an arm's length apart facing each other. The attacking side assumes the forward stance, while the defending side assumes the open-leg stance.
   (a) Attacking side delivers right reverse punch to the lower level.
   (b) Moving back two feet, attacking side now delivers right lunge punch to the lower level.

1(a)3 ⟶

1(c) ⟶

2 ⟶

2(a)

2(b)

(c) Attacking side moves back an additional two feet from the previous attack point. Straightening supporting leg, propel the body strongly forward, then deliver right lunge punch to the lower level.

(d) Attacking side retreats an additional two feet from previous attack point used in exercise (c). Straightening supporting leg, propel the body strongly forward. As right foot completes lunging step, simultaneously slide both feet forward, closing remaining gap between students, then deliver right lunge punch to the lower level.

(e) Straightening supporting leg, simultaneously slide left foot somewhat forward, repeating exercises (c) and (d).

(f) Repeat (a), (b), (d) and (e), with attacking side substituting the following attacks:
(1) left jab, upper level; right reverse punch, lower level
(2) right front kick
(3) left jab, upper level; right front kick, then right reverse punch, upper level

(g) In the event that attacker delivers a right lunge punch which falls short, he can then close the distance and continue the attack with one or more lightning-swift right reverse punches, each implemented by a simultaneous driving, pounding right step forward (the left foot should be drawn forward each time to maintain the proper interval).

2(f)1

2(f)2 →

2(f)3 →

2(h)1

→

(h) Repeat (g), substituting:
    (*1*) right back-fist strike
    (*2*) right bottom-fist strike
    NOTE: The entire spectacle (the expression, the step, the punching arm, etc.) must convey an overwhelming intensity.
    (*3*) Leaping forward onto the right foot execute:
        (*a*) left front kick
        (*b*) left side-thrust kick
        (*c*) repeat (*a*) and (*b*), adding right front kick to each
        (*d*) repeat (*a*)–(*c*), adding right reverse punch to each
    NOTE: The kick is initiated with the commencement of the leap and must be landed a split second after the right foot touches the ground. The lower the leap the greater the distance that can be spanned. During forward leap, right knee must be raised high to protect abdomen against kick.
    (*4*) With a low leap forward onto the right foot, simultaneously withdraw the left fist to a point above the hip and immediately execute the left reverse punch.
    (*5*) Rapidly advance using short staccato-like steps while keeping left foot forward; pause for an instant immediately before penetrating within danger zone; then leap forward, executing right front kick and right reverse punch.
    NOTE: This technique is intended to force the opponent to block or attack prematurely, thus rendering his defenses vulnerable.
(Left Forward Stance)
    (*a*) With low forward leap, reverse foot positions, landing in the forward stance; quickly execute right front kick, followed by right reverse punch.
    (*b*) With low forward leap, reverse foot positions, landing in the forward stance; execute the right lunge punch.
    (*c*) With low forward leap onto right foot, simultaneously execute right reverse punch while raising left foot to opposite knee; lower left foot forward, simultaneously executing left reverse punch, upper level, then right reverse punch, lower level.

2(h)5a ⟶

2(i)3 ⟶

(d) With low forward leap onto right foot, simultaneously execute right reverse punch, upper level; left reverse punch, lower level, and simultaneous left front kick; right side-thrust kick.

NOTE: (a), (b), (c), and (d) effectively place the student well within his opponent's danger zone.

(Forward Stance)

(i) (1) *Attacker:* Delivers right lunge punch to the upper level, stopping just short of contact.

(Open-Leg Stance)

Defender: Remains motionless with gaze fixed on attacker's eyes. Does not blink or flinch. While the body remains motionless defender's feeling is "forward."

(2) Repeat (1), with attacker adding left reverse punch, lower level.

(3) Repeat (2). Immediately upon completion of right lunge punch, upper level, pivot slightly counterclockwise on ball of right foot, simultaneously sliding left foot to the right; execute left reverse punch, lower level.

SPARRING **339**

(4) *Attacker:* Feints right reverse punch; executes left lunge jab; pivots slightly counterclockwise on ball of left foot, simultaneously sliding right foot forward to the right oblique, and executes the right reverse punch, lower level; right sweeping kick to defender's left foot and simultaneous left reverse punch, upper level; then right reverse punch, lower level, simultaneously lowering right foot forward or backward.

(j) Feint right reverse punch; execute right reverse punch; left reverse punch and simultaneous right front kick; right, then left reverse punch; right reverse punch and simultaneous left front kick; left, then right reverse punch.

NOTE: This technique is especially effective against the student who relies solely upon the counterpunch since he may well be overwhelmed by the constant barrage of hand and foot attacks.

(k) A growing laxity manifesting itself in uncontrolled hand attacks is becoming increasingly evident at various tournaments. Where once this could be attributed to inexperience, we now find increasing numbers of brown- and black-belt holders displaying an almost arrogant lack of control. Contestants realize that to score a point in a match they must land an attack which combines the essentials of power and judicious spacing. Oftentimes students who are ostensibly high ranking reveal poor training in either punching rashly through to score the coveted point or in delivering a hand attack which falls far short of its mark. To rectify this growing deficiency, the following exercise should be practiced.

(Forward Stance)

Attacker: Delivers alternate, unbroken right, then left lunge punches to the lower level, stopping just short of contact.

Defender: Does not block but instead slide-steps in any direction at his own discretion, even at times remaining motionless, forcing a series of adjustments in attacker's direction and range.

NOTE: In turning the body to cope with a new line of attack, the attacker must most emphatically align his body squarely behind the attacking hand.

(l) When the distance between opponents is greater than normal the following technique may be utilized to advantage:

Close the distance up to the "danger zone" with swift running steps, stopping abruptly; stamp the floor loudly with the left foot and immediately execute the right front kick, then right reverse punch.

NOTE: To close the distance, to penetrate an opponent's defenses while successfully evading his counterattack, is admittedly a tough assignment. Its effectiveness will hinge upon repetitive drill and the perfecting of a wide range of combinations of single techniques.

2(i) ⟶

1(a) ⟶

THROWING TECHNIQUES

(Forward Stance)

1. (a) *Attacker:* Delivers right lunge punch to the upper level.

   Defender: Keeping left foot in place, slides right foot to left; then quickly executes left outward block and simultaneous left sweeping kick to attacker's right ankle; grasps attacker's right sleeve pulling forward and down, simultaneously delivers right palm-heel attack or ridge-hand strike to left side of his face, then right reverse punch downward.

(b) *Attacker:* Delivers right lunge punch to the upper level.

Defender: Executes left outward block, then left sweeping kick to attacker's right ankle, and simultaneously grasps his right sleeve, pulling forward and down. Drives right foot forward, hooking leg behind attacker's right knee; quickly executes right palm-heel attack to left side of attacker's face, simultaneously thrusting right leg backward and up, then delivers right reverse punch downward.

2. *Attacker:* Delivers left lunge jab to the upper level.

Defender: Executes left rising block, then immediately grasps attacker's left wrist, pulling forward and down. Pivoting counterclockwise on ball of left foot, drives right foot forward, hooking leg inside of attacker's left knee while continuing downward pressure on his arm. Thrusts right leg backward and up, then delivers right reverse punch downward.

3. *Attacker:* Delivers right lunge punch to the upper level.

Defender: Executes left rising block, then immediately grasps attacker's right sleeve pulling forward and down. Drives right foot forward, hooking leg behind attacker's right knee. Quickly delivers right forward elbow attack to right shoulder, simultaneously thrusting right leg backward and up, then delivers right reverse punch downward.

4. *Attacker:* Delivers right lunge punch to the upper level.

Defender: Executes left rising block, then immediately grasps attacker's right wrist, pulling forward and down. Drives right foot forward, hooking leg behind attacker's right knee, simultaneously delivering right knife-hand strike to left side of his neck. Quickly thrusts right leg backward and up, then executes right reverse punch downward.

NOTE: In exercises 3 and 4 if attacker's balance is intact after hooking technique is applied, then, maintaining hold of arm or training uniform, quickly return right foot to original position and execute either right front or knee kick.

1(b)

2

4 →

5 ⟶

5. *Attacker:*   Delivers right front kick.
   Defender: Slides left, then right foot forward and slightly to the right, hooking left arm beneath kicking leg. Drives right foot forward through attacker's legs, hooking leg behind left knee. Immediately retracting left arm, delivers right palm-heel attack to attacker's face, simultaneously thrusting right leg backward and up, then executes right reverse punch downward.

6. *Attacker:*   Delivers right front kick.
   Defender: Slides left, then right foot forward and slightly to the left, hooking right arm beneath kicking leg. Drives right foot forward, hooking leg behind attacker's left knee. Lifts right arm, simultaneously thrusting right leg backward and up, then executes right reverse punch downward.

7. *Attacker:*   Delivers right lunge punch to the upper level.
   Defender: Slides left, then right foot forward and slightly to left into side straddle-leg stance, simultaneously delivering left knife-hand strike to the throat (avoiding contact) which blocks attacking hand as well; quickly hooks right arm behind attacker's right knee, lifting up and, at the same time, pushing back with the left arm; then executes right reverse punch downward.

8. (a) *Attacker:*   Delivers left lunge jab to the upper level.
   Defender: Left slide-steps backward and slightly to the left, executing right knife-hand block, then immediately grasping attacker's left sleeve, pulls forward and down; drives left foot forward, hooking leg behind attacker's left knee, simultaneously executing left knife-hand strike to the neck. Maintaining pressure against neck with left hand, simultaneously thrusts left leg backward and up, then executes right reverse punch downward.

6 ⟶

7 ⟶

8(a) ⟶

8(b)

(b) *Attacker:* Delivers right lunge punch to the upper level.

Defender: Executes left outward block and simultaneous right side-stamping kick to attacker's right knee or below; immediately grasping attacker's right hand with both hands, pivots one hundred and eighty degrees counter-clockwise, placing kicking foot beside attacker's right foot, then pulls him vigorously forward, throwing him to the floor.

9. *Attacker:* Delivers right reverse punch to the upper level.

Defender: Right slide-steps forward, executing left rising block, then immediately grasps attacker's right sleeve pulling forward and down. Delivers right knife-hand strike or right inner forearm attack to attacker's neck. Maintaining pressure against neck with right hand, simultaneously left slide-steps to the rear, causing attacker to lose balance, then executes right reverse punch downward.

NOTE: Pull on arm or sleeve continues until attacker is thrown.

10. *Attacker:* Simultaneously feints upward with hands and kiais. Quickly slides feet forward, wrapping arms around defender's right knee; drives right foot forward between defender's legs, hooking leg behind his left knee; pulling inward with both arms, thrusts right leg backward and up, at the same time ramming right shoulder forward.

11. *Attacker:* When defender is in open-leg stance, half left, then right slide-steps forward, wrapping arms around defender's knees; pulling arms inward, rams right shoulder forward.

9 ⟶

10 ⟶

11 ⟶

12 →

12. *Attacker:*   Delivers right lunge punch to the upper level.
    Defender: Executes left outward block or rising block; immediately grasping attacking arm, pulls forward and down; quickly grips attacker's throat with right hand; drives right foot forward hooking leg behind attacker's right knee; maintaining pressure on throat, thrusts right leg backward and up, then executes right reverse punch downward.

13. (a) *Attacker:*   Delivers right lunge punch to the upper level.
    Defender: Half left slide-steps forward, simultaneously executing left palm-heel block, sweeping attacking arm across chest; drives right foot forward, hooking leg behind attacker's right leg, simultaneously gripping his throat with right hand; thrusts right leg backward and up and, maintaining pressure on throat, executes left reverse punch downward.

   (b) *Defender:*   Executes left palm-heel block, sweeping attacking hand across chest and simultaneously driving right foot forward, hooking leg behind attacker's right knee; executes right downward knife-hand strike to his left collarbone, simultaneously thrusting right leg backward and up, then executes right reverse punch downward.

(Left Forward Stance)

14. *Attacker:*   Right jab and a simultaneous left slide-step forward; holding right arm rigid, executes right sweeping kick to back of defender's left foot, simultaneously pushing backward with right arm; left reverse punch downward.

    Defender: Assumes forward stance.

NOTE: Use extreme caution when practicing any of the throwing techniques. Do not actually complete the throw unless a mat is used.

13(b) ⟶

14 ⟶

▪ Multiple Opponents

1 ⟶

Exercises depicting defense against multiple opponents are a highly effective method of indicating to the student the range of his potential in defending himself.

1. Defender is held around neck by attacker behind him while second attacker attacks from front with right lunge punch. Defender executes right backward elbow attack and simultaneous right front kick.
2. Defender's wrists are held out laterally by two attackers, one on either side. Defender executes right side-thrust kick to the side and over attacker's arm; return kicking foot alongside opposite knee and, pivoting counterclockwise on ball of left foot, executes right front kick, followed by right reverse punch.
3. Defender's wrists are held out laterally by two attackers, one on either side, while third attacker attacks from front with right lunge punch. Defender executes right front kick, right side-thrust kick to the side and, with low hop to the left, places right foot in space vacated by the left, immediately executing left side-thrust kick to the left.

4. *First Attacker:*   Delivers right lunge punch from right side.
   Defender: Executes right side-thrust kick to right side, maintaining observation of other attacker.
   Second Attacker: Closes distance from the front and delivers right front kick at momentarily distracted defender.
   Defender: Drops to left side, supporting himself on hip and forearm, executing right rising block and simultaneous right side-thrust kick.
   NOTE: When confronted by multiple opponents, rather than becoming involved in a punching exchange it is best to stress the more powerful foot attacks. Although a wall at defender's rear eliminates attack from that direction, it will hamper freedom of movement. Do not stay on the defensive, for this permits your opponents to close in, attacking at will. It becomes necessary to shift around rapidly in an effort to keep all opponents in front and to one side. To avoid entrapment, quickly move through opponents and reverse direction.
5. *First Attacker:*   Right slide-steps forward, grasping defender around upper body pinning arms to his sides, encircling body from rear.

(Open-Leg Stance)
   Defender: Left slide-steps backward, simultaneously executing left backward elbow attack.
   Second and Third Attackers: From defender's front and left, simultaneously deliver right lunge punches to the upper level.
   Defender: Executes left front kick, then immediate left outward block and simultaneous left side-thrust kick to the side.
   Fourth Attacker: From defender's right, delivers right lunge punch, upper level.
   Defender: Hopping low, places left foot in space vacated by the right, immediately executing right outward block and simultaneous right side-thrust kick to the side.

4 ⟶

5 ↓

6

6. Defender's wrists are held out laterally by two opponents, one on either side, while third and fourth opponents deliver simultaneous right lunge punches from front and rear respectively.

Defender executes right front kick, without lowering foot; right rear kick, without lowering foot; right side-thrust kick to the right, and with low hop to the left, places right foot in space vacated by the left, immediately executing left side-thrust kick to the left.

NOTE: These are trite situations which in all probability would never occur in the manner described above. Yet for purposes of building coordinated reactions to compound situations they will be of value.

The following free-style sparring exercises are for advanced students only.
(Forward Stance)
1. Student engages two opponents simultaneously.
2. Student engages three opponents simultaneously.
The beginning positions should be as follows:

. .   . . .
   .   .

■ Contest Rules

In public demonstrations participated in by one or more karate clubs, the atmosphere should reflect considerably more formality than during the frequent contests held at individual training halls.

The contest area is usually twenty-four feet square and covered with white matting on which the boundaries are clearly marked. A contest is halted when one or more of the contestants steps outside the boundary. A "time out" is then called by the referee, until both participants return to the center of the contest area. If a participant retreats outside the contest area too frequently, he should be first warned, then, at the next repetition, penalized.

In free-style sparring contests the standard flag system is used. There are four judges subordinate to one referee assisted by two scorekeepers and a timekeeper.[1] The most suitable attire for presiding officials is a plain dark suit, white shirt, and tie. The referee will remove his suit coat to facilitate the movement necessary in officiating, while with the judges it is optional. The referee remains in the contest area while the four judges sit one at each corner. These four judges each have a whistle and two flags, one red and the other white.[2] Each contestant will have either a red or white ribbon fastened to his belt.

The participants will approach the referee and, at a point six feet apart from each other and equidistant from the referee, execute a standing bow.[3]

The participants will then turn to face each other and, at the referee's command, repeat the standing bow. The referee will then

---

[1] The judge-referee system used in free-style sparring events was commenced at Waseda University by Tsutomu Ohshima in 1952, during the Keio and Waseda University training sessions.

[2] The use of whistles is arbitrary but has proven effective.

[3] To show respect for the referee the bow to him should be made with hands dropped at the sides, fingers straight. Contrastingly, the bow to an opponent, which need not be so low, is usually performed with clenched fists.

give the command to begin the contest.[4] If the contest is interrupted for any reason, the standing bow will be repeated by the contestants before resuming sparring. Upon completion of the contest, the students will bow to each other, and finally to the referee, prior to leaving the area. Because of the inherent nature of karate, it behooves us to remain constantly alert. When bowing to each other during sparring, do not allow yourself to get into the habit of bending the body or head so that the vision centers upon the lower half of your opponent. Never leave yourself in a position where your attention does not center on your opponent's eyes. If you cannot see your opponent's eyes, it may be difficult to judge his intentions at the instant he attacks.

Points are awarded for attacks that are strongly delivered in sufficient proximity to certain areas, provided they are judged potentially serious or disabling. These strategic locations include the face, head, and body from the groin up. When one has developed sufficient control to be able to direct a potentially damaging attack to these areas, it is acknowledged that he would be able to attack any given area with precision. The referee decides when a point or half point has been scored. If a point has been scored and he is not in a position to see it, then any one of the four judges who has observed it will

[4] That fleeting instant at the end of the referee's command to begin (Hajime!) may be put to devastating use. An alert student may have chosen his form of attack and so can proceed directly into it catching his opponent completely unprepared.

unhesitatingly blow his whistle and raise the flag corresponding to the scoring contestant's ribbon. The referee will then question him and the other judges as to the nature of the attack before rendering a decision. If as many as three judges signify having observed a point or half point, the referee (having determined that the judges had observed the identical technique) unhesitatingly awards the point (or half point) even though it had escaped his own observation.

The referee may consult with any one or all four judges regarding anything of which he is doubtful. If no point has been awarded by the end of the match, the referee calls for a decision in this fashion: he blows his whistle, terminating in a brief high note, which signals the judges to raise their flags in unison. This simultaneous action eliminates the possibility of improper influence. To indicate a tie a judge will raise both flags crossed at right angles to each other. In this event both contestants are permitted a brief rest period after which the match will resume. This procedure will be repeated until a decision has been reached. When observing a successful attack the referee should halt the match and indicate that the contestants face each other in front of him. Then, in an emphatic manner, the referee announces the point-winning attack, thrusting his arm (palm open) down to the winner's side. At the match's conclusion, the referee will render a decision by announcing the winning point or points as he thrusts his arm (palm open) up to the winner's side. Should there be a tie the referee will signal it with arms raised and crossed at right angles.

A referee who truly fulfills his duties is not going to view a contest objectively as a detached observer; he must bring to bear an intensity, a focusing of the mind with its accompanying physical tension which will highlight the action before him. In this way it would be difficult to overlook potential points. If, at the conclusion of a series of matches, a referee does not feel drained of energy, it is a fair indication that he was derelict in his obligations.

Karate inherently requires the utmost effort from each student participating in free-style sparring regardless of weight. Therefore pairs of contestants will be selected mainly on the basis of rank.

By means of the point system, the competition in forms is judged using a somewhat different procedure. In this pursuit, the referee sits at an edge of the contest area while the four judges sit one in each corner. In place of the flags previously noted, each judge holds ten cards with faces turned inward. Each bears a single number from one through ten. All decisions in this case are made on the basis of a tabulation of cards.

When a contestant has finished performing the prescribed form, the referee will give a long, slow toot on his whistle (again terminated by a sharp note), at the conclusion of which each of the judges simultaneously lifts one of his cards in the air, turned outward for the scorekeepers to record. An arbitrary number, say five, will have been agreed upon beforehand as representing the norm.

If a contestant has committed an error during his presentation of a form, the referee will, before using his whistle in the prescribed manner, announce the deduction of one or more points. Each judge will then mentally make the deduction before choosing his card. A contestant compiling the largest aggregate of points will be declared the winner.

The judge's decision should not be greeted by any outward display of emotion by either the winner or the loser. The audience should not be able to determine the winner by looking at either contestant. Neither should there be shouted encouragement from teammates on the sidelines.

NOTE: Black-belt holders should be thoroughly indoctrinated in the techniques of judging prior to service in that capacity.

The tournament provides an excellent showcase for reaching mass audiences. The very nature of karate is bound to produce a kaleidoscope of lightning swift clashes which overwhelm the laymen with an awesome spectacle of deadly maneuvers. The beginner's most cherished dream may be to compete one day in this glamorous arena. It must be said that after the fervor and shouting have died away the tournament is not an entirely valid vehicle to demonstrate karate as a science. The scoring of a point during the fleeting moments of a single encounter is no broad indication of overall technical competence; it merely attests to the effectiveness of a specific maneuver at a given time.

Viewed in the narrow context of a colorful sport or competition, karate finds its most apt vehicle in the tournament. To be pursued in depth, however, it must be undertaken as a meticulous and exacting science and will ultimately reveal itself as a way of life.

■ Forms

Forms, although constituting just one-third of our training endeavor, are the acknowledged backbone of karate. At one time forms and basic training comprised a greater portion of karate, but when Master Funakoshi synthesized his experience under the name "Shotokan," he added basic sparring as another essential. Originating centuries ago, forms have changed very little with the passage of time. Besides being a splendid example of dynamic tension, when done properly these forms provide an excellent workout benefiting the entire physique.

If a student who has already learned some forms finds it impossible to continue his membership at a training hall, all is not forfeited. He will never have to purchase exercise equipment or join a health club to remain in top physical condition. Neither will it be necessary to transport any apparatus nor seek a gymnasium if he travels. Thirty minutes in daily practice of forms will provide a substantial workout and, at the same time, develop basic stances, blocks, and attacks.

In general these inflexible patterns of movement, simulating defense and attack as they do, are similar to shadow boxing, except that in each case several opponents attacking from different directions are envisioned. Briefly, a series of blocks and attacks has been put together in a predetermined manner in which each student imagines multiple opponents. Each form is of approximately one-minute duration. Emphasis is placed upon concentration of effort and development of conditioned responses.

Forms supplement basic training in the development of positive equilibrium under combat conditions. Learning proper balance, including the ability to change direction without losing it, is a karate essential. Maintenance of balance must be a target of concerted effort at all levels of proficiency. Beginning students must therefore practice basic training and forms exclusively before moving into sparring. To expedite progress concentrate on a single form, repeating a minimum of fifteen times during each workout. Each movement within the form demands the student's most intensive concentration.

He must not allow himself to think ahead too far or else his performance will be weakened.

Beginning students and those having difficulty maintaining a low stance should perform numerous repetitions of Heian 1, greatly exaggerating a low forward stance. This puts tremendous stress on the leg muscles, conditioning them so that the proper forward stance becomes easier to hold.

The student should guard against the favoring of one particular form since this will result unavoidably in a proportionate slighting of the others. He should work toward the maximum development of all forms before allowing himself the "luxury" of a favorite one.

A useful exercise for the development of concentration under adverse circumstances consists in the class performance of forms, each student assigned a different one. Simultaneous execution of dissimilar forms requires intensive concentration.

In the same manner, an exercise helpful in the development of prolonged endurance should be included in the training program: the uninterrupted repetition of a single selected form with an eventual goal of fifty. It is best to begin gradually, attempting no more than five continuous repetitions. After the class has learned thoroughly all forms, it should perform twice over the entire group of fifteen consecutively without pausing. This, together with opening and closing calisthenics and several strengthening exercises, could well constitute an entire training session.

BASIC SHOTOKAN FORMS	HEIAN[1]	TEKKI[2]	INDEPENDENT
Number of forms	Five	Three	Seven
Number of opponents	Four	Three	Maximum of eight
Comment: To pass the Black Belt First-Degree examination, it is necessary to be well versed in all of Heian through Tekki, and to be able to give a demonstration of at least one form chosen from the Independent group.	"Form of Peace" Includes all basic blocks and attacks.	"Form of Riding a Horse" Favorites of Master Funakoshi. Deceptively simple, yet they build needed power.	Bassai—"Breaking out of an enclosure." Kanku[3]—"Looking at the sky." Empi—"Flying swallow." Gankaku—"Crane on the rock." Jitte—"Ten hand." Jion—Name of priest. Hangetsu—"Half moon." Combines the techniques involved in Heian and Tekki, and develops speed, agility, and power.

[1] Heian forms are performed within a limited circumscribed area, reflecting their secret development in closed and shuttered rooms during the Japanese occupation of Okinawa.

[2] Master Funakoshi practiced the three Tekki forms exclusively for ten years before he felt that he had mastered them.

[3] Master Kwang Shang-fu considered that of all the forms kanku was the most useful and practiced it exclusively. Its inclusiveness, he felt, equipped him to deal with multiple opponents. He was the first to bring this form to Okinawa from China, in approximately A.D. 1800.

Throughout the Orient there are countless variations of the forms. However, in the Shotokan school there are fifteen basic ones, which are grouped into three separate sections known as Heian, Tekki, and Independent. It should be understood that the mere mechanical accumulation of numerous forms, as an end in itself, is not desirable. It is far better practice to concentrate one's entire attention and devotion on the performance of a basic group of forms at a consistently high level.

The reader may wonder why no attempt has been made to include photographs of the various forms. It should be self-evident that still photography cannot convey the very necessary and precise changes in tempo which occur in every form. Nor can it impart adequately the rise and fall of muscular tension. Actually it can do little more than suggest the outward posture. In short, still photography cannot produce a total picture of the intricate fluctuations within each form. It would, however serve as a memory aid regarding the unfolding progression of each form.

■ Conclusion

The author has treated the material throughout with emphasis on its functional application. However, since so much inherent in karate is purely abstract, it has been incumbent upon him to include certain of these ideas. Technical mastery alone would deprive the student of the growth in character which molds "the whole man." The positive qualities which new students bring to karate will be strengthened and enhanced in this way. By the same token any objectionable traits will normally be discouraged.

When in a tournament do not become disturbed at losing a match or overly elated when winning. Either outcome should require only temporary adjustment. Remember, a loser need not be one forever, neither is the winner beyond all possibility of defeat. One's attitude should allow him to profit from each error, thereby turning momentary miscalculations to advantage.

For maximum proficiency, concentrate one training session on basic training and forms and the next on basic training coupled with sparring. The basic training may be comprised entirely of repetitive drill in one specific movement rather than in a broad grouping.

By way of review it is appropriate to redefine and perhaps elaborate upon the essentials in the performance of karate. The basic techniques to be acquired diligently and applied exactly are:

> Stance
> Blocking and attacking
> Breath control
> Kiai
> Distance between opponents
> Closing the distance
> Creating an opening

In the broader sense the components of karate are:

Basic training—teaches correct techniques

Forms—combine techniques

Theory—provides the explanation for each technique

Special Exercises—strengthen specific areas of the physique

Sparring—synthesizes through practical application the entire training experience

Mental Conditioning—the catalyst that fuses all other components

There is a growing lack of concern in many quarters regarding karate expressed in such matters as training uniform, student attitude, and application of technique. These incongruities become displayed on a grand scale during the many demonstrations and tournaments being held throughout the country. Since, as has been mentioned, the various competitions bring these peculiarities before the public, karate may appear to some to be a potpourri of loosely interpreted techniques rather than a group of formal, well-defined disciplines.

The mode of dress has undergone certain disturbing changes in some quarters; currently there have been made available a number of alternatives to the traditional training uniform. The instructor should be aware that any attempt to dramatize the visual spectacle of karate by the use of extraordinary colors does not reflect an acceptable approach. The wearing of tennis shoes (seen quite frequently of late) is likewise not proper.

The qualified karate instructor deserves and most certainly should be accorded unconditional respect. The general behavior of the student is mirrored in the quality of the student-instructor relationship, and if disrespect is evident the resultant level of achievement will unquestionably suffer.

Every effort should be made to execute precise techniques in the area of free-style sparring. Participants may be tempted to believe that a careless ill-defined exchange of attacks will provide an easy victory. Indeed one sees evidence of this kind of thinking in many tournaments. As a result of strict adherence to good form, victory should come ultimately to the advanced student; the beginner who utilizes the same discipline, while yet experiencing defeat, will develop heightened determination in the quest for his long-term goal.

There is a nebulous quality that fashions masters of a precious few and an impetus that makes it impossible for these few not to go forward even when the pinnacle of achievement may have been reached in the eyes of his fellow karateist. Lacking this quality others should nevertheless cultivate an awareness of being constantly in transition toward an ever higher level.

The karate master will have entered into what is best described as a condition of "pure mind," in which there are no debilitating states of hostility or fear, or the inability to clear his thoughts of worldly influence.[1] He then becomes capable of spontaneous and superlatively fluid movement. This "pure mind" state we know to be the outgrowth of strict adherence to a positive training program. His response to challenge has become reflexive rather than contemplative after countless repetitive drills. Fear, the destroyer of initiative and courage, yields to serenity when one is confident of his potential. With "pure mind" an interesting phenomenon occurs: an assailant's movements unfold almost as if in slow motion with a clarity which makes countermoves simple; on the other hand the timid, agitated mind will view the adversary's moves as a lightning-swift series of bewildering thrusts and blows with which he is incapable of dealing.

A final reminder to alert the student to a common pitfall along the way: When a karateist has attained his black belt, he has just made perhaps the most difficult transition of all. If we liken his progress to that of a bold adventurer attempting to scale the loftiest peak, we may discover something of value. Our new black-belt holder, his view obscured for the moment in the swirling mists and clouds of self-adulation and excessive pride at his accomplishment, may relax his efforts. He may seem on solid footing, with the most arduous part of his journey past. This is a precarious moment; now he must humbly renew his zeal and his dedication. There remain still more challenging heights to scale, and he would do well to remind himself that those below him who are attempting to follow in his footsteps are dependent upon his prowess and example.

[1] In Japan the "pure mind" state is variously known as "mind like water" and "mind like the moon."

■ Appendices

1. CHRONOLOGY OF THE DEVELOPMENT OF KARATE

India
ca. 2600 B.C.   Findings indicate evidence of ancient rudiments of unarmed self-defense.

China
ca. A.D. 525   The Buddhist monk Bodhidharma (*J.* Daruma Taishi) went to China from eastern India. He introduced Zen with karate training. He is believed to have written the *Ekkin Sutra* (the first karate book).

Ryukyu Islands
(Okinawa)
ca. 1429   General Sho Hashi became the ruler of the Ryukyus. To tighten his control he confiscated all weapons and issued the "No Weapons" edict. Training secretly in their homes, the natives began to improvise techniques of unarmed self-defense. They were greatly influenced by martial arts experts from the coasts of southern China, and also by Okinawan and Chinese pirates.

ca. 1480   A group of Okinawans went to China to study Chinese boxing, returning five years later to contribute their knowledge.

ca. 1650   The Satsuma clan in Kyushu became the rulers of Okinawa and renewed the "No Weapons" edict.

1690   Shimazu Iehisa, a Japanese feudal lord from Kyushu, conquered Okinawa and placed even firmer restrictions on weapons. The natives responded by hard training, thereby improving the unarmed self-defense techniques originally imported from China.

ca. 1700   Master Sakugawa of Shuri, Okinawa, went to China to study Chinese boxing and later returned to teach it.

ca. 1790   The Chinese Master Kwang Shang-fu (*J.* Ko Sho-kun) went to Okinawa with several students.

1805   Soshu Matsumura was born.

1827   Anko Azato was born.

1830   Anko Itosu was born.

ca. 1850   Chinese military attaches, experts in Chinese boxing, traveled to Okinawa.

1852   Kanryo Higaonna was born.

1868   Gichin Funakoshi was born.

1889   Kenwa Mabuni was born.

1905   Gichin Funakoshi, together with several karate experts, demonstrated karate to the public.

1906   Anko Azato died.

1915   Anko Itosu died. Kanryo Higaonna died. Kambun Uechi returned from China.

Japan
1916   Gichin Funakoshi demonstrated karate in Butokuden, Kyoto.

1922   Gichin Funakoshi introduced karate in First National Sports Exhibition in Tokyo. Published *Ryukyu Kempo, Karate.* Opened Meisei-juku (shotokan-ryu).

1924   Gichin Funakoshi established Karate club at Keio University, Tokyo, the oldest university karate club in Tokyo.

1934   Chojun Miyagi (goju-ryu) went to Hawaii to teach karate. Kenwa Mabuni opened Yoshukan (shito-ryu) in Osaka.

1935   Gichin Funakoshi published *Karate-do Instruction Manual.*

1952   Kenwa Mabuni died.

1953   Chojun Miyagi died.

1957   Gichin Funakoshi died.

369

2. OUTLINE OF THE DEVELOPMENT AND SPREAD OF KARATE

KEY:
- - - ➤ Influence of master or short periods
       of practice with master
——➤ Direct teacher
C   Chinese origins
O   Okinawan origins
J   Japanese origins

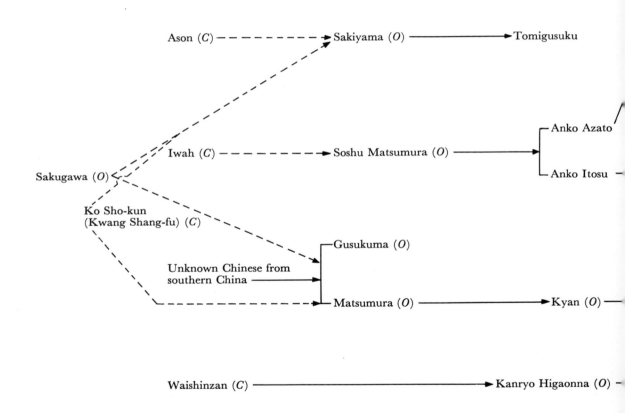

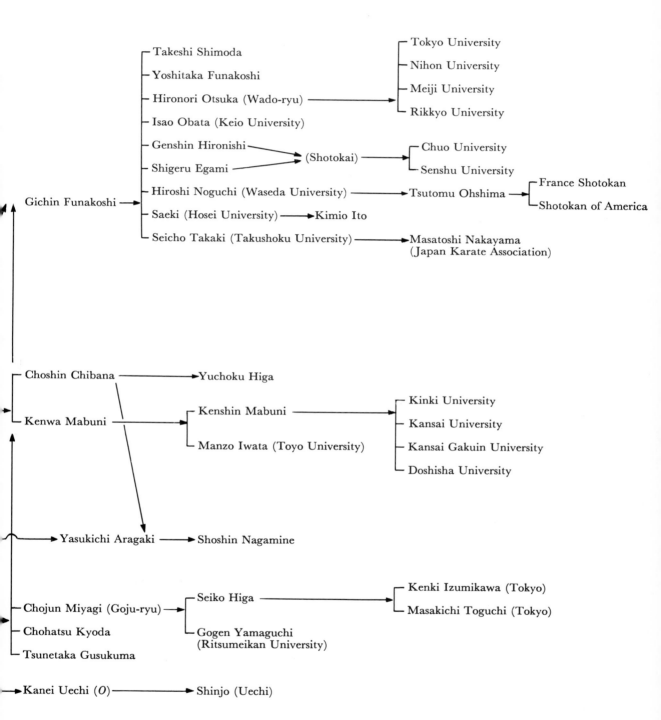

■ Training Hall Glossary

Note: Pronunciation of Japanese terms is given in parentheses.

Numbers

one	*ichi*	(ee-chee)
two	*ni*	(nee)
three	*san*	(sahn)
four	*shi*	(shee)
five	*go*	(goh)
six	*roku*	(roh-koo)
seven	*shichi*	(shee-chee)
eight	*hachi*	(hah-chee)
nine	*ku*	(koo)
ten	*ju*	(joo)

General

assume stance   *kamaete* (kah-mah-eh-teh)
at ease   *yasume* (yah-soo-meh)
basic training   *kihon* (kee-hohn)
black-belt rank   *dan* (dahn)
board breaking   *tameshi wari* (tah-meh-shee wah-ree)
escape methods   *torite* (toh-ree-teh)
formal exercises/forms   *kata* (kah-tah)
good afternoon   *konnichiwa* (kohn-nee-chee-wah)
good-by   *sayonara* (sah-yoh-nah-rah)
good evening   *kombanwa* (kohn-bahn-wah)
instructor   *sensei* (sehn-seh-ee)
master   *shihan* (shee-han)
maximum physical/mental concentration   *kime* (kee-meh)
meditate   *mokuso* (moh-koo-soh)
pivot/assume opposite direction   *kaete* (kah-eh-teh)
please teach me   *onegai shimasu* (oh-neh-gah-ee shee-mah-soo)
punching board   *makiwara* (mah-kee-wah-rah)
ready   *yoi* (yoh-ee)
response   *hen-o* (hehn-oh)
standing forms   *tachikata* (tah-chee-kah-tah)
thank you very much   *domo arigato* (doh-moh ah-ree-gah-toh)
throwing techniques   *nagewaza* (nah-geh-wah-zah)
training hall   *dojo* (doh-joh)
training uniform   *keiko-gi* (keh-ee-koh-gee)
training uniform belt   *obi* (oh-bee)
vocal expulsion of air   *kiai* (kee-ah-ee)

373

white/brown-belt rank *kyu* (kyoo)
you are welcome *doitashimashite* (doh-ee-tah-shee-mah-shee-teh)
your training hall senior *sempai* (sehm-pah-ee)

Stances *dachi* (dah-chee)
back stance/weight rearward *kokutsu-dachi* (koh-koo-tsoo dah-chee)
cat stance *neko-ashi-dachi* (neh-koh-ah-shee dah-chee)
close-leg stance *heisoku-dachi* (heh-ee-soh-koo dah-chee)
forward stance/weight forward *zenkutsu-dachi* (zehn-koo-tsoo dah-chee)
half-front facing stance *hammi-dachi* (hahm-mee dah-chee)
immovable stance *fudo-dachi* (foo-doh dah-chee)
open-leg stance *hachiji-dachi* (hah-chee-jee dah-chee)
straddle-leg stance *kiba-dachi* (kee-bah dah-chee)

Blocking *uke* (oo-keh)
cross-arm block *juji uke* (joo-jee oo-keh)
downward block *gedan-barai* (geh-dahn bah-rah-ee)
foot-edge block *sokuto-osae uke* (soh-koo-toh-oh-sah-eh oo-keh)
grasping block *tsukami uke* (tsoo-kah-mee oo-keh)
inward/outward forearm block *ude uke* (oo-deh oo-keh)
knife-hand block *shuto uke* (shoo-toh oo-keh)
palm-heel block *teisho uke* (teh-ee-shoh oo-keh)
pressing block *maeude deai osae* (mah-eh-oo-deh deh-ah-ee oh-sah-eh)
rising block *age uke* (ah-geh oo-keh)
sweeping block *te-nagashi uke* (teh-nah-gah-shee oo-keh)
two-hand grasping block *morote-tsukami uke* (moh-roh-teh-tsoo-kah-mee oo-keh)

Hand Attacks *te waza* (teh wah-zah)
close punch *ura-zuki* (oo-rah zoo-kee)
double punch *morote-zuki* (moh-roh-teh zoo-kee)
hook punch *kagi-zuki* (kah-gee zoo-kee)
jab *kizami-zuki* (kee-zah-mee zoo-kee)
lunge punch *oi-zuki* (oh-ee zoo-kee)
palm-heel *teisho-zuki* (teh-ee-shoh zoo-kee)
reverse punch *gyaku-zuki* (gyah-koo zoo-kee)
rising punch *age-zuki* (ah-geh zoo-kee)
straight punch *choku-zuki* (choh-koo zoo-kee)
vertical punch *tate-zuki* (tah-teh zoo-kee)

Combination Techniques *renzoku waza* (rehn-zoh-koo wah-zah)
consecutive punching/alternate hands *ren-zuki* (rehn zoo-kee)
consecutive punching/same hand *dan-zuki* (dahn zoo-kee)
lunge punch/reverse punch/reverse punch *sanren-zuki* (sahn-rehn zoo-kee)

Elbow Attacks *empi uchi* (ehm-pee oo-chee)
backward elbow attack *ushiro-empi uchi* (oo-shee-roh-ehm-pee oo-chee)
downward elbow attack *otoshi-empi uchi* (oh-toh-shee-ehm-pee oo-chee)
forward elbow attack *mae-empi uchi* (mah-eh-ehm-pee oo-chee)
upward elbow attack *tate-empi uchi* (tah-teh-ehm-pee oo-chee)

Striking Techniques *uchi waza* (oo-chee wah-zah)
back-fist strike *uraken uchi* (oo-rah-kehn oo-chee)
bottom-fist strike *tettsui uchi* (teht-tsoo-ee oo-chee)
knife-hand strike *shuto uchi* (shoo-toh oo-chee)
  forearm *ude* (oo-deh)

fore-fist   *seiken* (seh-ee-kehn)
fore-knuckle fist   *hiraken* (hee-rah-kehn)
inner forearm   *nai wan* (nah-ee wahn)
middle finger knuckle fist   *nakadaka ken* (nah-kah-dah-kah kehn)
one-knuckle fist   *ippon ken* (eep-pohn kehn)
outer forearm   *gai wan* (gah-ee wahn)
ridge-hand   *haito* (hah-ee-toh)
spear-hand   *nukite* (noo-kee-teh)
two-finger spear-hand   *nihon nukite* (nee-hohn noo-kee-teh)

Kicks *ashi waza* (ah-shee wah-zah)
combination kicks   *renzoku-geri* (rehn-zoh-koo-geh-ree)
double front kick   *nidan-geri* (nee-dahn-geh-ree)
flying front kick   *tobi-geri* (toh-bee-geh-ree)
flying side-thrust kick   *tobi yoko-geri* (toh-bee yoh-koh-geh-ree)
front kick   *mae-geri* (mah-eh-geh-ree)
front kick/front leg   *mae-ashi-geri* (mah-eh-ah-shee-geh-ree)
front-thrust kick   *mae-ashi kekomi* (mah-ee-ah-shee keh-koh-mee)
rear kick   *ushiro-geri kekomi* (oo-shee-roh-geh-ree keh-koh-mee)
round kick   *mawashi-geri* (mah-wah-shee-geh-ree)
side-snap kick   *yoko-geri keage* (yoh-koh-geh-ree keh-ah-geh)
side-thrust kick   *yoko-geri kekomi* (yoh-koh-geh-ree keh-koh-mee)
stamping kick   *fumikomi* (foo-mee-koh-mee)
sweeping kick   *aori-geri* (ah-oh-ree-geh-ree)
　　ball of foot   *koshi* (koh-shee)
　　foot edge   *sokuto* (soh-koo-toh)
　　heel   *kakato* (kah-kah-toh)
　　kneecap   *hizagashira* (hee-zah-gah-shee-rah)

Sparring *kumite* (koo-mee-teh)
continuous punching attack   *renzoku-zuki uchi* (rehn-zoh-koo zoo-kee oo-chee)
five attacks   *gohon kumite* (goh-hohn koo-mee-teh)
free style   *jiyu kumite* (jee-yoo koo-mee-teh)
one attack/basic   *kihon ippon kumite* (kee-hohn eep-pohn koo-mee-teh)
one attack/semifree style   *jiyu ippon kumite* (jee-yoo eep-pohn koo-mee-teh)
three attacks   *sambon kumite* (sahn-bohn koo-mee-teh)
　　begin   *hajime* (hah-jee-meh)
　　bow   *rei* (reh-ee)
　　distance between opponents   *ma* (mah)
　　draw   *hikiwake* (hee-kee-wah-keh)
　　end of match   *sore made* (soh-reh mah-deh)
　　half-point   *wazari* (wah-zah-ree)
　　head   *jo-dan* (joh-dahn)
　　lower body   *ge-dan* (geh-dahn)
　　middle body   *chu-dan* (choo-dahn)
　　one more time   *mo ichido* (moh ee-chee-doh)
　　point   *ippon* (eep-pohn)
　　referee   *shimpan* (sheem-pahn)
　　simultaneous points by both opponents/self-canceling *aiuchi* (ah-ee-oo-chee)
　　stop   *yame* (yah-meh)
　　team captain   *taicho* (tah-ee-choh)
　　team contest   *shiai* (shee-ah-ee)
　　two half-points equal one point   *wazari awasete ippon* (wah-zah-ree ah-wah-seh-teh eep-pohn)

■ Index

forearm, 66
forearm attack, 122
forearm strengthening, 256
fore-fist, 66
forehead, 66
formalities, 33–34
forms, 359–61; chart of, 360
forward stance, 82–83
front kick, 146, 172, 226
front-thrust kick, 159, 172
Funakoshi, Gichin, 21–22, 41, 267

gi. *See* uniform
grading. *See* rank structure

half-front facing stance, 83
hand techniques: back-fist strike, 110; bottom-fist strike, 110; close punch, 100; combinations, 112; double close punch, 111; double reverse punch, 112; double straight punch, 111; elbow attack, 118–20; extended lunge punch, 118; extended reverse punch, 118; forearm attack, 122; hook punch, 108; jab, 114; knife-hand strike, 122; lunge jab, 116; lunge punch, 102–8; palm-heel attack, 122; reverse punch, 100–102; ridge-hand strike, 124; rising punch, 108; straight punch, 100
hook punch, 108

index finger, 66
index-knuckle fist, 66
instructors, hints for, 230–31
inward block, 93

jab, 114

karate, derivation of the term, 22; history of, 21–24
kata. *See* forms
kempo, 21
kiai, 26, 70, 229
kicking, development of, 172–76
knee, 66
knee kick, 178
knife-edge of foot, 172 n
knife-hand, 66
knife-hand block, 94–96, 263
knife-hand strike, 122
knuckle fist, 66
kumite. *See* sparring

kung-fu, 21

legs, special exercises for, 252–54; stretching of, 257
lunge jab, 116
lunge punch, 102–8, 226–27, 304

ma. *See* distance control
middle-knuckle fist, 66
multiple opponents, 350–54
muscle tone, exercises to develop, 261–62

neck exercises, 254

Ohshima, Tsutomu, 22–24
Okinawa-te, 21–22
open-leg stance, 81
outward block, 92

palm-heel attack, 66, 122
palm-heel block, 98
power, consistent level of, 308; maximum focus of, 181; reservoir of, 233
pressing block, 98
promotional examination, 38–41; sample of form used in, 41
punch development, 232–40
punching board, construction of, 240; use of, 240–41
punching combinations, 112
punching power, development of, 233–34, 250; principle behind, 232
"pure mind," 364–65

rank structure, 36–41
Rasch, Dr. Phillip J., 26
reaction speed, development of, 242–44
rear kick, 170, 226
reverse punch, 100, 227
ridge-hand, 66
ridge-hand strike, 124
rising block, 92
rising punch, 108
round kick, 168, 226; variation of, 180
rules of conduct, 30–31

side-snap kick, 167
side-thrust kick, 159–67, 172, 226; variation of, 180
Southern California Karate Association, 22, 24, 41